SYMBOLS AND ABBREVIATIONS

A = Present value of an annuity; flows are recurring

AS = Total assets

b = Earnings retention rate

B = Bonds; total value of bonds

C = Capital structure

CON = Convertible securities; also represents conversion value

CS = Common stock; total dollar value of common stock

CSD = Common stock dividend

D = Expiration point of a convertible security as a fixed income obligation

DBT = Supply of external funds

E = Earnings, both total and per share

EAI = Pretax earnings after interest

EBIT = Earnings before interest and taxes; this is operating income

E/P = Market capitalization rate; inverse of the *price* to *earnings* ratio; cost of common equity, $K_{CS} + K_{RE}$

F = Fixed operating costs

g = Growth rate

H = Call price of a bond

I = Interest amount

i = Interest rate

K_B = Cost of bonds

K_C = Cost of capital; made up of (all after tax) K_B, K_{CON}, K_{CS}, K_{PS}, K_{RE}

K_{CON} = Cost of convertibles

K_{CS} = Cost of common stock; same as E/P

K_{PS} = Cost of preferred stock

K_{RE} = Cost of retained earnings; same as E/P

$\hat{K}_{RE}$ = Cost of retained earnings before taxes

L = Leverage; same as B/C (*debt* to *equity* ratio)

M = Number of payments in 1 year

MC = Margi~~~

MC_b = Margi~~~

ME = Margin~~~

MT = Marginal tax rate

n = Number of periods (days, years, etc.)

NCI = Net cash inflow

NCO = Net cash outflow

NS = Number of shares

P = Market price

Q = Bond redemption value at maturity ($1,000), par value

P/E = *Price* to *earnings* ratio; inverse (E/P) is cost of common equity ($K_{CS} + K_{RE}$)

PS = Preferred shares; total dollar value

PSD = Preferred-share dividend

r = Rate of return (discounted cash flow); same as return on equity

R = Sales revenue; sales at break-even point

RE = Retained earnings

ROI = Return on investment; ΔROI is change of return after tax

S = Present value of a single lump sum

SC = Stock cost

SE = Stockholders' equity (CS + RE); same as book value

T = Tax amount

t = Tax rate

V = Variable costs; cost of accelerating inflows

v = The portion of the sales dollar that covers variable costs; $(1 - v)$ is *profit* to *volume* ratio

X, x = Any unknown, such as immobilized funds

Z = P/E adjustment factor

Δ = Change in value

σ = Standard deviation

Decision
Strategies
in Financial
Management

Decision Strategies in Financial Management

Donald Hart Shuckett
Edward J. Mock

 A DIVISION OF
AMERICAN MANAGEMENT ASSOCIATION

Figures 4-2, 4-3, 8-6, 9-1, 9-2, 9-3, 9-4, and 9-6 are copyright © 1968 by International Textbook Company. Reprinted from *Basic Financial Management: Text, Problems, and Cases*, by Edward J. Mock, Robert E. Schultz, Raymond G. Schultz, and Donald H. Shuckett, by permission of Intext Educational Publishers.

International standard book number: 0-8144-5300-7
Library of Congress catalog card number: 72-75468
First printing

Preface

A number of outstanding books on finance are now available. None of these, however, presents the strategies involved in decision making. This book explores financial strategy by discussing the tools used to make decisions, and by showing how those tools are applied to specific problems. After much experimentation and consultation, three areas were selected for coverage: treasurer strategies, controller strategies, and merger strategies. Within each area a special topic has been selected for intensive investigation. For example, within treasurer strategies, cost of capital is examined and strategies are developed for its optimum use.

We have simplified the approach to the presentation of these tools and their application by breaking down the components into their fundamentals and developing the more complex theories from these bases. This book also introduces new tools, which the financial manager will find both practical and necessary if he is to compete successfully with business rivals. These tools apply to every size and kind of business, from the small company to the large corporation.

For the reader's convenience, a list of symbols and abbreviations used in the book is given on the endpapers.

The authors wish to acknowledge the valuable assistance provided by many people in areas where they have high professional expertise. Special thanks go to Wayne R. Wilson and James A. Dickson, who assisted us in formulating the materials in Chapter 14. Finally, the authors wish to acknowledge the invaluable and patient assistance of Helen Mauger, who typed the numerous drafts of the manuscript.

DONALD HART SHUCKETT
EDWARD J. MOCK

Contents

1. Organizing the Financial Function   1

PART I: *Treasurer Strategies*

2. Economic Factors   11
3. Cash Management   22
4. Cost of Capital   41
5. Dividend Policy and Stock Valuation   70
6. Treasury Stock   84
7. Convertible Bonds and Warrants   93

PART II: *Controller Strategies*

8. Financial Analysis and Return on Investment   109
9. Cost-Volume-Profit Analysis   130
10. Financial Planning and Budgeting   144
11. Capital Budgeting   165
12. Leasing   186

PART III: *Merger Strategies*

13. Legal, Tax, and Dilution Aspects of Mergers   197
14. Valuing Acquisitions   206

APPENDIX   223

INDEX   235

CHAPTER 1

Organizing the Financial Function

Financial management evaluates how funds are used and procured. In all cases it involves sound judgment combined with a logical approach to decision making. The purpose of this book is to present the tools used by financial management to make major strategic decisions.

Evaluation. Evaluation requires planning the selection of investments and managing company assets. The financial manager must have plans of fund flows, as well as asset requirements, in order to determine the fund requirements and their allocation. Comparison of actual performance with the plan is the measure of management's abilities to plan and manage.

Procurement. After deciding upon the asset requirements, funds must be raised to acquire them. The financial manager must be familiar with the various forms, instruments, and techniques of finance, and must know their cost and flexibility. The terms must be tailored to fit the short- and long-run needs of the firm, but they also must be attractive enough to induce investment by suppliers of funds. This demands awareness of current conditions in the money and capital markets and accessibility to the institutional sources of funds. In many instances, continuing relationships can be established, which will enable the firm to develop relatively permanent sources of funds. In other situations the financial manager will have to negotiate specific agreements. One financial organization for a large corporation is illustrated in Figure 1-1.

From the example of a large corporation, the financial organization can be generalized down to the medium-size and smaller company. In very small companies, the finance, production, and marketing functions are all concentrated in one man. A medium-size company may have the financial organization shown in Figure 1-2. A small firm may have the financial organization shown in Figure 1-3.

Needless to say, certain of the responsibilities shown on the organization charts depend a great deal on the degree of decentralization. Figures 1-1, 1-2, and 1-3 picture a centralized finance function. With decentralization two changes occur. First, financial functions are set up in each of the decentralized profit centers. Normally, their direct responsibility is to the profit center, with only indirect responsibility to the corporate finance function. Second, certain responsibilities are delegated to the decentralized function, such as credit and collections, general accounting, and cost accounting. The actual organization of the finance function depends to a great degree on size and decentralization.

DEVELOPMENT OF FINANCIAL MANAGEMENT

Financial management has undergone considerable change in recent years. The traditional approach emphasized the procurement of external funds, with little attention given to their allocation. Over the past few decades there has been a major shift in emphasis from the raising of funds to the management of assets because of the growing demand of investors for soundly managed companies. This has resulted in the development of various analytical techniques to judge management's effectiveness.

The traditional role of the treasurer was to maintain contact with external suppliers of funds. As this need declined because of the growing incidence of mature firms able to finance their growth internally, the treasury function received less top-management attention. His secondary function was to serve as custodian of liquid resources that, although of increasing importance, did not require continuous high-level management. Thus, the keystone of the treasurer's function developed into an episodic rather than a continuing function.

While the treasurer raises capital, the controller continually evaluates its utilization. The techniques of the controller have become more and more important, since he has assumed responsibility for an information system necessary to evaluate performance and plan future strategies. However, his burden has been lightened considerably by the computer, which has transformed the job of record keeping from a burdensome task to one that can be performed quickly and with precision. Therefore, the controller can now devote his time to the decision aspects of finance.

FIGURE 1–1   Organization of the finance function in a large corporation.

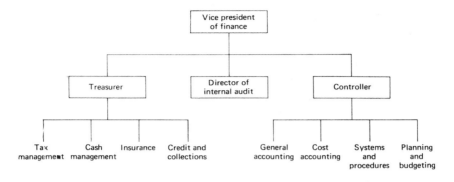

FIGURE 1–2   Organization of the finance function in a medium-size corporation.

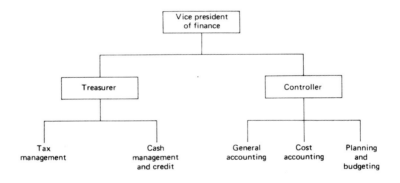

FIGURE 1–3   Organization of the finance function in a small corporation.

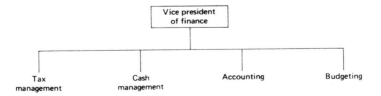

The functional areas of business operations are production, marketing, and finance. Of these, production and marketing are the most critical, for they determine the firm's very existence—its ability to sell competitively priced goods at a profit. Finance integrates these two functions. The relationship of the finance function to the overall corporate structure is depicted in Figure 1-4, which shows a highly centralized organization structure that fits a small company. If the structure is decentralized on a product line basis, the structure may look like Figure 1-5, with the dashed lines representing indirect authority. In large corporations, more staff-type functions are normally added, but the structure is basically similar to that of Figures 1-4 and 1-5, depending upon the degree of decentralization.

The core of financial policy is to maximize earnings over the long run and optimize them in the short run. This requires evaluation of the monetary advantages of alternative fund uses, as well as the allocation of resources after considering production and marketing interrelationships. For example, the decision to purchase a capital asset is based on expected net returns from its use. This cannot be determined by the financial manager alone and he must consult other disciplines such as marketing,

FIGURE 1-4   Organization of centralized small company.

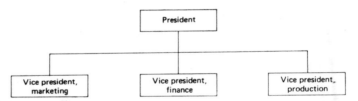

FIGURE 1-5   Organization of decentralized medium-size company.

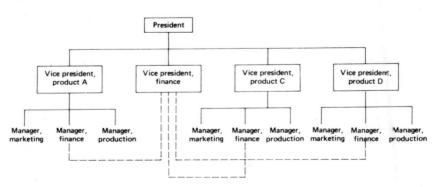

production, accounting, engineering, personnel, and research and development. Since the financial decision cuts across functional boundaries, the financial manager works as a part of the total management team.

CRITICAL FINANCIAL DECISIONS

What problems does the financial manager face? We start with four:

1. What expenditures should the firm make?
2. What volume of funds should the firm commit?
3. How should the required funds be financed?
4. How can the firm maximize its profits from existing and proposed commitments?

The decision-making approach, illustrated in Figure 1-6, considers business as an action system. The firm makes a series of strategic decisions that are determined by the company's objectives. This is the core which gives the firm its purpose. Determination of how funds will be used depends upon matching their projected return with their cost. The unifying principle of the use of funds is the expected return; and of the source of funds, the concept of comparative cost. These two concepts are

FIGURE 1–6   Decision-making approach to finance.

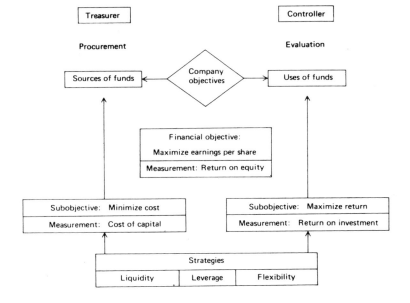

related because the overriding objective of financial management is to maximize profits by maximizing return and minimizing cost.

It is now possible to become more precise in defining the broad financial objectives of the firm. For example, it is reasonable for the firm to attempt to gear operations to the accomplishment of specific use strategies. The use strategy might be growth in sales of 10 percent per year, growth in earnings per share of 15 percent per year, or return on investment of 15 percent. The firm may also have an earnings utilization strategy for retention and reinvestment or acquisition of its own common stock.

The three basic areas of specific source strategies are liquidity (for example, the current ratio should not be less than 2:1), leverage (debt/equity ratio should be 0.9:1), and flexibility (all bonds issued should have call provisions; assets should be leased rather than owned).

At best, illiquidity will prevent a firm from taking advantage of certain opportunities. At worst, it could cause reorganization or bankruptcy. Excess liquidity, on the other hand, can reduce return on investment. The financial manager must compromise in his approaches to liquidity and profit maximization. A similar situation prevails with the capital-structure risks involved in leverage. Long-term debt financing can usually be carried out with a lower cost of funds than alternative types of financing. However, long-term debt incurs fixed charges for interest and possible sinking-fund payments so that the firm is much more vulnerable to failure if future earnings decline or fluctuate.

Another strategy may be to achieve as much flexibility as possible in both raising and using funds. Future flexibility may be provided by devices such as convertible features, call provisions, or contingent (income bonds) charges, by the use of conversion and option rights, and by flexible sinking-fund payments. However, many of these provisions—for example, conversion and option rights—carry with them the risk of diluting common-stock interests at a later date. Others, such as contingent charges, might afford the financial manager some flexibility, but will cost more. A flexible dividend policy may be desirable to handle cash-flow problems, but the market standing of the firm's common stock may suffer. Thus, although financial flexibility is desirable in practice, it carries certain risks and costs.

FINANCIAL OBJECTIVES

Figure 1-6 illustrates the formulation of rational decisions on the optional source and use of funds. This implies two major decisions: financing and investment.

Cost of capital. Cost of capital is the rate that must be paid to obtain funds for a company's operations. It must not exceed the return to be earned from the use of the funds; at a minimum it must equal the return on the investment being made. It is the cutoff point for investments. There are many sources of capital, from trade credit to bank debt to bonds to stock. Each of these sources has an independent cost, but the total cost is interdependent. The use of any one source of funds changes the conditions and the cost under which other sources of funds can be used, so that the cost of capital varies with the amounts and kinds of funds passed by a firm. Initially, the more debt, the lower the cost and the higher the leverage.

Return on investment. Return on investment can be measured in two ways: as a return on a firm's asset investment base (ROI) or as a return on the stockholders' investment (or net book value r). ROI is the best measure of management's past performance in handling the assets entrusted to it. It measures the profit the company is able to generate for each dollar invested in its assets. Past performance is the basis for analyzing future performance. ROI analysis, when combined with projected future investments, assists in selecting the best alternative in a capital-rationed environment.

Return on equity, r, is the single most important measure in finance because it measures the success of the firm in meeting its primary objective of maximizing shareholders' wealth. In other words, it measures how well the stockholders' money has been managed. There are two major ways in which it can be improved—by maximizing ROI or improving the capital structure of the firm.

Integrating example. A simple example illustrates the meaning of a more efficient capital structure. Assume firms ABC and XYZ have the income statements and capital structures shown in Table 1-1.

Note in Table 1-1 that the interest expense on the $200,000 debt changes the ROI for firm XYZ from 10 to 8.8 percent, but lesser use of ownership funds in XYZ meant a sharply higher r. In effect, firm XYZ borrowed at 5 percent ($10,000 interest divided by $200,000), or $2\frac{1}{2}$ percent after taxes, whereas it was able to earn 20 percent before interest and taxes on assets ($80,000 divided by $400,000) and 8.75 percent after interest and taxes.

This example points up the fact that as long as after-tax interest costs are less than the rate of return on assets, the rate of return r on the owners' investment can be increased by increasing the proportion of borrowed money to ownership funds. Or, if assets can be made to earn more than the cost of borrowed money, financing through debt is profitable to the owners.

TABLE 1-1   Examples of capital structure.

	Firm ABC	Firm XYZ
INCOME		
Sales	$1,000,000	$1,000,000
Earnings before interest and taxes	80,000	80,000
Interest	—	10,000
Earnings before taxes	$ 80,000	$ 70,000
Taxes (50%)	40,000	35,000
Earnings after taxes	$ 40,000	$ 35,000
CAPITAL STRUCTURE		
Total debt	—	$ 200,000
Owners' investment	$ 400,000	200,000
Total assets	$ 400,000	3 400,000
Return on investment	10%	8.8%
Return on equity	10%	17.5%

However, an infusion of debt increases not only leverage but also risk. If the cost of taking on additional debt (marginal cost) exceeds the average cost of capital, the firm is in danger of going beyond the optimal capital-leveraged structure. The marginal cost of capital is the change in ROI with varying debt.

PART I
Treasurer
Strategies

CHAPTER 2

Economic
Factors

The American businessman, politician, and consumer have witnessed an acceleration in the inflationary trend of the economy, and it is unlikely that government 'or consumer spending will dramatically change in the near future. Since this accelerating inflationary trend is of prime importance to the financial executive, this chapter presents some techniques for analyzing the state of the economy and for anticipating inflation, recession, and interest costs. Because inflation has been and will continue to be the most pervasive economic force, we examine the importance of net financial position during inflation as a criterion of financial policy.

BUSINESS CYCLE INDICATORS

Management has tools available that indicate turning points in the business cycle. Since these indicators are generally accepted, their movements assure their own fulfillment. There are also indicators that anticipate interest-rate fluctuations.

A company's susceptibility to business cycles depends upon its nature. Companies producing postponable purchases (durables) are less stable than those producing necessities (nondurables). Consumer-oriented companies are more stable than industrially oriented enterprises. A change in consumer demand can bring about a greater than proportionate change in business investment because of the acceleration principle.

Acceleration Principle

One of the tools management uses as an indicator of increased investment activity is the acceleration principle. In effect, the principle operates in the following manner:

> So long as substantial excess industrial capacity exists, businessmen will be slow to invest in new plant and equipment. However, as the gap between capacity and output narrows, a dramatic response in investment activity becomes likely. A sort of "flash point" is approached, in other words, at which something like an investment explosion takes place.
>
> This interpretation of investment behavior rests on an assumption, seemingly reasonable, that the typical business firm tries to maintain a fixed relation between its capital equipment and what it regards as the normal demand for its products. Unless it judges demand to be heading for a permanently higher level, the firm is likely to confine new investment to meeting replacement needs. When the firm's managers become convinced, however, that a new and lasting element of demand for their products is emerging, they will step up their investment outlays so as to assure the maintenance of the desired capital output ratio.
>
> The results that this turn of events can produce are evident from a simple hypothetical example. A firm that has been using 100 units of machinery may have been replacing ten units a year (reflecting, say, an average machine life of ten years). If it should decide at some point that a permanent increase of 5 percent in product demand is coming, it would then need 105 units to carry on its operations. Its total demand for new equipment in the single year in which the reassessment of prospects occurred would jump from the pattern of ten units per year to fifteen per year, an increase of 50 percent.
>
> When the theoretical "flash point" is reached in any given enterprise, the percentage change in investment demand can thus be far greater than the change in underlying product demand.[1]

In booms, business expenditures for fixed capital will jump, but in recessions the converse is true.

The Leading Business-Cycle Indicators

Eight indicators predominate in signaling when the economy is on the verge of changing direction. All revolve around companies' future

---

[1] "The Theory Behind the Tax Cut," *The Morgan Guaranty Survey,* January 1964. Reprinted with permission from *The Morgan Guaranty Survey,* p. 5.

expectations, but only the first six reflect investment commitments. These leading indicators are:

1. Number of new incorporations
2. Manufacturers' new orders for durable goods
3. Industrial-stock prices
4. Wholesale prices of basic commodities
5. Commercial and industrial-construction contracts (floor space)
6. Residential-construction contracts (floor space)
7. Average workweek, manufacturing
8. Business failure liabilities

New businesses are incorporated and established concerns build new buildings or order new equipment because they think they can continue to make profits and avoid an expected price rise. Investors in corporate stock expect improved earnings, and home builders become active when they expect a strong market for housing. On the other hand, fewer new companies are incorporated, fewer current companies invest in plant, equipment, or inventories, and fewer persons buy corporate stock or build new homes when the business outlook seems poor. A company's first step toward expanding or curtailing production is generally to lengthen or shorten its workweek. This is done before employees are laid off. It adds or lays off workers, usually, only when workweek adjustments have proved to be inadequate.

Before a recession there is a tendency for costs to increase and profit margins to narrow, and inventories are reduced. This drives many marginal firms out of business. Conversely, expectation of a revival produces sufficient demand to save many marginal firms.

The Coincidental Business-Cycle Indicators

The eight leaders listed above are augmented by eight coincidental indicators, which identify the turning point by statistics that measure fluctuations in broad phases of economic activity or in relation to the transporting or financing of the goods in the economy. The coincidental indicators are:

1. Production (Federal Reserve Board Index)
2. Nonagricultural employment
3. Unemployment
4. Bank debits (outside New York City)
5. Freight carloadings

6. Wholesale prices (excluding farm and food products)
7. Corporate profits
8. The gross national product

Business-Cycle Laggers

The five lagging indicators confirm the new phase of the cycle and signal a new chance for a reversal. The laggers are:

1. Personal income
2. Retail sales
3. Consumer installment debt
4. Bank interest rates on business loans
5. Manufacturers' inventories

Personal incomes (wages, salaries, and dividends) are tied directly to production and employment, but their increase or decrease lags because layoffs, wage changes, and similar adjustments do not occur until a trend is under way. Dividend reductions or deferments are postponed as long as possible.

Retail sales trail the cycle because their major determinant is personal income. Consumer installment debt lags because repayments on debts incurred during prosperity do not immediately catch up with new credit extensions when the cycle begins to decline, and may still exceed new credit extensions after the cycle has begun to rise.

Interest rates on bank loans lag because money becomes easy or tight only after a downswing or upturn is well under way. Interest rates rise in booms and fall in recessions.

Since effective demand falls below production when a contraction begins, inventories tend to rise for a time after business turns downward. And since production does not catch up immediately when demand increases, inventories decline during the beginning of an expansion. In an upturn, on the other hand, speculative buildups of inventories may override consumer demand and cause a corrective recession. This corrective recession could cause an excessive inventory decrease, which could result in a future recovery.

INFLUENCE OF MONETARY POLICY ON THE BUSINESS CYCLE

Government fiscal and monetary actions indicate business conditions. For example, if government fiscal action results in a surplus, it means that less money is being put into the economy than is being taken out. This is anti-inflationary and would slow down a boom, indicating a business downturn. On the other hand, a budget deficit stimulates the economy and indicates a business upturn. Generally, the government tries to manage its fiscal policy to maintain steady growth, and therefore fiscal policy is not always a clear indicator of business conditions.

Monetary Theories

Government monetary policy with regard to money supply is important not only for determining business turns but also for anticipating the cost of money. Official actions revolve around three basic monetary theories: interest rate, quantity, and availability of credit. The interest rate theory assumes that as interest rates increase, the demand to spend money decreases, savings increase, and the economy becomes less active. The more money and credit available, the lower the interest rates and the more active the economy becomes. The quantity and credit theories say that economic activity is independent of interest rates, but the effects on the economy are the same, since the interest rate depends on the availability of money and credit. The government's pressure on interest rates, money supply, and credit availability is against the banks, since the banks are the only financial institutions that can create credit and money.

Monetary Policy

The government controls the cost and supply of money through the Federal Reserve System, which is responsible for implementing monetary policy. This affects money supply and cost because banks must hold reserves against their deposit liabilities in the Federal Reserve bank. Banks create money through the fractional reserve system. The Federal Reserve influences monetary policy by regulating bank reserves. It does this in three ways: reserve requirements, open-market operations, and rediscounting.

Reserve requirements. If the Federal Reserve changes the reserve ratio, this changes the amount of reserves the banks must keep idle in the form of deposits with the Federal Reserve bank. An increase in the reserve requirements will reduce the money-creating ability of the banks and tend to be recessionary. The Board of Governors of the Federal Reserve System, legally, can vary reserve requirements only within the following limits:

Demand Deposits	Percent
City banks	10–22
Country banks	7–14
Time deposits (all banks)	3– 6

Open-market operations. Open-market operations affect not only reserve requirements and money supply but also interest rates. Open-market operations are conducted in the money market by buying or selling Treasury bills. If the Federal Reserve buys Treasury bills, it will tend to bid up the price and lower the interest rate. The Federal Reserve buys from the public, paying with a check drawn on itself. Once the public deposits the check in a bank, reserves are created and the banks can increase the supply of money. The opposite will occur if the Federal Reserve sells Treasury bills. An increase in the Treasury bill rate indicates a tightening in the money market.

Rediscounting. The Federal Reserve serves as a banker to the commercial banks. Banks may borrow reserves to make up reserve deficiencies, paying interest (discount rate) to the Federal Reserve. The Federal Reserve can discourage or encourage the borrowings by changing the discount rate. This affects not only the availability of credit but, since the banks will pass on discount-rate variances to their customers, the interest rate as well. An increase in the discount rate signals government pressures to slow the economy.

Indicators

All these tools for market control are not used simultaneously. Changes in the Reserve requirements or discount rates are secondary. Primary pressure is applied through open-market operations. This affects the interest rate on Treasury bills. Changes in the reserve requirements or discount rates support open-market operations. Since bank reserves are the key to monetary policy, there is a bank net-reserve position that can be used along with the rate on Treasury bills, reserve requirements, and discount rates to determine monetary policy. The greater the banks' net reserves, the less susceptible the banking system is to the Federal Reserve tools.

The banks' net reserves are excess reserves less borrowings from the Federal Reserve bank. If excess reserves exceed borrowings, the banks have positive net reserves and are free to make loans. When borrowings exceed excess reserves, the net reserves are negative and banks must begin to retrench. The higher the level of excess reserves, the greater the monetary flow; the higher the level of borrowed reserves, the greater the restraint.

It is important to note that interest rates, both long (capital market) and short terms, are related to the Treasury bill rate on the money market. If the short-term rate increases relative to the long-term rate, funds will flow to the money market from the capital market, and the selling or capital market investments will increase the yield and cost. This is particularly important if the rediscount rate changes.

INFLATION AND NET FINANCIAL POSITION

A debtor gains real wealth during inflation while a creditor loses. Business firms as debtors (monetary liabilities exceed monetary assets) would gain while creditors (monetary assets exceed monetary liabilities) would lose.

Accounts on the balance sheet can be classified between monetary and real items. Net financial position is the excess of an organization's monetary assets over its monetary liabilities, or

Monetary Assets		*Monetary Liabilities*	
Cash		Accounts and notes payable	
Marketable securities	*less*	Accruals	
Receivables		Income taxes payable	= *Net financial*
		Bonds and long-term debt	*position*
		Preferred stock	

Monetary items are fixed dollars and are not affected by price-level changes. For example, if the price level rose by 10 percent, a $1 million obligation would still be paid with $1 million cash; however, in real terms, the cash is worth only $909,090 of its former purchasing power. The remainder of the items in an organization's balance sheet are classified as real assets or liabilities. These are tangible items that maintain their real value during period-changing prices, and their monetary value fluctuates according to the price level.

Problems in Determining Monetary Items

Three basic problems exist in determining monetary items: convertibility of bonds and preferred stock, investment in common stock of other companies, and obtaining information.

Nonconvertible preferred stock and bonds are fixed in amount, terms of ownership, and annual payments, and therefore are classified as monetary items. If bonds or preferred stock held for investment are convertible into common stock, the investment may be a real or monetary asset, depending on the net financial position of the organization whose common stock is acquired. The effect of convertibility must consider conversion price, timing, probability of conversion, and effect of net financial position.

If marketable securities are composed of government securities, they are monetary assets. Securities representing long-term investments in another company's common stock must be more clearly defined. If the common-stock investment is in a company that is a net monetary creditor, then that company will lose during inflation and will gain during deflation. Therefore, for each common-stock investment, the amount of its possible gain or loss due to price-level changes must be determined.

Investments in the common stock of other companies, which are not held for control purposes, are important because the composition of the investment portfolio could maximize expected gain or could be used as a hedge against price-level changes. Since the composition of an investment portfolio in common stock can be a dependent decision variable, the investments should be excluded from consideration.

Many difficulties arise in obtaining appropriate information with which to determine net financial position. Use of the balance sheet can be misleading because assets are reported at historical costs. Current values should be used in determining net financial position. Also, "off balance sheet" items such as leases can affect net financial position. A lease with option to purchase may be classified either as a real or as a monetary asset. By exercising the option, the property will be purchased at the option price, thus converting the property into a real asset. If there is no option to purchase, then, since the service potential remains constant, the asset leased will be a real asset until the lease is renegotiable. A lease liability is a monetary item unless it contains some rent escalation clause.

Net Financial Position Model

To illustrate the importance of net financial position as a financial management-decision tool, an example is given in Table 2-1 to show the effect of a 10 percent price increase on the ABC Company (a net monetary debtor), the DEF Company (a net monetary creditor), and the GHI Company (a neutral, that is, a company whose monetary assets equal monetary liabilities). Table 2-1 assumes no real earnings, dividends, or change in mix of monetary items.

To summarize the results of Table 2-1, ABC Company was a net monetary debtor with monetary liabilities exceeding monetary assets, and since monetary items are fixed in amount while the value of the dollar has decreased, the real value of ABC Company's liabilities decreased more than its assets. This resulted in a gain of $1,363 in real dollars. This amount will be reflected in the income statement in monetary dollars and consequently will affect total earnings, earnings per share, and in some measure the market value of the stock.

The DEF Company was a monetary creditor, with monetary assets exceeding monetary liabilities. Since monetary items are fixed in amount

TABLE 2-1   Importance of net financial position.

	Beginning of Year	End of Year Monetary Dollars	Deflator	End of Year Real Dollars
ABC Company				
Real assets	$100,000	$110,000	1.10	$100,000
Monetary assets	5,000	5,000	1.10	4,545
	$105,000	$115,000		$104,545
Monetary liabilities	$ 20,000	$ 20,000	1.10	$ 18,182
Common equity	85,000	95,000	1.10	86,363
	$105,000	$115,000		$104,545
DEF Company				
Real assets	$ 10,000	$ 11,000	1.10	$ 10,000
Monetary assets	95,000	95,000	1.10	86,363
	$105,000	$106,000		$ 96,363
Monetary liabilities	$ 60,000	$ 60,000	1.10	$ 54,545
Common equity	45,000	46,000	1.10	41,818
	$105,000	$106,000		$ 96,363
GHI Company				
Real assets	$ 45,000	$ 49,500	1.10	$ 45,000
Monetary assets	60,000	60,000	1.10	54,545
	$105,000	$109,500		$ 99,545
Monetary liabilities	$ 60,000	$ 60,000	1.10	$ 54,545
Common equity	45,000	49,500	1.10	45,000
	$105,000	$109,500		$ 99,545

while the value of the dollar has decreased, the real value of the DEF Company's assets decreased more than its liabilities. This resulted in a loss of $3,182 in real dollars for DEF Company. This also will be reflected in monetary dollars in the income statement, earnings per share, and possibly in the market price of common stock.

Finally, GHI Company was neutral, and since monetary assets equal monetary liabilities, a decrease in the value of the dollar decreases the real value of the liabilities. Thus, the neutral firm has no change in total real value due to price-level changes.

The summaries of these three financial positions are tabulated below, where loss in real dollars is indicated by parentheses.

	ABC	DEF	GHI
Equity at end of year (monetary value)	$95,000	$46,000	$49,500
Equity at end of year (real value)	$86,363	$41,818	$45,000
Equity at beginning of year	85,000	45,000	45,000
Net gain or (loss) in real dollars	$ 1,363	($ 3,182)	$ 0

A decline of 10 percent in price levels will have the reverse effect, that is, the net monetary debtor will lose in real value, as the following tabulation shows.

	ABC	DEF	GHI
Equity at end of year (monetary value)	$95,000	$46,000	$45,000
Equity at end of year (real value)	$85,000	$45,000	$45,000
Equity at beginning of year	86,363	41,818	45,000
Net gain or (loss) in real dollars	($ 1,363)	$ 3,182	$ 0

Market Valuation

The preceding illustration employed book values. The effect of the changes in price level will influence earnings per share. Assuming no change in the *price* to *earnings* ratio, it follows that the gain in real value should be reflected in the market value of the stock.

Empirical studies[2] have produced overwhelming evidence that net financial position is important to market valuation of stock. These studies indicated that market value of net monetary debtor's stock gained during inflation and lost during deflation relative to stock of net monetary creditors. In stable periods, there were virtually no differences. These tests were affected by earnings and changes in net financial position within a firm, but the variation attributed to the net financial position was statistically significant. During the period 1940 to 1952, when the wholesale price index increased by 218.6 percent, net debtors' stock values increased by 593 percent, in contrast to 446 percent for net creditors. In real terms, the increases were 172 and 104 percent, respectively, or a net gain of approximately 66 percent by debtors over that of creditors. Over a 12-year period, this 66 percent represents a gain of 4.5 percent compounded annually, whereas the wholesale price index increased by 6.5 percent compounded annually. These results were constant during periods of inflation and deflation, and were consistent among companies listed on different stock exchanges and within different industries.

The results of the studies imply that there is a bias in interest rates and that they do not properly reflect anticipated price-level changes. If a 6 percent increase is anticipated in the price level, the "rational" lender would not lend money at 6 percent because he would merely break even in real terms. Examination of Figure 2-1 indicates that interest rates do not properly anticipate inflation. If a firm becomes a net debtor during anticipated stable prices, it may have borrowed money at 4 percent; if, at

[2] Armen A. Alchian and Reuben A. Kessel, "Redistribution of Wealth Through Inflation," *Science* (September 4, 1959), pp. 535–39.

FIGURE 2–1   Price-earnings ratios, interest rates, and inflation.

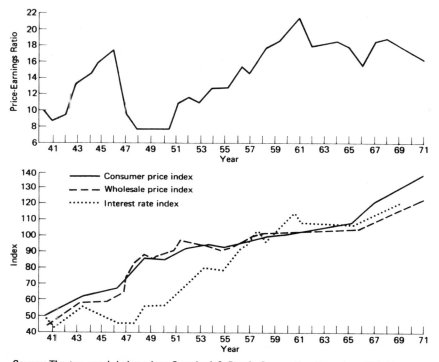

Source: The top graph is based on Standard & Poor's Corporation Report on 500 common stocks, 1971. The bottom graph is based on statistics in "Annual Report of the Council of Economic Advisers," *Economic Report of the President* (Washington, D.C.: U.S. Government Printing Office, 1971), Tables C-45, C-48, C-57; pp. 249, 252, 264. Figures have been converted from a 1967 base to a 1957–1959 base.

a later date, a 2 percent rise in the price level is anticipated, the interest rate should—but will not—rise to yield the same real value to the lender, assuming no bias in interest rates. The net debt position, then, at the time of change in the anticipated price level, would not be affected by the change. However, regardless of any interest bias, there will always be some effect, since all monetary items (for example, accruals, some accounts payable, and federal income taxes) are not interest bearing.

CHAPTER 3

Cash Management

Cash management involves the weighing of two priorities: (1) the firm's need for cash balances, and (2) the risk and cost of inadequate or excessive cash balances. Firms determine the amount of funds available for investment through cash budgeting, an integral part of financial planning. However, a firm's cash flow cannot always be forecast with complete accuracy. The greater the variation in the timing of cash flows, the greater the cash or near-cash investments a firm has to maintain. The priorities for weighing the need against the cost of excessive or inadequate cash has to be made by management. This chapter describes some of the tools available to conserve cash by increasing velocity; it also discusses investment alternatives and suggests a method for investing excess funds.

INCREASING VELOCITY

Increasing cash velocity allows companies to reduce the amount required to support a given level of operations. This not only allows each dollar to earn more income through profitable investment, but also reduces the company's dependence on outside sources of financing. The financial manager who has acquired the ability to "stretch" the working ability of each dollar need not rely on external sources in periods of tight money, when interest rates are increasing and banks are becoming more selective in granting loans. Figure 3-1 illustrates the methods of increasing velocity.

The velocity of corporate funds may be increased by accelerating cash inflows and delaying cash outflows. The two most common methods of increasing the availability of receipts are the use of lockboxes and the establishment of a system of concentration banks.

The Lockbox Technique

The purpose of the lockbox is to eliminate the time delays caused by long-distance mailing. This technique involves setting up a combination of post office boxes and depository accounts with one or more banks, geographically located so that remittances from customers will take no more than one day in transit. Customers mail remittances to a lockbox in the post office that services the company's regional bank. The bank collects from the box several times a day, deposits the checks, and credits the company for the amounts collected. Thereafter, depending upon the

FIGURE 3–1 Methods of increasing velocity.

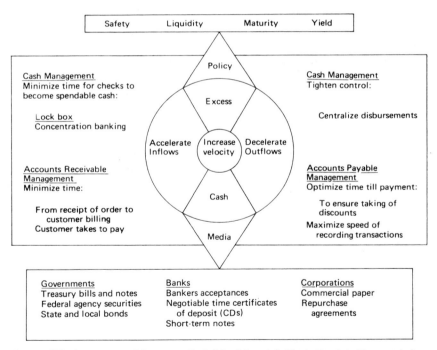

Source: "The Investment of Corporate Cash," by Edward J. Mock. Reprinted by permission of *Management Services* (September–October 1967). Copyright 1967 by the American Institute of CPAs.

arrangements with each regional lockbox bank, funds in excess of the minimum balances maintained to cover costs either are transferred automatically to the company headquarters bank or, less frequently, are drawn off by the financial manager at his discretion.

The lockbox is most useful for companies whose accounts receivable are centralized. Decentralized companies, in which local treasurers are responsible for their own credit collections and investments, cannot ordinarily use lockboxes to channel receipts to headquarters. The principal advantage of the lockbox is that funds are available from one to three days earlier than if collections had been made centrally. Faster collections may lower the need for seasonal bank credit and may also permit the earnings of additional short-term interest. Moreover, when the value of collections is sufficiently large, the use of a lockbox system can reduce company costs by using the bank's staff instead of a company's clerical force.

Despite the advantages, there are some problems in the use of the lockbox system. Notice of payments, forwarded by the regional bank, arrive at company headquarters a few days after checks have been received and deposited by the regional banks. Therefore, some of the information required for credit control is not available immediately. If customers are operating under uncertain financial circumstances, it is important to know whether or not their account status is current before any additional deliveries are made. To minimize this deficiency in the lockbox system, it may be advisable to maintain company credit men at each collection point when the volume of collections is sufficiently large to warrant immediate processing.

There may also be customer resistance to lockbox systems. They may insist on sending checks directly to company headquarters, in spite of requests that remittances be forwarded to the lockbox, in order to take advantage of their float. The use of the lockbox means that they must have bank balances to cover such remittances no later than one day after the check is mailed.

The lockbox is also expensive. There must be a sufficient volume of checks if the system is to be economically feasible, and the amounts of the individual checks must be large enough to justify the cost of processing them. One typical bank requires an average daily balance of $70 per check to cover the cost of processing. This daily balance requirement, of course, ties up otherwise usable cash. Another bank charges a minimum of 10 cents per check, plus 2 cents for clearing. Lockboxes should not be used unless a substantial number of remittances are from sources more distant than overnight mail. In addition, the amount of the average check should be large.

Concentration Banking

In concentration banking, local company units collect and deposit remittances in local banks from which the funds are transferred to the corporate headquarters banks. Concentration banking may be coupled with the lockbox system to increase velocity, or it may be used in lieu of a lockbox system. If it is combined with the lockbox system, it is used as an "automatic" mechanism to transfer cash from the local to the home office bank.

Rapid transfer of funds is accomplished through interbank wire transfer or bank drafts. Ideally, the local manager deposits daily collections and simultaneously draws a depository transfer draft in favor of the headquarters bank for the amount deposited. These funds are available the day following the receipt of the draft. Each draft has a stub that the local financial manager mails to headquarters, where it is compared with the deposit advices. Drafts are sometimes preferred to wire transfers because of this measure of control and their lower cost. However, the wire transfer of funds is faster not only because of their immediate transmission but also because they, unlike drafts, need not be cleared through the Federal Reserve System and therefore are considered collected on receipt.

One company, for example, utilizes its headquarters bank in connection with a system of automatic balances. Each area branch has its own bank account, with a working balance predetermined on the basis of its activity. Area funds are collected and deposited locally, and amounts in excess of the fixed maximum account balance are automatically transferred to the headquarters concentration bank. Similarly, if a local balance declines below a predetermined level, funds are automatically transferred from the headquarters bank to rebuild the local working balance. This company has recaptured for investment approximately $8 million that was previously spread over the country in a number of banks.

Special Techniques

Aside from the lockbox and similar collection systems, unusual techniques are sometimes employed, particularly for collection of a large single item. One such device is airmail pouch service, which is a superfast form of airmail. For example, an employee places a customer's check on a domestic flight from Chicago to the Los Angeles bank on the same day that it is received. Time-consuming postal handling from downtown to the airport is eliminated at both ends.

As another example, a messenger is sent to pick up a large check. In one case a check for nearly $25 million was to be mailed by a customer on Friday. The receiving company elected to fly a man from New York to Chicago to pick up the check personally and bring it back to New

York, where it was deposited immediately. This saving of two days' time resulted in a return, net of air fare, of approximately $6,000.

The advisability of adopting any system to accelerate cash inflows depends in part on the current dollar amount of the immobilized funds. This amount may be determined by multiplying daily receipts by the number of extra clearance days gained. By applying the investment rate of return to that amount, the opportunity cost benefits may be compared with the actual dollar cost of employing the system. The company should investigate methods of accelerating inflows, as long as

$$\left(\frac{n}{365}\right) (\text{ROI}) > XV$$

where n = number of days gained
ROI = return on investment
X = immobilized funds
V = cost of accelerating inflows

Control of Cash Outflows

The velocity of corporate funds can also be increased by controlling cash outflows. Three steps control cash outflows: deceleration of payments, centralization of disbursements, and the use of float.

Bills should be paid only as they come due. The cash temporarily conserved can be used for other purposes, such as short-term investment. Slowing down payments should not, of course, be carried to the point of losing cash discounts. One company follows a policy of never mailing a check for payment until after 3 P.M. on the day the bill is due. Alternatively, a few companies pay large sums by bank drafts made payable to the drawee on the day payment is due. With a draft, payment is not made and cash need not be in the bank until the draft is presented for acceptance, which may take an additional three days. Some companies pay vendors through small banks in remote geographic areas because these banks are not members of the Federal Reserve System. This further delays the time for a check to clear.

Centralized Disbursements

When the cash function is decentralized, controls are required to ensure that discount opportunities are not lost. The tendency of local company units to hold bills for verification of the quantity of merchandise received may result in forfeiture of the discount. Some companies avoid this by vouchering and paying bills from reliable vendors without waiting for such verification. When adjustments are necessary, they are made against future payments.

However, the primary advantage of centralization is the concentration of cash that would otherwise be frozen at the local level. This idle cash can be invested in marketable securities. Moreover, when disbursements are centralized, company headquarters can control divisional commitments. This system also forces more accurate cash budgeting by division and subsidiary controllers because divisions or subsidiaries usually operate on small working balances, either imprest funds or automatic balances, and all bills except local expenses are paid by company headquarters. A local zero-balance disbursement account can be maintained to pay local vendors. In these accounts, no running balance is maintained. All funds are held in the headquarters general account and funds are transferred to each zero-balance account as checks clear.

Float

Float, or "outstanding checks," arises from the delay between the time a check is written and the time it clears the bank. For example, a check of $10,000 drawn in New York on January 1 may not clear the FRS and reach the payee's bank in Miami, Florida, until January 5. During these four days the funds are unused, but they could become productive by investment on a day-to-day cycle.

The size of the float can be estimated by accurately predicting when checks will clear. A negative book balance can be maintained and the float invested day to day. This requires centralized management.

Compensating balances are the balances that banks ask their corporate customers to maintain in their checking accounts in return for a line of credit. The banks regard them as compensation for comparatively low interest rates. This balance is usually 20 percent of the line the bank has agreed to extend, and increases the interest cost for the line by the same percentage. The amount of funds freed for investment are available only up to the amount of the compensating balance. The cost of maintaining a compensating balance is the amount that investment earnings on these unavailable funds exceeds the interest rate on the line of credit.

INVESTMENT ALTERNATIVES

Short-Term Investments

An integrated cash management system increases the velocity of corporate funds by improving the collection process, controlling disbursements, and investing the excess cash generated. The alternative money-market (short-term debt versus long-term debt and equity in the capital market) investments utilized to invest excess cash are listed in Table 3-1.

TABLE 3-1   Principal short-term corporate investment alternatives.*

Securities	Unit Traded	Comments
Treasury bill, 91-day maturity, issued weekly.	$1,000	The most popular investment, since they combine safety with liquidity (due to the frequency and regularity of their issuance).
U.S. Treasury notes, certificates of indebtedness, and tax anticipation certificates: more than 91-day but less than 5-year maturities.	$1,000	Also popular, these are useful for companies that wish to invest to meet specific cash requirements (dividends, taxes, and capital expenditures).
Federal agency securities: offerings of five federally sponsored credit agencies (banks for cooperatives, federal land banks, federal intermediate credit banks, Federal Home Loan Banks, Federal National Mortgage Assn.) that issue their own securities and borrow directly from the public. Most corporate portfolios are restricted to 9-month to 1½-year maturities.	$1,000 to $5,000	These securities are not guaranteed by the federal government, and their yield is generally just above that of Treasury securities. However, they are very safe investments.
Public Housing Authority notes issued to finance various government land-development projects. Most corporate portfolios are restricted to one-year maturities.	$1,000 to $5,000	These securities have the double advantage of being tax exempt. The latter feature makes the effective yield to a corporation roughly double that quoted. The strong demand for these notes makes them very liquid in the secondary market.
State and local bonds: one-year and longer maturities. (A number of states will provide almost any maturity required by a corporate buyer.)	$1,000	Those rated AA and AAA are considered very safe investments. Their tax-exempt status makes them the highest-yielding security in the money market. They are sometimes used to meet specific cash requirements.
Bankers' acceptances: one-month to six-month maturities (usually three months).	Not less than $2,000	A banker's acceptance is a time draft drawn on a large bank by a trader. It becomes a negotiable instrument and can be discounted for resale to investors. It is considered very safe.
Time certificates of deposit (CDs): activity is generally restricted to prime certificates with a maximum maturity of 90 days. However, maturities of up to a year are available.	$1,000,000	The current maximum rate for certificates over $1 million is 5%. Market rates for prime certificates are often ¼% higher than rates for Treasury bills of comparable maturity.

Table 3-1 continued

Securities	Unit Traded	Comments
Finance company paper: short-term maturity, usually 90 days (a number of finance companies will provide almost any maturity required by the corporate buyer).	$5,000	These obligations of companies financing consumer appliances and automobiles are reasonably safe, but much depends upon the reputation of the issuing company. They are traded on the secondary market, and maturity dates are usually very flexible. Yield of this investment is generally high.
Commercial paper: usually four-month to six-month maturities, but sometimes as short as five days (purchasers usually intend to hold such obligations until maturity).	$5,000	Commercial paper today consists mainly of short-term, unsecured promissory notes issued by a relatively small group of highly rated companies. The yield is usually the highest of those that can be obtained from any short-term security except those which are tax exempt.

* Listed in order from lowest to highest yield.

The usual practice of companies with excess short-term cash is to invest in securities of the United States Treasury (Treasury bills and certificates of indebtedness), the short-term offerings of the five federally sponsored credit agencies (federal land banks, banks for cooperatives, federal intermediate credit banks, Federal Home Loan Banks, and the Federal National Mortgage Association), bankers acceptances, commercial paper, and state and municipal securities. Of these, Treasury bills are the most popular, not only because of their safety of principal, but also because they are traded in an active and relatively liquid market. This liquidity is due to the large amount of bills outstanding and the regularity of issue, which narrows the spread between the bid and ask prices.

The Treasury also issues tax-anticipation bills to raise funds when tax receipts are behind cash outlays. These obligations mature several days after the date on which corporate income taxes are due, and their face value (price paid plus interest) is accepted in payment of taxes. Thus, a few days' free interest is earned.

In the past few years three new forms of short-term investment that have been introduced offer flexibility as well as higher yields for the adventuresome. They are repurchase agreements, negotiable time certificates of deposit, and short-term notes of commercial banks. In the first of these, the repurchase agreement, a security dealer sells his securities to the corporate lender and simultaneously buys them back at the same price plus accrued interest. Payment is made at some future maturity date that can be tailored to the lender's needs. The agreement may be overnight with renewal possible, an open transaction that remains in effect until terminated by either of the parties, or a fixed-date agreement ordinarily covering a longer period of time.

The agreement offers the lender not only a tailored maturity but also a higher rate of return than he would earn if he had bought the short-term government obligations outright. The interest advantage derives from the spread between the maximum and minimum rates of interest that govern the price. The maximum rate is governed by the rate charged by New York banks for financing government security dealers. The minimum rate is influenced by the going rate on short-term Treasury bills.

In 1961 a new instrument, the negotiable time certificate of deposit (CD), was issued by a New York bank. The CD is a receipt given by a bank for a time deposit of money. The bank promises to return the amount deposited, plus interest, to the bearer of the certificate on the date specified. The certificate is transferable and may be traded prior to its maturity date. There is a fairly well established market in CDs, since dealers in government securities will buy certificates offered.

Although CDs are very flexible, the denominations offered are large ($1 million minimum). This is to keep the banks' cost-free demand deposits from flowing into CDs. There is also limited protection ($20,000) offered by the Federal Deposit Insurance Corporation. This restricts investment to large sums of money and makes the size and reputation of the issuing bank important criteria. Although the yield of CDs has been as much as 0.40 percent above that of Treasury bills, the discount earned on bills is exempt from state income tax, whereas interest on CDs is not.

Commercial bank short-term notes are a recent money market innovation. In 1964 a Boston bank arranged to borrow money by issuing its own unsecured notes. At the same time the First Boston Corporation agreed to make a market in these notes. Unlike CDs, these notes are not subject to Regulation Q of the Board of Governors of the Federal Reserve System, which sets a ceiling on rates of interest that banks may pay on deposits. This form of financing did not provoke the response that was expected, however, because the Federal Reserve liberalized the ceiling on rates payable on CDs in late 1964. Moreover, there is doubt about its legality in New York state.

INVESTMENT CRITERIA

With the many different types of investments available, it is not surprising that portfolios vary. In order to formulate a plan for the investment of excess cash, the financial manager must first determine the minimum amount of cash needed to meet operating requirements. This includes balances necessary to compensate banks for services and a small buffer against unexpected seasonal or cyclical requirements.

From the cash budget the company can determine how much, when, and how long excess cash will be available for investment. All three items of information are vital to the formulation of an investment plan because the financial manager must not only determine the dollar amount available for investment, but he must also select maturities. Since many of the investments are only a temporary utilization of cash earmarked for dividends, interest, federal income taxes, and large capital expenditures, financial managers attempt to match maturity with disbursement dates. This practice reduces the risk of having to liquidate a security in a technically weak market.

The criteria for the selection of investments are safety of principal, liquidity or marketability of the security, maturity, and yield. The most basic objective is ensuring the safety of principal. To accomplish this, many financial managers restrict themselves to a type of marketable investment that remains relatively stable in price. If liquidation becomes necessary, risk of capital loss is minimized. As an alternative, some portfolio managers purchase only those securities they intend to hold to maturity.

Another important criterion of safety is the financial stability of the organization issuing the security. Securities guaranteed by the U.S. government or issued by a government agency are the safest. The degree of safety of commercial paper, finance company paper, and certificates of deposit depends to a large extent on the size and reputation of the issuing corporation or bank.

Liquidity is the second most important consideration, since cash is available primarily for short-term investment. Furthermore, errors in cash budgets sometimes force financial managers to convert investments into cash on short notice.

The length of maturities selected depends upon the ultimate earmarking of the funds. Short maturities are preferable because most companies with excess cash intend to reinvest it in receivables and inventory, to make future payments with it, or to keep it as a hedge against the unexpected. However, the shorter the maturity, the lower the rate of return because of the great demand for the liquidity of short-term securities.

Some managers select a higher-yielding security with a longer maturity date coinciding with the date the cash is needed. Companies that carry a large cash cushion as a hedge against the unexpected invest a small portion in short-maturity, highly liquid securities and a greater portion in longer-maturity, higher-yielding, and more risky investments. Funds being accumulated for long-range purposes such as an expansion or acquisition program are invested in long-term securities.

Yield is fourth among the investment criteria. However, if the amount of excess cash is large and cannot be fully reinvested in the company in a short period of time, the pressure to earn a reasonable return on such funds is great. In such cases, yield is a significant criterion because of the additional yield to be gained through aggressive investment practices. For example, an increase of only one basis point (0.1 percent) can have a major impact on a corporation with excess cash of $25 million.

INVESTMENT MODEL

To evaluate a security in terms of these four criteria—safety, liquidity, maturity, and yield—a company might develop a model such as that illustrated in Table 3-2. This model is essentially a point system for ranking the securities. The points are assigned subjectively and their gradation in this model is in increments of 1; the more points, the higher the value of the security. The elements of Table 3-2 represent the following equation:

(Security factor) × (factor value) = weighted security-factor value

Each of the four investment criteria is given a subjective value of 1 to 4. These will differ for different companies and for the same company at different times. Yield, the least important criterion, is given the lowest factor value of 1. Then the principal types of money-market securities are ranked in relation to each other for each of the four criteria. Finally, the security rank is multiplied by each of its factor values to obtain a tabulation of weighted security-factor values. The total of the weighted values represents the relative strength of each security; the higher the total, the stronger the security.

The ranking of the securities depends on the current yield rates and the extent to which the securities meet other investment criteria. The length of the maturity was evaluated by giving the shorter maturities the higher value. To evaluate liquidity and safety, the considerations mentioned in the preceding section were used.

A way of comparing the total yields from portfolios of varying composition is shown in Table 3-3. In this matrix of alternative portfolios the percentage of a given investment to the whole portfolio is multiplied

TABLE 3-2 Value of securities as related to various factors.

SECURITY'S RELATION TO FACTOR

	Factor				Adjusted Yield
Security	Safety	Liquidity	Maturity	Yield	(Before Tax)
Treasury bills	7	9	7	1	5.22%
U.S. Treasury notes	6	8	1	2	5.36
Federal agency securities (FHLB)	3	6	2	4	5.55
FHA notes	5	7	4	8	6.66
State and local bonds (tax free)	4	5	3	9	7.50
Bankers' acceptances	2	2	7	5	5.65
Time certificates of deposit	2	4	6	3	5.45
90-day finance-company paper	1	1	7	6	5.88
Commercial paper	2	3	5	7	6.00

TIMES (×) VALUE OF FACTOR

Factor	Value
Safety	4
Liquidity	3
Length of maturity	2
Yield (before tax)	1

EQUALS (=) WEIGHTED SECURITY-FACTOR VALUES

	Factor					
Security	Safety	Liquidity	Maturity	Yield	Total	Rank
Treasury bills	28	27	14	1	70	1
U.S. Treasury notes	24	24	2	2	52	3
Federal agency securities	12	18	4	4	38	5
FHA notes	20	21	8	8	57	2
State and local bonds	16	15	6	9	46	4
Bankers' acceptances	8	6	14	5	33	8
Certificates of deposit	8	12	12	3	35	6
90-day finance-company paper	4	3	14	6	27	9
Commercial paper	8	9	10	7	34	7

by the applicable yield to derive the weighted yield factor for that investment medium. The weighted portfolio return for a given investment program is determined by summing the weighted yield factors. The elements of Table 3-3 represent the equations

(Composition (%) of portfolio) × (percent of yield) → weighted yield factor

$\sum$ weighted yield factor = total weighted return on portfolio

TABLE 3-3 Matrix of alternative portfolios.

Program	Percentage Composition of Portfolio								
	TB	TN	CD	FHLB	BA	CP	PHA	TE	Total
A	30%	30%	10%	10%	5%	5%	5%	5%	100%
B	25	25	10	10	10	5	10	5	100
C	20	20	10	10	10	10	10	10	100
D	20	15	10	10	10	10	15	10	100
E	15	10	5	10	10	20	15	15	100
F	10	10	10	10	10	10	20	20	100
G	10	5	5	10	10	10	25	25	100
H	5	5	5	5	10	10	30	30	100

TIMES (×) YIELD

TB (U.S. Treasury bills, 91-day maturity) = 5.22%
TN (U.S. Treasury notes) = 5.36
CD (Negotiable time certificates of deposit) = 5.45
FHLB (Federal Home Loan Bank bonds) = 5.55
BA (Bankers' acceptances) = 5.65
CP (Commercial paper) = 6.00
PHA (Public Housing Authority bonds) = 6.66
TE (Tax-exempt securities) = 7.50

YIELDS (→) WEIGHTED YIELD FACTOR

Program	TB	TN	CD	FHLB	BA	CP	PHA	TE	Total Weighted Yield on Portfolio
A	1.566%	1.608%	0.545%	0.555%	0.282%	0.3%	0.333%	0.375%	5.564%
B	1.305	1.340	0.545	0.555	0.565	0.3	0.666	0.375	5.651
C	1.044	1.072	0.545	0.555	0.565	0.6	0.666	0.750	5.797
D	1.044	0.804	0.545	0.555	0.569	0.6	0.999	0.750	5.862
E	0.783	0.536	0.272	0.555	0.565	1.2	0.999	1.125	6.035
F	0.522	0.536	0.545	0.555	0.565	0.6	1.332	1.500	6.155
G	0.522	0.268	0.272	0.555	0.565	0.6	1.665	1.875	6.322
H	0.261	0.268	0.272	0.277	0.565	0.6	1.998	2.25	6.491

Source: Adapted from Table 4 in Money Market Investments: The Risk and the Return, Morgan Guaranty Trust Company of New York, 1964, p. 56.

The eight investment programs presented in Table 3-3 demonstrate the corporate investment policies and decisions behind the percentage composition of the portfolios. Programs A and B represent conservative portfolios for a company mainly concerned with security of principal. This company maintains primary reserves in the form of Treasury bills and notes, to provide funds for unforeseen disbursements on short notice or to meet unexpected variations in operating cash requirements.

Programs C and D are still conservative, with 40 percent of the funds in Treasury bills and notes for program C and 35 percent for program D, but they strike more of a balance between short- and long-maturity investments, thus increasing the yield. A company could invest 40 percent in certificates of deposit, Federal Home Loan Bank bonds, Public Housing Authority notes, and tax-exempt securities for the primary purpose of meeting a particular predictable future cash need—for example, dividends or plant expansion. Such securities are purchased to mature on or near the date of the cash need. This avoids the liquidity risk.

The emphasis in programs E and F is on medium-term maturity dates, with 40 percent invested in bankers' acceptances, Federal Home Loan Bank bonds, and commercial paper. This portfolio carries somewhat greater risk and therefore higher returns. For program E, 30 percent of the portfolio is in Public Housing Authority bonds and tax-exempt securities, and 40 percent for program F. A company with such a portfolio usually can predict its operating cash requirements with considerable reliability.

Programs G and H are the most dynamic. They are well balanced between medium-term and long-term maturities. Moreover, they provide for a short- and medium-range safety factor in the form of Treasury bills, notes, and negotiable certificates of deposit. Primary emphasis is on Public Housing Authority and tax-exempt securities, which produce the highest yields; about 60 percent of the portfolio is invested in these securities (50 percent for program G; 60 percent for program H).

The impact of increasing the return on an investment portfolio by a fraction of a percent is clear from the following calculation: A basis point of yield has a value of $1,000 per $1 million invested each year. This means that if a company were investing $20 million annually in the money market, there would be a difference of $185,400 in interest earned each year between programs A and H. This might be sufficient to pay the salary of a good portfolio manager and his staff.

Conservative versus Dynamic Programs

Investment policies fall into two distinct categories. The first is a program that may be labeled conservative. Financial managers in companies adopting this policy restrict investments to Treasury bills, purchased with the intention of being held to maturity but possessing high marketability if the company is forced to sell. Only on rare occasions do these companies purchase prime finance-company paper. The rationale of this policy is that because the dollar amount of the excess yield is small and can be reinvested in the company rather quickly, the additional income that could be derived from a more aggressive policy is not commensurate with the time and effort required. Some companies may pursue a conservative policy to offset the risks the company has assumed in the areas of production, distribution, and new-product development. They believe that they require a larger near-cash buffer to ensure solvency. Some financial managers are conservative because they operate under outdated investment policies, formulated when short-term interest rates were low. Finally, some managers have many duties in addition to the investment of surplus cash and are unable to devote the time required for adequate portfolio management.

The second category of program is more dynamic. Financial managers allocate a greater portion of their portfolios to higher-yielding investments such as certificates of deposit, commercial paper, federal agency securities, and tax-free municipal bonds. Financial managers in this group have found that only a relatively small portion of the total portfolio may have to be converted into cash on very short notice. They purchase only enough Treasury bills to achieve the liquidity desired and concentrate on the higher-yielding securities with the intention of holding them to maturity. Portfolios in this category require constant supervision, and the companies have staffs of money-market experts and portfolio traders.

Organizations that adopt higher-yielding investments concentrate on taking advantage of yield differences among maturities as well as among the various types of securities. They further increase yield by bidding directly on new issues of Treasury bills, riding the yield curve, playing the interest cycle, and utilizing repurchase agreements. For all their complexity, these trading techniques and the high-yielding securities they involve carry little additional risk. Thus, a company would be forgoing profits if it failed to hire a competent portfolio manager (at, say, $20,000 per year) who could increase profits by as little as $50,000 per year (which is a mere 0.05 percent on a $10 million portfolio).

Riding the yield curve means buying long-term maturities and selling them at a date nearer to maturity when the price rises and the yield rate is less. When the long-term rates are high, but are expected to decline, investors will favor long-term securities to guarantee a higher rate of return. At such times, long-term rates may fall below the short-term

FIGURE 3–2   Effect of shifting from long-term to short-term interest rates.

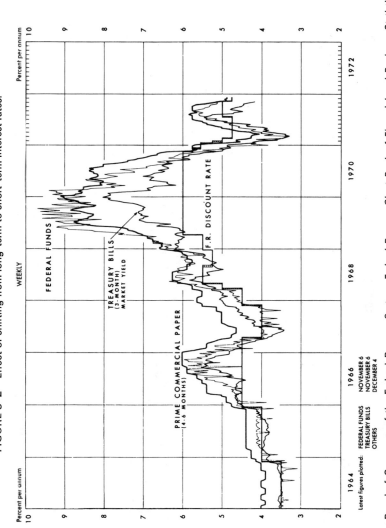

Source: Board of Governors of the Federal Reserve System, *Federal Reserve Chart Book of Financial and Business Statistics* (Washington, D.C.: U.S. Government Printing Office, December 1971). p. 24.

FIGURE 3–3 Yields on U.S. government securities (fully taxable issues).

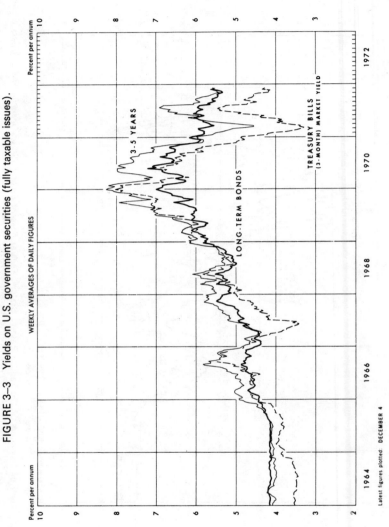

Source: Board of Governors of the Federal Reserve System, *Federal Reserve Chart Book of Financial and Business Statistics* (Washington, D.C.: U.S. Government Printing Office, December 1971), p. 25.

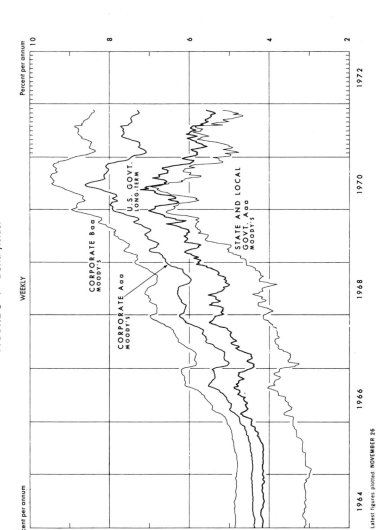

FIGURE 3–4 Bond yields.

Source: Board of Governors of the Federal Reserve System, *Federal Reserve Chart Book of Financial and Business Statistics* (Washington, D.C.: U.S. Government Printing Office, December 1971), p. 28.

rates. In this situation, successful portfolio management involves playing the interest cycle.

Playing the interest cycle involves shifting from long-term into short-term obligations when interest rates are low and prices high, on the assumption that sooner or later the rates will rise again. Interest-rate fluctuations are shown in Figures 3-2, 3-3, and 3-4. The financial manager protects his portfolio against the subsequent fall in prices because his short-term paper will mature at par. Then, of course, as rates rise, the financial manager moves into longer-term investments and holds them to the point where he judges rates to be at their high and prices at their low. This technique, however, carries with it a risk of loss. Care must be taken not to buy more long-term paper than can be held to maturity if interest rates do not perform as anticipated.

CHAPTER 4

Cost
of Capital

To make meaningful investment decisions, a firm must consider the cost of capital. This is the return that must be paid on all types of securities to induce investors to supply their resources to the firm. The cost, then, is the yield on debt, dividends on preferred stock, and anticipated earnings on common stock.

Capital consists of those items making up the financial structure of the firm, including long-term debt, capital stock, and surplus. However, there is no strict technical classification to determine the items included; rather, the nature of the business is the selective criterion for identifying the components of the capital base. For example, although bank credit is technically short term, practically it may be a supplement to long-term financing and be treated as part of capital.

The cost of capital is closely related to the breakeven point. The breakeven point relates to operating costs, while the optimum cost of capital is the financial breakeven point. This concept is also related to return on equity and to capital budgeting. The interrelationship is shown in Figure 4-1.

THE CONCEPT

The cost of capital is a tool to maximize wealth. It is the minimum rate of return required to maximize the net present worth of the owners. The price paid to capital suppliers must not exceed the returns to be received for capital utilization.

FIGURE 4–1   Interrelationship of cost of capital and other decision tools.

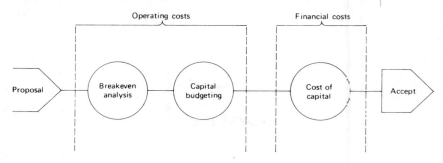

The cost of capital is the hurdle rate that must be cleared if capital is to be invested. We have assumed that the risks of the proposed capital projects are not only equal but are also at a level that would not change the capital suppliers' evaluation of the company's risk posture. Cost of capital is also an effective tool to plan the various components of the capital structure. At a given point in time, there is likely to be a specific capital structure that is better than any other, in terms of the lowest cost of capital.

Marginal Cost of Capital

We say a "given point in time" because there is not just one cost of capital but a series of higher and higher costs, since funds must be competitively lured away from other users. Marginal cost of capital initially decreases because lower-cost debt is used. After a certain point, however, marginal cost increases because an increasing *debt* to *equity* ratio increases the risk to debtors, raising the returns they will demand.

Some companies are not so fortunate as others because they are confronted with a declining product demand or a retarded development program. Their marginal-cost curve may intersect the marginal-revenue curve before internally generated funds are fully utilized (Figure 4-2). These firms must consider disinvestment by stock repurchase, dividend payments, or debt retirement.

On the other hand, some firms face an increasing product demand so that internally generated funds become exhausted before the marginal-cost curve intersects the marginal-revenue curve. They must raise external capital for additional investment. These more fortunate firms are dynamic in nature (Figure 4-3). Companies of this type are examined in Table 4-1.

The basic decision rule is that no capital project should be undertaken unless its expected discounted cash-flow rate of return (computed from anticipated cash outlays and inflows) exceeds the anticipated cost of

FIGURE 4–2   Capital pool of declining earnings company.

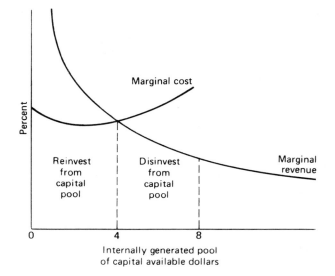

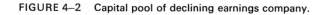

FIGURE 4–3   Capital pool of dynamic earnings company.

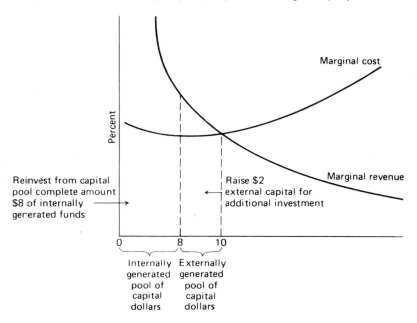

TABLE 4-1   Selected growth stocks (annual compounded per share growth rate; 10 years, 1960–1970).

Company	Percent
Xerox	47.3
Colt Industries	39.3
American Petrofina	32.0
Loew's Theatres	29.9
Gulf & Western Inc.	28.7
Pabst Brewing	26.2
Getty Oil	23.7
National Can	21.2
Polaroid	20.9
Avon	19.1
IBM	18.8
Briston Myers	16.9
Magnavox	13.0

Source: Reprinted from the 1971 *Fortune* Directory by permission.

capital by some factor; alternatively, the present value of the expected stream of net incremental cash inflows generated must be greater than the present value of the anticipated net cash outlays demanded by the investment, when both inflows and outlays are discounted at the cost of capital. Both decision rules yield the same result as far as the acceptance or rejection of investment decisions is concerned.

Marginal revenue can be shifted upward if the investment opportunities available to the firm represent opportunities for a greater rate of return. This is possible through new-product development or by acquiring or merging with companies offering new products or a greater rate of return. Marginal cost can be shifted downward if the cost of capital is decreased by changes in the capital structure.

COMPUTING THE COST OF THE VARIOUS SOURCES OF CAPITAL

We are interested in the after-tax cost of the individual sources of capital because the cost of capital will be compared with the after-tax rate of return or, alternatively, used when calculating the after-tax profitability index. Taxes are a cost of doing business and must be considered in measuring cost of capital.

Cost of Borrowed Capital

Calculating the explicit cost of most borrowed capital is a relatively simple task, since the terms are fixed by contract and are not generally subject to changes.

Short-term debt: trade discounts. Under normal conditions there is no explicit interest cost for accounts payable (trade credit). This cost is hidden in the price of the purchased materials.

However, the cost of a lost cash discount can be very expensive. If discounts are consistently missed, the explicit cost of accounts payable is computed by matching the discounts missed against the average amount of accounts payable outstanding during the year. For example, if discounts in the amount of $5,000 were missed and accounts payable averaged $20,000 for the year, the pretax cost would be 25 percent, or 12.5 percent after tax.

The cost of trade credit is $i(365/n)$, where i is the stated percent and n the additional days money is used. For example, if terms were 2/10, net 30, where a 2 percent discount was offered if paid in 10 days and the net amount was due in 30 days, the cost would be $0.02(365/20) = 36.5$ percent.

If payment were slowed down, the cost would drop. For example, if payment were made on the sixtieth day, cost would be 14.6 percent; if on the ninetieth day, 9.1 percent. This may, however, seriously impair a company's credit rating and the logistical support of production.

Short-term debt: bank loans. Banks offer various terms on their loans. One of the most common is *compensating balances.* The true cost is the stated interest rate adjusted by the compensating balance that must be kept idle. For example, if the rate of the loan is 8 percent and a 20 percent compensating balance has to be maintained, the true interest cost is

$$\frac{Xi}{\text{NCI}}$$

where X = amount to borrow
i = annual interest rate
NCI = proceeds

For example, if a company wished to borrow $500,000 at 8 percent but had to maintain a 20 percent compensating balance ($X - 0.2X = $500,000$), the amount borrowed would have to be $625,000 and the true interest cost would be

$$\frac{(\$625,000)(0.08)}{\$500,000} = 10.0\%$$

The cost of a compensating balance can be reduced by *link financing.* If a third party makes a deposit for the borrower (usually in the form of a certificate of deposit), the balance requirement is covered. The borrower pays the depositor, but pays at a rate less than the differential between the stated rate and true rate of interest.

Banks also may discount a loan by taking the interest off the loan immediately. If a bank offers $500,000 at 8 percent discount for one year, the true interest rate is

$$\left(\frac{I}{\text{NCI}}\right)\left(\frac{365}{n}\right) = \frac{\$40,000}{\$460,000} = 8.7\%$$

where I = interest cost in dollars
$\quad$ NCI = proceeds
$\qquad n$ = number of days loan is outstanding

There are two types of bank loans, unsecured and secured. Unsecured loans are either a line of credit or revolving credit. With a line of credit, the agreement is unwritten as far as the amount and time are concerned. The interest rate is not fixed. To eliminate the uncertainty of interest rate fluctuations, some companies would rather have revolving credit, where the interest rate and time are formalized. However, the bank must be paid a commitment fee for tying up a certain amount of capital, based upon the difference between the amount available and the amount utilized.

Loans may also be secured by accounts receivable and/or inventory. The costs vary with the terms; however, it is important to note that the amount loaned is usually about 75 percent of the face value of the accounts receivable and about 65 percent of the value of the inventory.

Short-term debt: notes payable. Short-term notes payable to commercial banks and other lenders have a stated interest rate. The dollar cost is a function of the interest rate and the time period of the borrowing. To measure cost, the interest paid must be matched against the net proceeds received.

For example, assume we issue a 5 percent note for $100,000 discounted to $95,000 payable in one year. The true rate of interest before taxes is 5.26 percent:

$$\frac{\text{Interest}}{\text{Net proceeds}} = \frac{\$5,000}{\$95,000} = 5.3\%$$

However, since interest is a deductible expense in computing federal income tax, each interest dollar reduces our tax bill by 50 cents $(1 - t = \$1 - \$0.50)$—assuming a 50 percent corporate tax rate—and only 50 percent of the interest paid constitutes a net cash outlay. Thus, the explicit after-tax cost of borrowing is 2.63 percent $[(1 - t)(5.26\%)]$. Table 4-2 ranks the advantages of various short-term financing alternatives; the higher the number, the more advantageous the alternative.

TABLE 4-2   Short-term financing alternatives.

Source	Cost of Funds	Risk of Payment	Flexibility	Availability	Convenience
Trade discounts					
2/10	7 (lowest)	1	7 (most)	7 (most)	7 (most)
Net 30	1	6	1	6	6
31–90	2	7 (lowest)	2	5	5
Bank loans					
unsecured	5	3	5	2	3
Bank loans secured					
A/R	4	4	4	4	2
Inventory	3	5	3	3	1
Notes payable	6	2	6	1	4

As can be seen from Table 4-2, there is a direct relationship between the cost and the flexibility of the funds. This correlation is inherent in the definition of the criteria, since those funds to which the firm has committed the least will also be those that are the most flexible. An inverse relationship can be seen between the risk of payment and the flexibility and cost of funds. Although trade credit is free during the discount period, and therefore the most flexible, it naturally carries the highest risk of payment. Once the discount period is missed, however, the cost—and therefore the flexibility—is the highest of any source; yet the risk of payment drops to its lowest point.

There is a general correlation between availability and convenience, especially in the "lower" ranges. The most available source will usually be the most convenient for the firm. However, the least available source will not be the least convenient, for if the source is unavailable to the firm, convenience cannot be measured.

Intermediate-term debt. The cost of intermediate-term debt is normally the stated interest rate, since most intermediate-term debt is executed at face value. The net cost is the stated rate adjusted to an after-tax figure. However, there is one exception and that involves installment debt.

Measuring the cost of installment debt is often confusing because of the declining outstanding loan balance. For example, assume borrowings of $10,000 repayable in equal monthly installments over a period of three years. Although the quoted rate is 6 percent, or 3 percent after tax, the lender multiplies it by the original balance of $10,000 to secure the total interest in dollars. This results in a pretax dollar interest cost of $1,800: 0.06×3 years $\times$ $10,000 = $1,800.

The formula for approximating the effective after-tax interest rate on installment contracts is

$$i = \frac{2mI}{\text{NCI}(n + 1)} (1 - t)$$

where i = effective interest rate
m = number of payments in one year
I = interest charge in dollars
NCI = proceeds
n = total number of payments

In the example, $m = 12$, $I = \$1,800$, NCI = $\$10,000$, and $n = 36$. If there are any charges involved with the credit, they should be added to the interest charges. Therefore,

$$i = \left(\frac{(2)(12)(\$1,800)}{(\$10,000)(37)} \right) (0.50) = \left(\frac{43,200}{370,000} \right) (0.50) = 5.8\%$$

The effective rate is almost double the stated rate. Throughout the period of the loan only about half the $10,000 was available because part of it was applied against installment payments; nevertheless interest was paid on $10,000.

Cost of Equity Capital

Long-term debt: bonds. The cost of bonds is a function of the net proceeds (net amount received per bond from the issue), maturity value, number of years to maturity, and cash payments for interest. If the bonds are sold below their face value, the effective yield to maturity will be greater than their coupon rate, and vice versa. However, if the bond is selling at face or par value, yield to maturity is the same as nominal yield.

For example, assume that a 20-year bond with a $1,000 face value, maturing in its entirety at the end of the 20th year and having a stated rate of interest of 6 percent, nets the firm $950. The bonds are not being retired gradually through a sinking fund and will not be called for redemption prior to maturity. The total cost of the bond to the firm is $60 per year plus a proportionate share of the $50 discount, amortized over the 20-year period, or $2.50 per year. This increases annual interest cost to $62.50. We must also determine the average amount of funds on which $62.50 is being paid. Initially, the firm received $950 in cash ($1,000 − $50 discount), but it must repay $1,000 at the end of 20 years. The average amount of funds available for use over the 20-year period is the average of $950 net proceeds and $1,000 face value (at maturity), or $975. This calculation assumes that the discount appreciates equally over the period of the loan. Dividing the average cost of borrowing, $62.50, by the average amount of funds available, $975, yields a cost of 6.4 percent before taxes. The after-tax cost can be expressed mathematically as

$$K_B = \frac{I + [(NCO - NCI)/n]}{(NCI + NCO)/2}(1 - t)$$

where K_B = yield to maturity of bonds after tax
I = annual interest in dollars
n = number of years to maturity
NCI = net proceeds per bond in dollars
NCO = maturity or face value of the bond in dollars

The preceding example can now be solved:

$$K_B = \left[\frac{\$60 + (\$1,000 - \$950)/20 \text{ years}}{(950 + \$1,000)/2}\right](0.0)$$

$$= \left(\frac{\$62.50}{\$975}\right)(0.50)$$

$$= (6.4\%)(0.50)$$

The after-tax cost is 3.2 percent.

The same procedure is followed when a bond is sold at a premium. However, the premium is deducted rather than added to the annual cash interest payments, since the borrower repays less than the initial net proceeds. The formula for this calculation is

$$K_B = \frac{I - [(NCI - NCO)/n]}{(NCI + NCO)/2}(1 - t)$$

Cost of preferred stock. Calculating the cost of preferred stock is less complicated because it normally carries a stated dividend rate, payable in perpetuity, which is not deductible for federal income tax purposes. The objective is to match the annual dividend requirement with the net proceeds to be received by the issuer. Although the preferred dividend is not a legally fixed obligation as in the case of bonds, most firms issue preferred stock with the expectation of making regular dividend payments. The formula for the cost of preferred stock is

$$K_{PS} = \frac{PSD}{P}$$

where K_{PS} = after-tax cost of preferred stock
PSD = annual cash dividend requirement per share, in dollars
P = net proceeds per preferred share, in dollars

To illustrate, assume we could receive $95 per share on an issue of preferred stock that carried an annual dividend requirement of $6 per share. The cost of preferred stock is

$$K_{PS} = \frac{\$6}{\$95} = 6.3\% \text{ after tax}$$

It is important to note that the dividend must be paid from earnings after corporate income taxes of 50 percent. Consequently, no tax adjustment is necessary.

Cost of common-stock equity. Determining the cost of debt and preferred-stock capital is relatively straightforward because of contractual agreements. However, it is difficult to estimate the cost of common-stock equity (common stock and retained earnings).

We use anticipated rather than current earnings because investors buy common stocks in terms of expectations. Therefore, earning forecasts are necessary, and these are relatively uncertain. Some firms are dynamic and seem to have brighter prospects than others. Still other firms are stable and have less optimistic prospects.

A dynamic firm is one in which the capitalization rate is less than return on equity. A stable firm is one in which the capitalization rate exceeds the return on equity. In other words, if the ratio of return on equity over cost of capital is greater than 1, we have a dynamic firm; if less than 1, we have a stable firm.

With this distinction in mind, we have another consideration. Common-stock equity is supplied through the sale of new securities (external) and the reinvestment of earnings (internal). Thus, we treat separately the external cost of common stock and the cost of retained earnings. For those firms that are not publicly traded, we use the rate of growth of earnings after taxes and preferred dividends, plus dividends per share divided by book value per share.

External equity: stable earnings firm. The cost of new equity capital assumes that these funds will yield a rate of return greater than that earned if the investment proposal had not been made; without them, there will be earnings dilution. Our purpose is to increase earnings per share. Thus, the cost of external equity funds is the capitalization rate:

$$K_{CS} = \frac{E}{P}$$

where K_{CS} = after-tax cost of common-stock equity

E = after-tax net earnings per share expected without the investment proposal being considered. (We have used present earnings because of the stable nature of the firm. For dynamic firms we shall modify this by a growth factor.)

P = net market value (net proceeds after flotation costs) of existing ownership rights

Assume that we have prospective earnings of $4 million; one million shares are outstanding, there is no debt, and stock is presently selling at $35 per share. We wish to raise $6,400,000. Therefore, the market is currently capitalizing prospective earnings at 11.4 percent ($4/$35 = 11.4 percent). Assume that underwriting and other costs associated with the sale are $3 per share, so our net proceeds will be $32 per share. We shall have to sell 200,000 new shares to raise $6,400,000 ($6,400,000/$32 = 200,000 shares). Assume that earnings will be at least $4 per share from our investment on each new share, to avoid earnings dilution and maintain the investment of existing owners. Therefore, the cost of the common stock is

$$K_{CS} = \frac{\$4}{\$32} = 12.5\% \text{ after taxes}$$

We may prove that the new project will have to earn at least its cost of capital to preserve both the earnings per share, $4, and the present market value of the stock, $35, as follows:

Total number of shares outstanding after sale of common stock	1,200,000
Times earnings per share needed to maintain a market price of $35	× $4
Total earnings required after sale of common stock	$4,800,000
Less total earnings before expansion	4,000,000
Minimum required earnings from new project	$ 800,000

$$\text{Required rate of return on new capital} = \frac{\$800,000 \text{ required earnings}}{\$6,400,000 \text{ funds raised}}$$

$$= 12.5\%$$

The difference between the market capitalization rate (E/P) (11.4 percent) and the cost of new equity K_{CS} (12.5 percent) is due to the cost of flotation.

The cost of equity capital may now be defined as the minimum rate of return that the company must earn on an investment project in order to keep the market price of its common stock from declining. If projects were selected with an expected return less than the minimum required return, market price of the stock will decline.

Internal equity: stable firm. For the stable-earnings firm, a large portion of the required financing comes from retained earnings. When a company retains earnings, it merely reinvests them for stockholders instead of paying them out, and at first it may appear that such funds are cost-free. However, there is a very definite opportunity cost involved. This cost, simply stated, is the dividend forgone by the stockholders.

By adopting an opportunity cost concept, we are assuring that the minimum cost of funds retained and reinvested in capital projects within the business is the cost of equity capital, in the absence of taxation and flotation costs. Market price of the stock is used rather than net proceeds because flotation costs are not required for retained earnings. The cost of retained earnings, in the absence of taxation, becomes

$$\hat{K}_{RE} = \frac{E}{P}$$

where $\hat{K}_{RE}$ = cost of retained earnings before shareholders' taxes
E = net earnings per share, after tax
P = current market price per share

If the financial manager is unable to find investment opportunities that provide a minimum return of $\hat{K}_{RE}$, shareholders deserve the opportunity to find stocks of similar companies of equivalent risk which can provide such a return. Rather than retain the funds and invest in projects providing a return lower than $\hat{K}_{RE}$, the financial manager should distribute the earnings to the shareholders and allow them to invest in similar companies of an equivalent-risk class which provide greater returns.

Up to this point we have assumed the absence of personal income taxes. When taxation is taken into account, the shareholders will have the use of only that portion of dividends remaining after income taxes. Therefore, the cost of retained earnings must be adjusted to compensate for the taxes a stockholder has to pay on dividends received. Accordingly, the cost of retained earnings becomes

$$K_{RE} = \frac{E(1 - MT)}{P}$$

where MT = weighted marginal tax rate of all shareholders
K_{RE} = cost of retained earnings after shareholders' taxes

For example, if the weighted marginal tax rate of all shareholders is 30 percent, the shareholders will derive the use of only 70 percent of the funds received as dividends. If $\hat{K}_{RE}$ is 11.43 percent ($4/$35), the total return the shareholders are able to achieve by investing the dividends in a company of equivalent risk is 0.7 (0.1143) = 0.08. This is determined by

$$K_{RE} = \frac{E(1 - MT)}{P}$$

$$= \frac{\$4(1 - 0.3)}{\$35} = \frac{\$2.80}{\$35} = 0.08$$

You can well imagine the difficulty in determining the weighted marginal tax rate for all shareholders and the difficulty in resolving the differences among these tax rates. The amount of usable funds from the dividend will differ greatly, depending upon the individual tax bracket. In the case of some institutional investors, the tax bracket is often zero while the personal rates range from 14 to 70 percent. As you can see, the determination of marginal tax rates is quite difficult for a large public corporation.

This difficulty has encouraged the development of a second approach for estimating the cost of retained earnings. We can conceive of a pool of capital forthcoming from operations after our fixed commitments for interest, taxes, and sinking fund payments have been met. What rate of return should we demand for capital projects that will use a portion of this pool? Clearly, we can invest in other firms; we can retire our debt or preferred stock. Finally, we can disinvest by paying dividends to common-share holders or by repurchasing their shares. In keeping with our past treatment, all alternatives (including disinvestment) would be ranked and the available funds would be allocated among the most profitable opportunities available in relation to the risk involved. We are saying that the cost of funds reinvested in capital projects within our business is the return that must be sacrificed by not using the funds for some other purpose outside our firm. This is the cost of disinvesting.

The reinvestment concept is based on the notion that the financial manager must evaluate external investment opportunities as a use of retained earnings. Accordingly, the return available on such investments is the cost of retained earnings. Therefore, the investment rate of return should approximate K_{RE}, assuming equilibrium in the market between risk and return.

The investment criterion has the principal advantages of being broader in scope and of being unaffected by personal income taxes. Moreover, it represents an economically justifiable opportunity cost that can be applied consistently. According to the investment concept, the cost of retained earnings is determined by the return the financial manager is able to obtain on the investment of such funds. The former criterion is based upon what the shareholders are able to earn on other investments adjusted for the marginal tax rate of the shareholders.

External and internal equity: dynamic firm. The dynamic-earnings firm presents a more complicated problem. Retention of earnings necessarily implies that net assets and earnings after taxes are growing. Given the *price* to *earnings* multiplier, the market value of the common stock should be rising, since capital gains will be taken in lieu of cash dividends. In this case, the stock is likely to sell at a high price relative to current earnings. The resulting *earnings* to *price* ratio will provide an unrealistic cost criterion of equity capital on which to evaluate capital-investment opportunities.

This would paradoxically establish an artificially low cost of capital for companies that are earning unusually high rates of return on their investment. If such a procedure were followed, the growth company would quickly lose its growth characteristics as it accepted projects along its investment-demand schedule at this artificially low cost of capital. Therefore, an adjustment is required, to take into account the element of dynamic growth.

Various projects are likely to have differing rates of return. Capital-demand proposals are arranged in a descending order of expected rate of return, forming a negative-sloping demand schedule for capital. The supply of capital follows the principle of increasing cost, since more funds are provided by investors or diverted from other uses only when they are offered a higher price. The result is a positive-sloping supply curve (Figure 4-4).

FIGURE 4-4 Supply of and demand for capital.

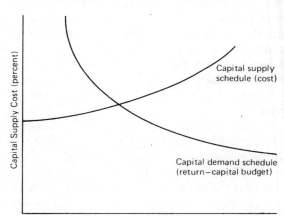

In short, the cost of capital varies with the amount of funds actually raised. Therefore, when we refer to cost of capital we are referring to various points on a positive-sloping supply schedule of capital costs, the amount of funds supplied. Likewise, the returns on the investment decrease with the amount of funds raised. In capital-budgeting theory we speak of this as riding down a negative-sloping demand curve, assuming equal risk, to the point where the marginal cost of additional capital from the positive-sloping supply curve is just covered by the marginal rate of return on the demand curve (Figure 4-4). The cost of common-equity capital is equal to the rate of return demanded by common-share holders. This return can be measured by determining expected future dividends and then comparing them with the present market value of the common stock. (See note 1 at the end of this chapter.) Therefore, the discount rate that equates future dividends for perpetuity to the market value of the stock is the cost of capital for common-equity capital. This can be solved mathematically:

$$K_{CS} = \frac{CSD}{P} + g$$

$$= \frac{E(1 - b)}{P} + br$$

where K_{CS} = cost of common equity after tax
  CSD = current dividend per share, or $E(1 - b)$
  P = current market price per share
  E = current earnings per share
  g = expected annual percentage rate of increase in future dividends, expressed as a decimal fraction. That is, $g = br$, where:

> b = proportion of earnings retained and reinvested (this must be a positive fraction smaller than unity); this is 1 minus the dividend payout ratio
> r = rate of return on the reinvestment of earnings

The cost of common equity K_{CS} is therefore equal to the current dividend yield plus the rate br at which the dividend stream is expected to grow. The growth rate depends upon the proportion of net earnings devoted to reinvestment and the rate of return achieved on these reinvestments.

Assume that a company's stock is selling at a price per share of P. It is currently earning E, $2 per share, and paying CSD, $0.50 per share in dividends. The company plans to retain and reinvest internally 0.75 of its earnings regularly. The fraction of earnings retained, b, is related to the internal investment-demand schedule discussed earlier. Assume further that dividends are paid and discounted continuously and that the reinvestment will grow continuously at a rate of $g = br$, where $g = 9$ percent. Therefore, the value of a share is

$$P = \frac{\text{CSD}}{K_{CS} - g} \quad \text{or} \quad \frac{E(1 - b)}{K_{CS} - g}$$

$$= \frac{\$0.50}{0.10 - 0.09} \quad \text{or} \quad \frac{\$2.00(1 - 0.75)}{0.10 - 0.09}$$

$$= \$50$$

This states that market value P is equal to the current dividend discounted at a rate $K_{CS} - g$. We assume that the growth rate g is smaller than the cost of common-equity capital K_{CS} or that stock price will be infinite.

This approach assumes a constant rate of growth in earnings and dividends, a constant retention rate, a constant dividend-payout rate, and a process in which investors exclusively value the expected stream of dividends. The critical assumption is that dividends per share are expected to grow continually at a compound rate of g. For K_{CS} the realistic expectations in the market must be such that dividends per share do in fact grow at rate g. The important factor is the measurement of growth in dividends per share. From an operational point of view we may be forced into estimating the future growth rate by relying on historical data. As such, we may find it necessary to rely on the earnings growth rate rather than on the dividend growth rate because in many instances the dividend-payout rate and the earnings-retention rate are not constant. Moreover, in estimating the growth rate, compound interest and/or present-value tables are helpful. Assume that a firm's dividends per share increase from $0.20 in year 1 to $1 in year 5. Employing either present-value or compound-rate tables, growth of earnings is approximately 19 percent.

Why do the stocks of companies that pay no dividends (supernormal growth firms) have positive market values? If the dividend–market value model is applicable, why would anyone pay such high prices for these stocks if they pay no current dividend? Finally, to sum up, how can this model be employed for measuring the cost of equity when a company pays no dividend or a negligible one? To use it, one would have to estimate the amount and timing of forthcoming dividends. Admittedly, this is a difficult task.

As explained earlier, the dividend–market value model encompasses both dividend and retained earnings. Retained earnings are the means to finance the future growth in earnings and dividends per share. In the valuation process, investors often view current market price as a combination of the present value of expected future dividends and a capital gain to be received at the time of sale of the security.

Investors who buy stocks that pay no current dividends expect to sell these stocks at some future date, at a price greater than they paid for them, and thereby generate a capital gain. Such investors rely not on dividend income plus capital gain but on capital gain alone. The capital gain in turn depends upon the expectation of the company to maintain the supernormal growth rate in earnings and market price. Ultimately, investors expect that at some time in the future the company will pay dividends, during normal growth, and they will receive a cash return on their investment. During the intervening period, many investors are content with the expectation of being able to sell their stock at some future date at a price greater than present market value. In the interim, the financial manager reinvests a portion of the earnings b at rate r and, hopefully, thus enhances the company's future earnings and dividends.

To illustrate the impact of a change in the growth rate on market price, consider the ABC Company with an expected future growth rate of 9 percent. Assume that dividends per share are $0.50, market price per share is $50, and earnings per share are $2. Given this information, the cost of equity capital is

$$K_{CS} = \frac{CSD}{P} + g$$

$$= \frac{\$0.50}{\$50} + 0.09$$

$$= 0.10$$

Since the company pays $0.50 per share in dividends and earns $2 per share, the retention rate is 0.75. The growth rate is 0.09 and the retention rate is 0.75, so the rate of return on reinvestment is 0.12, since $g = br$. Finally, assume that the measured costs in fact are true costs of equity capital for the company.

The point to be made is that as growth rate increases, market value will increase, and as growth rate declines, market value will decline. To illustrate, assume that dividend, risk posture of assets, and financing mix remain constant and that growth rate is revised downward by 10 percent because investors anticipate a recession. In reality, it is the reinvestment rate of return r that declines from 0.12 to 0.108 with a decline of 10 percent in the growth rate. Market price of the stock is

$$P = \frac{CSD}{K_{CS} - br}$$

$$= \frac{\$0.50}{0.10 - (0.75)(0.108)}$$

$$= \frac{\$0.50}{0.10 - 0.081}$$

$$= \frac{\$0.50}{0.019}$$

$$= \$26.32$$

Given a 10 percent decline in the growth rate (from 0.09 to 0.081), market value will decline from \$50 to \$26.32. This is a significant decline in market value. If we assumed that growth rate declined 20 percent, market price would be \$17.86. In 1968, Litton Industries (which pays no cash dividend) recorded a 10 percent decline in estimated growth rate, and market price dropped from \$104 to \$62 per share.

Consider the company that pays no dividend or a negligible one. How does one employ the dividend–market value models to measure the cost of common equity? The critical item we are concerned with is the rate of return demanded by investors on the equity-financed portion of the investments. The rate of return is what is expected to be received from the growth in earnings per share and market price in the future. We begin with past earnings per share and market price, and extrapolate these data into future earnings.

For example, if earnings per share and market price increased at the compound rate of 12 percent over the past five years, and it is probable that such a rate is representative of the future, this rate is then used to estimate K_{CS}. This approach is not precise, but estimates must be made. The important point is that we want to detect changes in the rate of growth as early as possible because of the dramatic impact on market price, a point that was demonstrated earlier. Second, we wish to estimate as accurately as possible the future growth rate of the non-dividend-paying company as viewed by investors today. There is a danger in extrapolating supernormal growth rates of the past into the future because few companies can continue to grow at these rates for long periods of time. Thus, it is a problem to estimate the duration of supernormal growth. In this case, the Soldofsky-Murphy[1] present-value tables are helpful.

Cost of Convertible Securities

The price at which the securities can be converted into common stock is known as the conversion price. For example, if a $1,000-face-value bond can be converted into eight shares of common stock, it has a conversion price of $125 per share: $1,000/8 = $125. Assume further that the present market price of the common stock is $100. The difference between the conversion price of $125 and the market price of $100, or $25, is known as the conversion premium, often expressed as a percentage. This premium is 25/100 = 25 percent. Since the convertible security is a delayed equity financing, its cost will be less than the cost of common stock, K_{CS}, because it represents the future sale of common stock at a price greater than the present market price. In our previous calculation of K_{CS} we employed a price of P. When a convertible security is involved, we should substitute the conversion price per share for P and then solve for K_{CON}, cost of the convertible. Since conversion price per share, $125, is higher than current market price, $100, the cost of a convertible security, K_{CON}, will be less than K_{CS}, the cost of common stock:

$$K_{CON} = \frac{E}{P}$$

$$= \frac{\$8}{\$125}$$

$$= 6.4\%$$

The computation of cost is not always that simple. Companies issue convertible securities with the complete expectation of conversion. However, the option to convert rests with the investor, and he will generally hold the debt or preferred-stock security because its price will increase as the price of the common stock increases. Moreover, his current yield on the convertible security will generally be higher than the yield on the common stock. Therefore, many investors will not convert unless forced to do so. Companies force conversion by insisting upon a call option on all convertible securities.

A 20 percent premium of conversion value over call price is a sufficient inducement for investors to convert. Using our previous example of a

[1] Robert M. Soldofsky and James T. Murphy, *Growth Yields on Common Stock: Theory and Tables* (Iowa City: Bureau of Business and Economic Research, University of Iowa, 1961).

conversion price of $125, and assuming a call price of $132, a 20 percent premium of conversion value over call price would result in a market price of common stock of $158.40 ($132 × 120%) per share. Such a price should assure a complete conversion because the investor would suffer a significant opportunity loss if he did not convert. If, however, the stock were called when the market price of common stock was approximately $132, many investors would choose cash at the call price, a certainty situation, rather than convert. If many select a call, the corporation would unwillingly have to redeem for cash. Moreover, the purpose of the original financing would be frustrated.

WEIGHTED COST OF CAPITAL

Now that we have measured the cost of the individual sources of funds, we must determine composite cost for our total capital structure. After determining the cost of each type of capital separately, we weigh the cost of each component of capital by the relative proportion of that type to the total amount of capital.

Two critical questions must be answered before we compute the weighted cost of capital: What are the appropriate weights to be assigned to the particular sources of funds? How do changes in the weights affect the weighted cost of capital; or, stated differently, how does the introduction of debt into the capital structure affect the combined cost of capital?

The Problem of Weights

In combining the capital segments to obtain the weighted cost of capital, we can employ either the present capital structure or an ideal optimum one. In theory we should employ the optimum capital structure because it gives us the true cost of capital. Because an optimal structure is seldom achieved and cannot be precisely determined, it is practical to use the present capital structure as the basis for estimating the weights, even though it may sometimes result in suboptimal investment decisions.

Three critical determinations must be made before weights can result in optimal investment decisions. First, present capital structure must not represent a serious deviation from other firms in the same risk class. Second, the firm must continue to raise funds over a period of time in approximately the proportions specified in the present capital structure. The raising of capital is a "lumpy" process, and strict proportions cannot be maintained at all times; therefore, true weighted cost of capital may differ slightly from that calculated and used in capital-investment decisions. The important point is that the firm's capital structure need not be optimal for the financial manager to employ the weighted cost of capital in capital-investment decisions, provided the weights take into consideration the future financing plans of the company. If these two factors are satisfied, the financial risk posture of the firm should not change, and capital investment decisions will be optimal. Third, investment decisions must not differ considerably from those comprising the existing portfolio of assets. Additions and deletions to the portfolio of assets must not alter the business-risk posture of the firm. In summary, if business and financial risk are expected to remain relatively constant, present capital structure may be employed as a basis for estimating weighted cost of capital, and weighted cost of capital will result in optimal capital-budgeting decisions.

Once weighted cost of capital has been decided upon, the next problem involves the values to be used. Should they be the book values or the present market values of the securities? Book values are based upon the actual balance sheet and represent historical costs. When the market value of any component differs from book value, weighted cost of capital will differ. When market value is greater than book value, weighted cost of capital using market-value weights will exceed weighted cost of capital using book-value weights.

Market-value weights should be employed because the financial manager is interested in the opportunity costs of his sources of funds and not in his historical costs. The cost of capital is its present acquisition cost rather than its cost at some time in the distant past. If we issue or retire securities, we do so at market values, not book values. Current costs should be used to make current decisions.

A more serious objection to the use of book values is that the market-equilibrating process is in market-value terms rather than in book-value terms. Therefore, the use of book values gives rise to an inconsistency in costing. Individual costs are measured in terms of market values and not in book values. The inconsistency becomes particularly apparent when market value is greater than book value. The important point to remember is that the objective of cost of capital is the maximization of market value and not of book value. Book-value weights can seriously understate the importance of equity capital in the capital structure. Thus, we use market values to weigh the costs of the various components in the capital structure.

Assume a yield to maturity of 5 percent on bonds, a 6 percent yield on preferred stock, and a cost of common-equity capital of 10 percent. We must make these three cost figures comparable. Cost of preferred and common is already computed at its after-tax value, but bonds require a tax adjustment. Therefore, a 5 percent yield on bonds corresponds to an after-tax debt cost of 2.5 percent.

	Market Value	×	Cost	=	Opportunity Cost
Bonds	$ 15,000		2.5%		$ 375
Preferred stock	5,000		6.0		300
Common equity	80,000		10.0		8,000
Total	$100,000				$8,675

Using the data provided in the accompanying tabulation, the capital structure and the weighted cost of capital can be computed as

$$\text{Weighted cost of capital} = \frac{\$8,675}{\$100,000} = 8.7 \text{ percent}$$

Restating the computation in equation form, we have

$$K_C = \frac{K_B(B) + K_{PS}(PS) + K_{CS}(CS)}{B + PS + CS}$$

$$= \frac{0.025(\$15,000) + 0.06(\$5,000) + 0.10(\$80,000)}{\$15,000 + \$5,000 + \$80,000}$$

$$= 0.08675 \quad \text{or } 8.675\%$$

where K_C = weighted average cost of capital after tax
K_B = after-tax cost of bonds
K_{PS} = after-tax cost of preferred stock
K_{CS} = after-tax cost of common equity
B = total dollar value of bonds
PS = total dollar value of preferred stock
CS = total dollar value of common-stock equity

The Problem of Capital Structure

A firm's optimal capital structure is the combination of equity and debt that minimizes weighted cost of capital (Figure 4-5), or identically where marginal cost (MC) of capital is equal to average cost of capital. Stated differently, a firm's optimal capital structure is the combination of inputs that will maximize the market value of the common-stock equity. One goal in determining such a structure is to maximize its value and obtain the lowest cost of capital available, consistent with the various financial constraints imposed by the external market.

FIGURE 4–5   Leverage and capitalization rates.

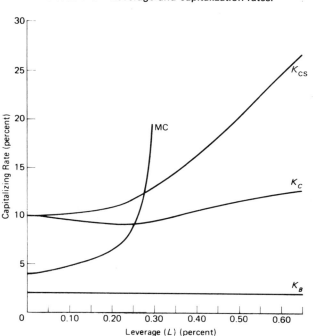

Leverage, the *debt* to *capital* ratio, is important in determining the optimal capital structure (Table 4-3). Utilizing leverage may initially result in increased earnings on equity through the assumption of additional debt risk. Cost of capital and the factors affecting it are illustrated in Figure 4-6.

However, once a firm's leverage position approaches the optimal, the average cost of capital begins to increase as both creditors and stockholders demand larger returns as compensation for greater risk. Therefore, the cost of future capital increments will have a higher cost and will thus increase K_B, K_{CS}, and K_C. When the cost of common equity increases, any increased future earnings will not be reflected in an increased market price of the common stock. See Table 4-3.

As the initial increment of debt, *B*, is introduced in the capital structure, the effects of leverage show as increases in the market value of common stock CS and total capital structure C. The average cost of capital K_C decreases from its original 10 percent. The respective trends continue until the third incremental increase in debt, after which the

TABLE 4-3 Effect of increasing leverage on cost of capital.

B	b	K_B	EBIT	I	EAI	E	K_{CS}	CS	C	L	K_C	MC_C
$ 0	0%	0%	$100	$ 0	$100.0	$ 50.0	10.0%	$500	$ 500	0.00%	10.00%	8.07%
100	2.00	2.00	140	4.0	136.0	68.0	10.5	648	748	0.13	9.36	8.55
200	2.00	2.00	180	8.0	172.0	86.0	11.0	782	982	0.20	9.18	9.05
300	2.10	2.03	220	12.2	207.8	103.9	11.5	903	1,203	0.25	9.14	20.40
400	2.25	2.08	260	16.7	243.3	121.6	13.5	901	1,301	0.31	9.99	
500	2.50	2.17	290	21.7	268.3	134.6	15.0	895	1,395	0.36	10.38	
600	2.90	2.29	310	27.5	282.5	141.2	17.0	830	1,430	0.42	10.86	
700	3.50	2.48	330	34.5	295.5	147.7	20.5	720	1,420	0.49	11.61	
800	4.25	2.68	350	43.0	307.0	153.5	25.0	614	1,414	0.57	12.42	
900	5.00	2.94	360	53.0	307.0	153.5	31.0	495	1,395	0.65	12.91	
1,000	7.50	3.40	370	68.0	302.0	151.0	39.0	387	1,387	0.72	13.34	

Notes:

B = amount of debt, at market value
b = after-tax marginal cost of debt
K_B = after-tax average cost of debt
EBIT = expected annual operating earnings, before tax and interest
I = annual interest charges
EAI = pretax expected earnings, after interest charges
E = net annual expected earnings
K_{CS} = capitalization rate (average cost of equity capital)
CS = market value of common stock
C = total capital of firm, at market value
L = leverage ($L = B/C$)
K_C = after-tax average cost of capital: $K_C = (CS/C)(K_{CS}) + (B/C)(K_B)$
MC_C = marginal cost of capital, adjusted for decline in equity position

market value of common stock decreases and average cost of capital K_C reaches its lowest point, 9.14 percent.

Optimum leverage L is approached at 0.25, with the average cost of capital declining from 9.18 to 9.14 percent. Cost of capital increases to 9.99 percent with the next incremental increase in debt.

Between leverage of 0.25 and 0.31, marginal cost of capital intersects average cost of capital K_C, representing optimum leverage. The marginal

FIGURE 4–6   Influence of growth on cost of capital.

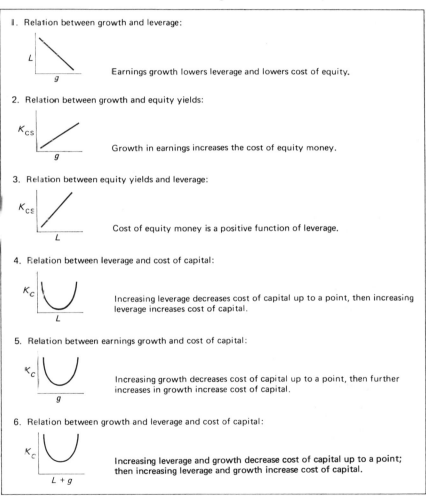

1. Relation between growth and leverage:

Earnings growth lowers leverage and lowers cost of equity.

2. Relation between growth and equity yields:

Growth in earnings increases the cost of equity money.

3. Relation between equity yields and leverage:

Cost of equity money is a positive function of leverage.

4. Relation between leverage and cost of capital:

Increasing leverage decreases cost of capital up to a point, then increasing leverage increases cost of capital.

5. Relation between earnings growth and cost of capital:

Increasing growth decreases cost of capital up to a point, then further increases in growth increase cost of capital.

6. Relation between growth and leverage and cost of capital:

Increasing leverage and growth decrease cost of capital up to a point; then increasing leverage and growth increase cost of capital.

cost of capital is the relationship between the added dollar costs and the added market value of the total outstanding securities. (See note 2 at the end of this chapter.)

Within limits, K_C can be lowered by substituting debt for equity, as indicated by the average cost of capital between leverage 0.0 and 0.25. Between leverage 0.25 and 0.31, our hypothetical firm reaches its optimal degree of leverage when marginal cost of capital and average cost of capital are equal. At optimal leverage, average cost of capital is at its minimum and market value of common-stock equity is at its maximum.

Up to this point we have introduced lower-cost debt, and the weighting process has lowered the average cost of capital and raised the market value of equity. It is interesting to note that the change in CS becomes negative at this point. If we exceed optimal leverage, marginal cost of capital rises rapidly, causing K_C to rise and CS to decline.

Between leverage 0.05 and 0.10, marginal cost of capital begins to increase, surpassing the average cost of capital in the general proximity of $L = 0.25$. At this point the value of common stock reaches its high and then decreases. This results primarily because risk-avoidance lenders influence the cost of increased debt, the external market increases debt, and the external market increases the capitalization rate of common stock.

It is difficult to judge how much a proposed debt issue or a different capital structure will change the cost of capital. This issue has not been resolved; in fact, it is probably the most debated issue in the field of finance.

TAX FACTORS FOR SMALL PRIVATELY HELD COMPANIES

The theory of the ideal capital structure, a great deal of debt and retention of earnings, is only part of the story. These types of decisions can be made for small privately held companies on a practical basis only if tax factors are considered. There are penalties for thinly capitalized corporations as well as for companies that unreasonably accumulate earnings.

Thin Capitalization

There are very definite financial advantages in using debt, such as leverage or trading on the equity. In addition, there are tax advantages such as the allowable deduction of interest on debt (dividends are not allowable) and payment on debt principal not being treated as income to the lender (distributions to common stockholders are taxable). For all these reasons, cost of debt to the corporation and lender is less than the cost of equity.

However, the Internal Revenue Service considers loans by shareholders to be capital contributions if the *debt* to *capital* ratio is excessive (generally 10–20:1) and the following conditions exist: no effort is made to collect the debt; there is no fixed maturity date; there is no fixed rate of interest; a normal, prudent outside investor would not have made such a loan; or the original capital invested to finance the business was not adequate. Note that this applies only to shareholders-creditors, that is, stockholders who are also lenders. If the courts decide that the loans were in fact capital, then interest payments will be disallowed as corporate deductions and treated as income to the shareholder-lender.

Unreasonable accumulation of earnings. Any corporation that retains its earnings in excess of $100,000 rather than distributing them to shareholders will face heavy penalties if the accumulations are unreasonable. A company with a past history of growth may retain its earnings without penalty if it can establish that this was a necessary action for its growth. The Treasury will also allow accumulation if it can be established that the accumulation is to be used for business expansion or replacement, to acquire other businesses, to provide for debt retirement, or to increase working capital.[2]

The accumulation may be treated as unreasonable if there are uncertainties or vagueness about the future needs, or if the plans are postponed.[3] They may also be treated as unreasonable if they are invested in properties or securities unrelated to the company's normal activities, or are loaned to shareholders for nonbusiness use.[4] Reasonableness, of course, depends upon individual circumstances. The criteria appear to be a high proportion of retained earnings to stock and unrepaid shareholders' loans. Although this can be avoided theoretically by declaring stock dividends, the act of capitalizing retained earnings may arouse suspicion by the Treasury. Practically, publicly held corporations are exempt from this tax. The tax is $27\frac{1}{2}$ percent on the first $100,000 of retained earnings considered to be excessive, and $38\frac{1}{2}$ percent of any amount exceeding $100,000.[5]

NOTE 1

To show this, it is convenient mathematically to assume that dividends are paid out and discounted continuously. If the initial dividend is CSD_1, and it is

[2] Internal Revenue Regulations (under the 1954 Code), 1.537–2(b).
[3] *Halby Chemical Co.* v. *U.S.* 180 Court of Claims 584—Int Rev 912,1471.
[4] Internal Revenue Regulations (under the 1954 Code), 1.537–2(c).
[5] Internal Revenue Code, 1954, Sec. 531.

expected to increase at the rate of g per year, then the dividend in year 2 (that is, CSD_2) will be

$$CSD_2 = CSD_1 E^{g_2}$$

By assumption, the current market price P_1 will be equal to the present value of this stream of expected dividends. If the (unknown) rate of discount is r, we can write

$$P_1 = \int_0^\infty CSD_2 E^{-r_2} CSD_2$$

Substituting and integrating, we have, provided $r > g$,

$$P_1 = \int_0^\infty CSD_1 E^2(g - r)CSD_2 = \frac{CSD_1}{r - g}$$

The expression in the text is found by rearranging terms from the expression

$$P_1 = \frac{CSD_1}{r - g} \quad \text{or} \quad P_1 = \frac{CSD_1}{K_{CS} - g} \quad \text{or} \quad K_{CS} = \frac{CSD_1}{P_1} + g$$

where $r = K_{CS}$.

NOTE 2

Marginal cost of capital between $L = 0.25$ and $L = 0.31$ is determined as follows:

$$L = \frac{\$300}{\$1,203} = (0.25 \text{ market value})(\text{after-tax rate}) = \text{dollar cost}$$

Debt, B	$ 300	2.03%	$ 6.10
Equity, CS	903	11.50	103.90
Total, C	$1,203		$110.00

Then

$$K_C = \frac{\$110}{\$1,203} = 9.14 \%$$

For $L = 0.13$,

$$(\text{Market value})(\text{after-tax rate}) = \text{dollar cost}$$

Debt, B	$ 400	2.0%	$ 8.30
Equity, CS	901	13.5	121.60
Total, C	$1,301		$129.90

Then

$$K_C = \frac{\$129.90}{\$1,301} = 9.99 \%$$

The marginal cost of additional financing is

	Market Value	Dollar Cost (After Tax)
$L = 0.31$	$1,301	$130
$L = 0.25$	1,203	110
Difference	$ 98	$ 20

so that

$$MC = \frac{\$20}{\$98} = 20.40\ \%$$

CHAPTER 5

Dividend Policy
and
Stock Valuation

One of the most important duties of the financial manager is the proper allocation of his company's assets. One decision he must make is whether to pay out part of these assets as dividends or to reinvest all or part of them. A company's success depends upon the amount of assets retained because this affects its ability to expand and modernize.

Shareholders may benefit immediately from dividends, not only from cash inflow but also from the effect on stock price. The price of the stock is rarely unaffected by the dividend policy; poor earnings and a high payout ratio may be as beneficial to stockholders as good earnings and a low payout.

This chapter is divided into two sections. First, the concept of a sound dividend policy is discussed. The second section examines a quantitative approach to this subject and introduces a valuation model that can be used to determine the appropriate dividend payment and its effect on the market price of the stock.

THE CONCEPT

The vast majority of corporations are aware of the importance of paying a cash dividend, and make a continual effort to maintain a record that will be beneficial to the shareholders in the long run. The two most significant reasons for such a policy are its investment attractiveness and capital-cost-reduction aspects.

1. *Securities become investment grade.* With a continuing dividend-payout policy, stocks win a reputation of being investment rather than speculative stock. This means that certain investors, such as institutions, will buy them. This broadens the market and gives stability to the stock price. Various state laws require an unbroken dividend record for a specific time period, such as five years, in order that a company's bonds may be purchased by banks and other fiduciaries in that state.

2. *Reduces cost of capital.* If a company meets the various state requirements, its bonds, which qualify as "legals," sell on a relatively low-yield and therefore a low-cost basis. Stock sells easier because of the broadened market. The stock will usually sell at a high price in relation to the dividend cost.

A company may not pay a dividend at all and still have a sound dividend policy if the company has investment opportunities that benefit the shareholder more than paying dividends. The factors behind a sound dividend policy differ from one company to another.

Features of a Sound Cash-Dividend Policy

The two fundamental features of a sound dividend policy are continuity and stability. Continuity is important because many shareholders depend upon dividends as a source of income, and good stockholder relations and investor confidence result from regularity of dividend payments. This is much more important among stockholders of well-established companies in mature industries. Most shareholders of "growth" companies are not interested in dividends. Additionally, a company's dividend record is a principal factor in the rating given to its shares by security analysts.

There is a strong incentive for a company to pay a stable dividend even though earnings may fluctuate from year to year. One of the factors used in rating a stock is the stability of the dividend record. A stable record increases the rating and price of the stock; conversely, a stock tends to sell at a lower price when the dividend record has not been stable.

Some companies will pay an extra dividend at the end of the year if earnings have been high enough to justify them. This extra dividend is better than an increase in the regular dividend because a stable conservative policy can be maintained. However, once the regular dividend payment is increased, there is a strong tendency to maintain the payment amount.

Legal Aspects

The various state legislatures as well as the courts have set up guidelines for the payment of dividends. These restrictions are designed to protect creditors and stockholders from—and hold directors and officers liable for—improper dividends that impair the firm's solvency and security holders' investments.

The firm's charter and bylaws generally prescribe the circumstances under which dividends may be declared. However, there are much more effective restrictions on dividend payments. Two general rules prevail in common law: Normally, dividends can be paid out only from the profits (past and present) of the business; and/or dividends can be paid out of the firm's capital only if all creditors have been satisfied or provided for first.

A firm may have substantially large previous deficits and no surplus, but may still declare a dividend if it makes a profit in the current year. Some states restrict dividends to earned surplus, while other state laws do not prescribe the source of eligible surplus. However, few states deny the firm the right to revalue its assets and/or capital account, thereby making it relatively easy for the firm to create surplus and use it to pay out dividends.

Legal recourse is available to damaged parties if dividends are declared and paid illegally or if dividends are not forthcoming under circumstances that clearly call for their payment. Directors are held liable under both civil and criminal law for the declaration of the improper dividends, since such payments would be fraudulent. Moreover, if stockholders are aware that they have received an illegal dividend, it may be recovered from them. If they receive the dividends in good faith and without knowledge of their illegality, such dividends cannot be recovered legally by creditors. On the other hand, stockholders who have brought equity suits to force the payment of dividends on their stock have been successful only in a few extreme situations. In the successful cases, stockholders have had to show that the company had ample profits to pay the dividends in question and that it declined to do so in order to compromise or prejudice the position of its stockholders. The directors of a firm are usually able to defend their actions on the grounds of financial expediency and discretion.

A company should consider the possibility of creditors' restrictions that would limit the amount of a dividend payment. Dividend restrictions can result from many types of debt. For example, a debenture or bank loan might stipulate that while bonds or loans of a certain class are outstanding, the dividend payment may not exceed a specified amount. Preferred shareholders are also frequently protected through the use of such provisions. Here, again, the directors are prevented from dissipating cash through excessive dividend payments or payments that would impair the liquidity position of the corporation.

Economic Factors

The age of a corporation is a factor influencing dividend policy. A young or small company, for example, usually cannot obtain additional capital through the sale of bonds in the securities market. Consequently, it may have to rely on retained earnings for needed capital. Such companies may have to refrain from paying a dividend, or at most pay a conservative amount, if additional assets are constantly needed for expansion.

Quite naturally, the nature of the business conducted by a company will affect the dividend policy. Certain industries characteristically have more stable earnings than others. For example, a mature company in a mature industry will typically have a high payout ratio, whereas low payout ratios predominate when earnings are commonly volatile, as they are likely to be in young companies in new fields of industry. Consequently, the nature of a business heavily influences the certainty of earnings, and the earnings dictate the possible dividend payment.

A number of economic considerations influence dividend policy. For example, in an inflationary period, a company must face higher costs for replacing assets, as well as higher interest rates and tight money. The cost is often higher than companies previously anticipated, and money is not only more expensive to borrow but also hard to acquire. Corporations can lessen the impact of high interest rates and inflationary periods by retaining their earnings. However, the stock market may penalize the stock for a conservative capital structure, especially if these retained earnings are not reinvested within a reasonable period of time.

Stock Dividends

The main reason for declaring a stock dividend is to conserve cash. It may supplement or be substituted for the cash dividend. Stock dividends ensure that assets remain in the business. Practically speaking, the amount of the stock dividend should not exceed the amount of the retained current earnings. Stock dividends have a tax advantage over cash dividends because they are taxed as long-term capital gains, whereas cash dividends are taxed as ordinary income. Depending upon the stockholder's tax status, stock dividends may offer him an advantage.

A company may use a stock dividend to increase the number of shares outstanding. A corporation, for example, may have to increase the total outstanding shares of stock to qualify for a listing on a stock exchange. A company may also wish to keep the market price of the stock within a desired low-price range, and might rather declare dividends than split the stock. Stock dividends should be considered when a dividend policy is formulated. Whether or not the stock dividend is incorporated into the policy will, of course, depend on the specific factors involved in each particular case.

THE MODEL

The ultimate responsibility of corporate management is to improve the position of the common-stock shareholders. The shareholders' position may be enhanced through total retention or through the distribution of earnings. The fundamental issue involved in the determination of a sound corporate dividend policy pertains to the establishment of the correct amount of earnings to be distributed to the common shareholders, if a dividend is to be paid at all.

Even though qualitative factors will influence the dividend policy, the actual retention rate will be determined by quantitative factors. A quantitative approach is essential in establishing the amount of the dividend that maximizes the interests of the common-share holders.

The Gordon Model

Myron Gordon[1] has developed a model for the valuation of a share of common stock. The financial officer can use this model to determine how much should be retained or paid out, and can also ascertain the subsequent effect on market price. He makes the assumption that the value of the share of stock is a result of its expected future dividends, discounted at the rate of profit required on the expectation. The Gordon valuation procedure assumes that the corporation engages in no outside financing and is expected to earn r on investments and retain fraction b of its income for every future period. The dividend expectation can be represented as its current value $(1 - b)E$ and its growth rate br.

The following application of the Gordon model expresses the relationship necessary between r and b before the market price P can be maximized.

[1] Myron J. Gordon, *The Investment, Financing and Valuation of the Corporation* (Homewood, Ill.: Richard D. Irwin, 1962).

If CSD = annual cash dividend
b = annual retention rate
E = earnings after taxes
r = return on equity investment
SE = stockholders' equity per share
g = growth rate br
K_{CS} = cost of common stock, the capitalization rate E/P
P_1 = market price before changes in r and b
P_2 = market price after changes in r and b

then $CSD = (1 - b)E$
$E = (r)(SE)$
$CSD = (1 - b)(r)(SE)$
$$P = \frac{CSD}{K_{CS} - g}$$
$g = br$
$$P = \frac{(1 - b)(r)(SE)}{K_{CS} - br}$$

We can now solve for r:
$$r = \frac{(K_{CS}P)}{b(P - SE) + SE}$$

The effect of changes in r and b or P can be ascertained in the following manner.

Assume that
$$SE = \$30.00$$
$$K_{CS} = 0.08$$
$$P_1 = \$50.00$$
$$P_2 = \$15.00$$

$$r = \frac{50(0.08)}{b(50 - 30) + 30} \qquad r = \frac{15(0.08)}{b(15 - 30) + 30}$$

At $P_1 = \$50$,
$$r = \frac{50(0.08)}{b(50 - 30) + 30}$$

and values for r and b are

r	b
13.3%	0.0%
11.4	25.0
10.0	50.0
8.9	75.0

At $P_2 = \$15$,

$$r = \frac{15(0.08)}{b(15 - 30) + 30}$$

and values for r and b are

r	b
4.0%	0.0%
4.6	25.0
5.0	50.0
6.7	75.0

Figure 5-1 is a graphic illustration of the relation between r and b and K_{CS}. Note that when $r/K_{CS} > 1$, the price remains constant with higher b as r decreases; when $r/K_{CS} < 1$, the price remains constant as r increases if b increases.

Several observations should be made with regard to this stock-valuation model: (1) The stock price (either 50 or 15) can be obtained under an infinite number of r and b combinations; (2) for any given level of b, the higher the rate of return becomes, the higher the price of the stock will be; and (3) as long as r is higher than 0.08 (the K_{CS}), the isoprice line will have a negative slope—as b rises, r can fall without affecting price. When $r > K_{CS}$, reinvested earnings will yield a higher return than shareholders could obtain elsewhere with equal risk. When $r < K_{CS}$, the isoprice line will be positive. Here, as b increases, a higher rate of return must occur to keep the price steady.[2]

FIGURE 5–1   Stock-valuation model.

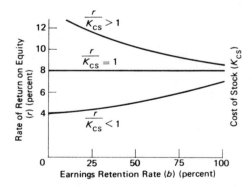

[2] Eugene M. Lerner and Willard T. Carleton, "The Integration of Capital Budgeting and Stock Valuation," *American Economic Review* (September 1964), p. 119.

The preceding application of Gordon's model illustrates important relationships among r, b, and K_{CS}. This form of analysis does not, however, tell us what the exact retention rate should be in order to maximize market price. A unique application of the Gordon model is presented in the following analytic chart system, and the dividend payment that maximizes market price is part of this discussion.

Chart System for Dividend Analysis

This analysis is an outgrowth of the formula $P = CSD/(K_{CS} - g)$, where the price of the common stock is a function of the dividend divided by the rate of discount applied by stockholders to the company's stream of dividends, less the company's growth rate. The chart system is a result of a series of simulations derived from empirical data (using the Gordon formula) and which are plotted by a computer.

A company's internal growth rate is a function of the internal rate of return on investment r multiplied by the earnings-retention rate b. Thus, $g = rb$. This is illustrated in Figure 5-2. The internal return for our purposes is the total expected value of all operations divided by the original investment.

While corporate decision makers can control the growth rate only indirectly through r, they exert direct influence on the earnings-retention rate.

Figure 5-3 illustrates how the total chart system works in actual practice. After the growth rate chart (Figure 5-2) is used to find g, Figure

FIGURE 5–2   Company's internal growth rate.

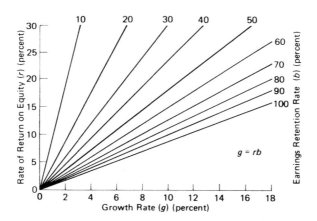

5-3(a) shows how g is integrated with K_{CS} to find $K_{CS} - g$, and finally market price is determined by Figure 5-3(b). Using this chart system it is possible to trace at a glance a change in one or more variables and measure the resulting impact on common-stock values.

Corporate policies on the earnings-retention rate normally have a direct influence on the firm's growth characteristics. Most growth companies retain a substantial percentage of their earnings. Additionally, these firms usually have *price* to *earnings* ratios higher than those of nongrowth, high-payout firms. Thus, it might appear that a high earnings-retention rate will automatically maximize common-stock values. This is not necessarily true, as Figure 5-4 illustrates. In this graph, common-stock values actually decline with an increasing retention rate when the internal return on investment is less than the stockholder discount rate K_{CS}. A partial explanation for this phenomenon is that a company is reinvesting funds at a rate below that which stockholders could receive from other sources, given commensurate risks. Conversely, with r above the stockholder discount rate, an increasing retention rate inflates the common-stock value. Further, the rise in P is accelerated in deference to the lower tax rate for capital gains relative to dividend income.

The validity of the foregoing chart system will now be tested with empirical data. Two companies are tested separately. The data used have been taken from annual reports to the stockholders. Pertinent information —such as the relationship between r and K_{CS}—accompanies the chart system. See Figure 5-5.

FIGURE 5–3   The total model.

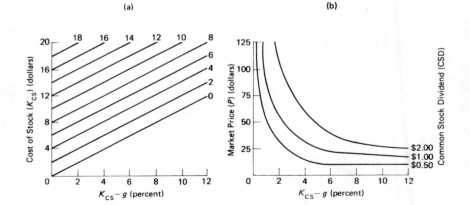

The actual market price is used to calculate the cost of equity; then the chart system is used for computing the market price at various dividend-payout ratios (Figure 5-6). The reason, of course, is to find the optimum-dividend payment. The dollar amount of the payment for the various retention rates accompanies the charts. The third and final graph (Figure 5-7) charts the relationship between market price and the various dividend-payout ratios.

Dravo Corporation. Dravo Corporation prides itself in being a company of uncommon enterprise.[3] The company consists of eight major divisions and nine subsidiaries. Dravo is involved in construction, mining, water and waste treatment, marine equipment, water transportation, and other unrelated activities.

Net income for 1967 of $7.2 million, equivalent to $3.51 per common share, was the highest ever attained by Dravo Corporation. These figures compare with $3.7 million, or $1.80 per share, in 1966. Both per-share figures are adjusted for a December 1967 stock split.[4]

In January, 1967, the quarterly common stock dividend rate was increased from 40 to 50 cents per share, resulting in a total of $2.00 declared during the year. Including the $2.00 per share on preferred stock, total dividends declared in 1967 amounted to $2,105,000. Following the December 1967 stock split, directors again increased the common stock dividend rate by

FIGURE 5–4   Common-stock values related to retention rate ($r < K_{CS}$).

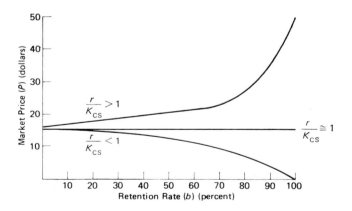

[3] *Annual Report to the Stockholders of Dravo Corporation,* 1967, p. 29.
[4] Ibid., p. 19.

FIGURE 5–5   The total model: market price, January 19, 1968 (Dravo Corporation).

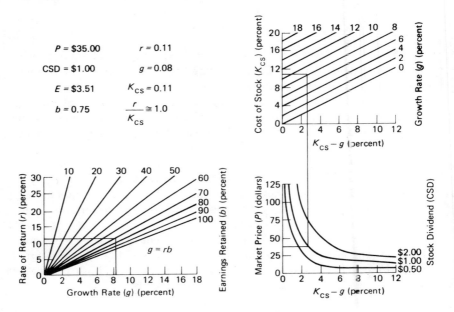

$P = \$35.00$ $r = 0.11$

$CSD = \$1.00$ $g = 0.08$

$E = \$3.51$ $K_{cs} = 0.11$

$b = 0.75$ $\dfrac{r}{K_{cs}} \cong 1.0$

$g = rb$

FIGURE 5–6   The total model: market price under various payout ratios (Dravo Corporation).

b	Dividend Payment
0.00	$3.51
0.10	3.15
0.20	2.80
0.30	2.45
0.40	2.10
0.50	1.75
0.60	1.40
0.70	1.05
0.80	0.70
0.90	0.35

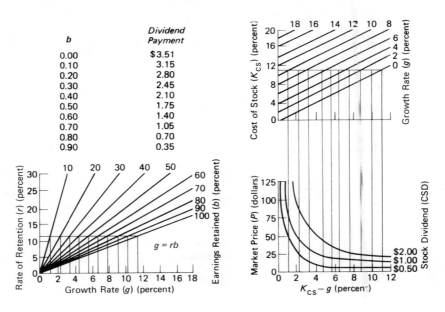

$g = rb$

FIGURE 5–7   Market price (Dravo Corporation).

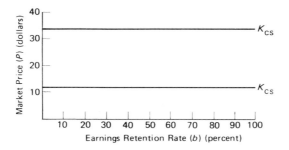

declaring, in January 1968, a quarterly dividend of 30 cents per share. This new annual rate of $1.20 is equivalent to $2.40 on shares outstanding prior to the split and represents a 20 percent increase over the previous rate of $2.00.[5]

Here is a 10-year dividend summary,[6] with the 1967 figure adjusted for the Dec. 29, 1967, two-for-one common-stock split.

1958	1959	1960	1961	1962
$0.50	$0.50	$0.50	$0.50	$0.50

1963	1964	1965	1966	1967
$0.87½	$0.82½	$0.92½	$1.00	$1.00

It is interesting to note that the market price found by using the chart system closely approximates the actual market price prevailing in 1958 (Figure 5-5). Dravo Corporation has a dividend policy that does not affect the market price of the stock. When the various payout ratios (Figure 5-6) are plotted, it is apparent that the market price (Figure 5-7) is indifferent to the various payout ratios.

Bankers Security Life Insurance Society. Bankers Security Life Insurance Society became the twenty-eighth life insurance company, among 1,700 in the United States, to be licensed to do business in all 50 states and the District of Columbia. This event, which occurred in 1967, was a fitting climax to a successful fiftieth anniversary year's operation.[7]

"Results of the year's operation were good. Net after tax earnings of $835,835 exceeded the prior year's net by 77 percent."[8] The earnings in

[5] Ibid., pp. 19–20.
[6] Ibid., pp. 26–27.
[7] *Annual Stockholders Report of the Bankers Security Life Insurance Society*, 1967, p. 3.
[8] Ibid., p. 5.

FIGURE 5–8 The total model: market price, January 1, 1968 (Bankers Security Life Insurance Society).

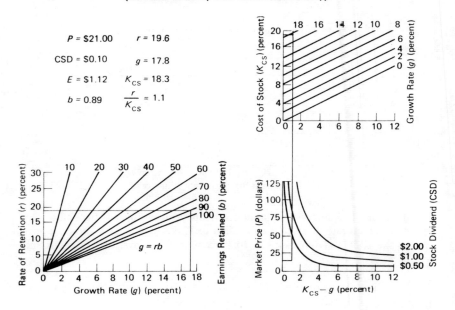

$P = \$21.00 \qquad r = 19.6$

$CSD = \$0.10 \qquad g = 17.8$

$E = \$1.12 \qquad K_{CS} = 18.3$

$b = 0.89 \qquad \dfrac{r}{K_{CS}} = 1.1$

FIGURE 5–9 The total model: market price under various payout ratios (Bankers Security Life Insurance Society).

b	Dividend Payment
0.00	$1.12
0.10	1.01
0.20	0.90
0.30	0.78
0.40	0.67
0.50	0.55
0.60	0.44
0.70	0.33
0.80	0.22
0.90	0.10
1.00	0.00

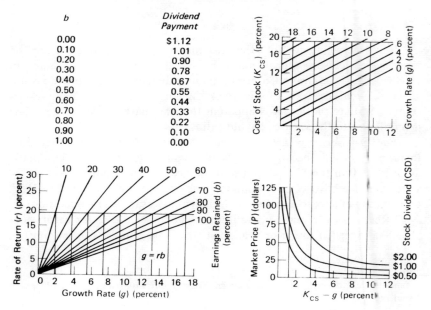

FIGURE 5–10   Market price (Bankers Security Life Insurance Society).

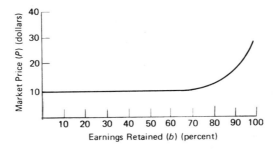

1966 represented an increase of 143 percent over the net earnings of 1965.

Bankers Security pays a $0.10 cash dividend. But Bankers Security *should not* pay a $0.10 cash dividend, and it should not be necessary to use the chart to learn this fact. When a company has a return on equity of 19.6 percent after taxes and a 77 percent increase in earnings, it is evident that the market price will be maximized when a dividend is not paid. See Figure 5-7. This fact is confirmed by the analysis presented in Figures 5-8, 5-9, and 5-10, using 1968 figures in the graphs.

Bankers Security will continue to pay a dividend of $0.10 per share. However, the retention rate will increase as the dollar amount of the dividend is held constant at $0.10 per share. This token dividend is paid because of stockholder pressure.

CHAPTER 6

Treasury
Stock

The rising trend of interest rates over the past few years had made it costly to hold cash idle. As a result, corporate financial managers have come under increasing pressure to manage their funds more effectively.

Corporate treasurers may invest their cash either externally or internally. External investment involves the purchase of marketable securities or investment in other companies offering opportunities for growth. Internal investment takes many forms, such as allocation of funds among accounts receivable, inventories, and fixed assets. This chapter examines another use for these funds, investment in treasury stock. (Treasury stock of a company is its own stock, either reserved and not offered for sale on the market or purchased from stockholders.)

Treasury stock is used to retire equity—thereby increasing the rate of return—and to pay for the acquisition of other corporations. We have formulated decision models for each of these situations. The last section of this chapter deals with the ethical problems involved in a stock reacquisition.

THE MODEL

Corporate Acquisitions

Once the decision has been made to acquire a corporation, it must be determined whether it is better to acquire it with cash or stock. A tax advantage can be given to the seller of a company, through deferment of the capital-gains tax, if stock is used to acquire either stock or assets under Section 368 (a) 1 of the Internal Revenue Code, 1954. This may work to the advantage of the acquiring company if it reduces the amount of funds that would otherwise be required to make the offer attractive to the seller. The first decision, then, is to decide between cash and stock.

The ABC Company wishes to acquire the DEF Company. Assume the owners of DEF wish to net $1 million from the sale of their company. They must receive $1,538,462 cash in order to net $1 million.

Let CS = cost if stock is used in the acquisition
NCO = cost if cash is used in the acquisition
X = cash payment in excess of tax-cost base
t = individual capital-gains tax rate of 35 percent has been used, although in 1973 and following years the rate is 25 percent on the first $50,000 and 35 percent on the excess of $50,000. Corporate capital-gains tax rate of 30 percent would be used if the seller were a corporate entity.

Thus,

$$X - 0.35X = \$1,000,000$$

$$X = \$1,536,462$$

If the company is acquired with cash, an additional 54 percent will have to be paid to cover seller's capital-gains tax. If stock is used, there will be a deferment of the capital-gains tax. The $1 million of stock would be equivalent to $1,538,462 cash to the seller.

The decision is to acquire with stock if

$$(NCO)(1 - t) > CS$$

It will be more profitable for the acquiring company to purchase with stock if the capital-gains tax to the seller is more than the costs incurred to acquire this stock. This emphasizes that stock may be used as a form of scrip whose value differs because of tax considerations.

If it is decided that it is better to issue stock rather than use cash, a second decision must be made. What type of share should be used, treasury or unissued?

Let E = earnings after tax before acquisition
ROI = return on acquired company after tax
K_C = cost of capital after tax
P = market price of acquiring company's shares
NS_1 = number of shares outstanding prior to any transaction
NS_2 = number of shares to be issued in the acquisition

If new stock is issued, the effect on earnings per share is

$$\frac{E + (\text{ROI} \times P \times \text{NS}_2)}{\text{NS}_1 + \text{NS}_2}$$

Earnings of the corporation will be increased by $\text{ROI} \times P \times \text{NS}_2$ when shares that could be sold on the market for P are used to acquire a company that is earning a return on investment, ROI.

If treasury stock is purchased, the effect on earnings per share is

$$\frac{E - (K_C \times P \times \text{NS}_2)}{\text{NS}_1}$$

Earnings of the corporation will be decreased by $K_C \times P \times \text{NS}_2$ as funds earning the return open to the corporation are given up to acquire treasury stock. Then, the alternative that yields the best return to the stockholders should be undertaken. Treasury stock should be used if

$$\frac{E + (\text{ROI} \times P \times \text{NS}_2)}{\text{NS}_1 + \text{NS}_2} < \frac{E - (K_C \times P \times \text{NS}_2)}{\text{NS}_1}$$

Given that $E = \$4,400,000$
$\text{ROI} = 7\%$
$K_C = 6\%$
$P = \$20$
$\text{NS}_1 = 2,000,000$
$\text{NS}_2 = 200,000$

we find that for treasury stock,

$$\frac{\$4,400,000 + \{0.06\,[\$20(200,000)]\}}{2,000,000} = \$2.08$$

and for unissued stock,

$$\frac{\$4,400,000 + \{0.07\,[\$20(200,000)]\}}{2,000,000 + 200,000} = \$2.13$$

Therefore, since $\$2.08 < \$2.13$, unissued stock should be used to make the acquisition.

Retire Equity

The effect of a reduction in equity capital is shown in Figure 6-1. Various amounts of stockholders' equity, SE, are represented along the horizontal axis by the distances SE_1, SE_2, SE_3. For each specific capital structure there is a supply curve of external funds DBT. These curves

FIGURE 6–1   Supply of outside funds as the amount of equity varies.

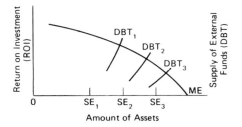

are DBT_1, DBT_2, and DBT_3. If a company reduces its equity base by contracting from SE_2 down to SE_1, the supply of external funds also shifts to DBT_1. The supply of external funds also becomes more inelastic because of the increasing proportion of debt, and thus risk, in the capital structure.

The downward-sloping, marginal rate-of-earnings curve ME assumes physical or competitive difficulties that make it difficult for additional assets to continually earn the same rate of return. The purchase of treasury stock will move a company farther up the ME curve. This is partially due to increased leverage (since debt is constant but equity is reduced) and partially due to the elimination of assets that earn a rate of return lower than that earned by investing in one's own stock.

A growth company should not acquire treasury stock because its earnings are low in relation to market price, and the company is able to earn more from other investments. However, companies no longer experiencing growth are faced with the choice of investing in low-yield negotiable securities, purchasing treasury stock, paying out large dividends, or just accumulating vast amounts of funds. Their decision should be based upon the effect on the common-stock holder. For example, treasury stock should be purchased if

$$\frac{E + (ROI \times NS_2 \times P) - (K_C \times P \times NS_2)}{NS_1} < \frac{E - (K_C \times P \times NS_2)}{NS_1 - NS_2}$$

where E = earnings after tax
ROI = return on investment after tax
K_C = cost of capital after tax
P = market price paid for stock
NS_1 = number of shares outstanding
NS_2 = number of shares purchased by treasury

Treasury-stock purchases are attractive if earnings per share on reinvested funds are less than the earnings per share on the reduced equity base.

Assume that the company has two choices: (1) buying 200,000 shares at the market price of $20 per share, or (2) earning a return on other investments of 7 percent. Also assume that the cost of cash is lost opportunity cost, or cost of capital.

Given that $E = \$4,400,000$
$$\text{ROI} = 7\%$$
$$K_C = 6\%$$
$$P = \$20$$
$$\text{NS}_1 = 2,000,000$$
$$\text{NS}_2 = 200,000$$

we find that for investment earnings,

$$\frac{\$4,400,000 + \{0.07[\$20(200,000)] - 0.06[\$20(200,000)]\}}{2,000,000} = \$2.22$$

and for purchase of treasury stock,

$$\frac{\$4,400,000 - (0.06)(\$20)(200,000)}{2,000,000 - 200,000} = \$2.31$$

Therefore, since $\$2.22 < \$2.31$, treasury stock is the preferable investment.

The practice of buying treasury stock to reduce capitalization and to increase book value, earnings per share, and return on investment is gaining favor among corporations. In the recent stock market decline, the dividend yield on some companies' shares was significantly greater than the yields in the bond market. In many cases, companies intentionally reduced their outstanding shares as a means of using excess funds and/or marketable securities to enhance the earnings and market price of their stock. In effect, these monies were passed on to shareholders as capital gains. If the total dollar amount of dividend payment is reduced more than the interest income received from marketable securities, any excess cash or marketable securities a company may use to purchase its own shares may save a great amount of money, since interest received on marketable (U.S. government) securities is taxable, whereas a company pays no tax on the dividends saved by buying its own stock.

For example, after Brown Shoe sold its G. R. Kinney Corporation subsidiary for $45 million in 1963, the company found that it had more cash than it could normally invest. In October 1963, Brown made a tender offer to buy 300,000 of its own shares. Shareholders actually tendered 157,000 shares and Brown Shoe bought another 110,000 in 1964 on the open market and in private transactions. Brown's profit for the fiscal year ending Oct. 31, 1964, increased 0.5 percent over fiscal year 1963 profit, but per-share earnings increased 12 percent.[1]

A somewhat spectacular example of this policy was the classic action in 1950 of Colt Manufacturing Company. The effect of reducing its stock and surplus by almost 50 percent is shown by Table 6-1, which gives an analysis of the company's capital structure.

The decision whether to invest available funds in treasury stock or whether to pay them out as dividends depends on the effect on the stockholder. Treasury stock should be purchased if

$$\frac{NCO}{NS} (1 - MT) < \Delta E_1 \frac{P}{E} \left(1 - \frac{MT}{2}\right)$$

where E = earnings after taxes

$\quad E_1$ = earnings per share before treasury stock acquisition

$\quad \Delta E_1$ = change in earnings per share effected by treasury stock purchase

TABLE 6-1   Change in capital structure of Colt Manufacturing Company, 1949–1950.

Item	1949	1950
Capital stock (par $25)	$ 5,000,000	$ 5,000,000
Retained earnings before earnings for year	7,762,726	7,874,833
Earnings for year after tax	519,497	944,117
Total net worth	$13,282,223	$13,818,950
Less reacquired stock at cost	109,174	6,653,174
Net stock and surplus	$13,173,049	$ 7,165,776
Number of shares outstanding	195,900	71,073
Book value per share ($)	67.24	100.82
Earnings per share ($)	2.65	13.28
Market price ($)		
High	44.50	66.75
Low	33.75	39.75
Moody's 125 industrial common-stock average ($)		
High	52.28	64.46
Average	46.88	57.83
Low	43.46	52.58

Source: Moody's Industrial Manual, 1951, p. 701.

[1] "Investing in Yourself," *Wall Street Journal* (June 30, 1965), p. 8.

NCO = funds available
MT = marginal tax rate of the average stockholder
MT/2 = capital-gains tax rate
P = market price per share
NS = number of shares outstanding
P/E = *price* to *earnings* ratio

In order to make treasury-stock purchases attractive, the return of the dividend must be less than the gain on increased stock price after taxes.

Given that E = $4,000,000
E_1 = $2
NCO = $4,800,000 with which to buy 200,000 shares
P = $24
MT = 30%
NS = 2,000,000
P/E = 12

and earnings per share after treasury-stock acquisition is

$$E_2 = \frac{\$4,000,000}{1,800,000} = \$2.22$$

the change in earnings will be

$$\Delta E_1 = \$2.22 - \$2.00 = \$0.22$$

Using the preceding formula,

$$\frac{\$4,800,000}{2,000,000}(1 - 0.3) = \$1.68$$

and

$$(\$0.22 \times 12)\left(1 - \frac{0.3}{2}\right) = \$2.24$$

Therefore, since $2.24 > $1.68, the acquisition of treasury stock is more attractive to the common-stock holders than is the payment of a dividend.

A somewhat spectacular example of this program was that of Paramount Pictures, Inc., which used a 15-year reacquisition program to maintain its $2 annual dividend rate. This seemed unlikely in 1949 when the old Paramount Pictures, Inc., left the new company with 33 million shares outstanding and with motion pictures producing only half of its former business income. The company decided to reacquire stock to maintain its $2 annual dividend. Through several tender offers and an open-market purchase program, Paramount reduced its outstanding shares by 1964 to about 1,560,000 and maintained the dividend.[2]

There are many alternative methods for acquiring stock, among which are block purchases of stock from individual shareholders, purchase in the open market, and tender offers. The opportunities available to buy large blocks are rare, and even rarer is the coincidence of availability at the specific time the purchase is to be made. For the purchase of large blocks of shares, tender offers are less costly, more flexible, and less risky than purchase on the open market. Open-market purchases tend to bid up the price of the stock, especially if large numbers of shares are to be acquired. The tender offer hedges the purchase because its exercise is contingent on the corporation's receiving the number of shares sought. It is also faster, since purchases do not have to be arranged in a time pattern that will disturb the market.

ETHICAL PROBLEMS

Whenever the corporation becomes involved in a program of treasury-stock reacquisitions, ethical and legal problems arise. Historically, management has taken a professional outlook toward the company, but with the separation of management and ownership, conflicts may arise between their respective goals. In a reacquisition, management will attempt to buy the stock at the lowest price while stockholders seek to sell at the highest. The problems that may arise revolve around insider information and its effect on the investing public.

The Securities and Exchange Commission (SEC) has established legal restrictions that apply to treasury-stock transactions. These laws say little about stock promotion. Their main thrust is against stock promotion that might affect the sales of securities in a public offering or which are blatantly dishonest. It is important in any stock exchange transaction to avoid violating the anti-manipulation provisions in the Securities and Exchange Act of 1934. There are certain guidelines to follow, such as buying each week only a reasonable percentage (10 to 15 percent) of the present average weekly trading volume, not opening daily trading, and being certain that the purchase price and number of shares bought in any transaction are not greater than the price and quantity of the last sale. Companies subject to provisions of the Securities and Exchange Act must file Form 8-K if the number of shares purchased is more than 5 percent of previously outstanding shares. Corporations listed on the New York Stock Exchange must file with the Exchange quarterly reports of all such

[2] Ibid.

purchases. In all cases, it is advisable that the corporation adopt a formal program. This program, approved by its board of directors, should specify the number of shares authorized (or the maximum amount of money to be paid), the maximum price to be paid, and the method (tender, open market, or negotiated block purchase) to be employed.

The SEC restrictions emphasize the effects of treasury-stock reacquisitions on the public's investment decisions: whether to acquire, dispose of, or retain its stock. Any question of impropriety is usually based on the dissemination of less than complete truths to induce unsuspecting investors to buy, or stockholders to sell, too soon.

The Cady, Roberts and Company decision[3] in 1961 emphasized both the materiality of the information and the effect of disclosure, or lack of it, on a reasonable man's investment decision. In a reacquisition it is important to present information that a prudent investor ought to have before purchasing the security, information which would materially affect the decisions of the other party, and information which might be expected to have an effect on the market. These guidelines transcend the basic goals of the corporation—maximization of stockholder wealth. It is the public at large and the effect of a treasury-stock acquisition on it, coupled with the effect on present stockholders, that must be considered. The Cady, Roberts and Company case also held that the nondisclosure of material information, coupled with insiders or their privies taking advantage of it unwittingly or otherwise, was a violation and subject to prosecution.[4]

Problems of this sort can be avoided by proper disclosure. The stockholder who sells and the individual who buys must have done so as if they knew that the corporation were the purchaser and as if they were in possession of all material information. It is quite difficult for the corporation to know whether it is in possession of material information not generally known to its shareholders, since a corporation will inevitably be better informed of its affairs and future prospects than will its public shareholders. Also, it may be unwise to make this information public, for competitive reasons. However, it is advisable that if the developments pending are significant enough to affect the price of the stock, purchases of the stock should be held in abeyance until after a public announcement has been made.

[3] In the matter of Cady, Roberts & Co. Sec. Exch. Act Reg. No. 6668, 40 S.E.C. 907, CCH Fed. Sec. L, Rep. 9176,803 (1961).
[4] Richard L. Baker, "Non-Dilutive Stock Benefits," *Business Lawyer* (January 1967), p. 440.

CHAPTER **7**

Convertible
Bonds
and Warrants

Prior to 1940 the convertible bond was used to make offerings of debt more palatable than they would be as straight issues. Companies with an unacceptable credit standing had to add a little "sweetener" to arouse investor interest. In more recent times, however, convertible securities have been issued by all types of companies, even those with the highest of credit ratings, because the conversion option is now being used as a mechanism for increasing the common stock of a company rather than for facilitating the issuance of funded debt.

Although warrants first appeared in the financial world in 1911, they were seldom used before the bull market of the 1920s. In the middle 1920s, however, they began to develop into a financial instrument of major importance. Since the market prices of separable warrants usually swing more widely than the price of the underlying common stock, warrants appeal to investors because the profit percentage is much higher than that of the stock. The central question to face in valuing warrants is the size of the premium between the price of the warrant and the price of the common stock. Term warrants have stock purchase privileges, which permit purchase at a price much lower than the prevailing market price.

THE CONCEPT

Both bonds and warrants have dual natures, each of which has unique advantage. Bonds may be "straight" or convertible; warrants may be time-limited options to buy the stock to which they are attached or they may be detachable and separately salable.

Convertible Bonds

The most important point that must be remembered about convertible bonds is that they *are* bonds. For this reason, a *convertible* bond has an "investment value," which is the price at which it would sell as a straight bond. The same investment attitude and the same general method of quantitative and qualitative analysis applied to the straight bond must be applied to the convertible bond. In many cases it is the very strength or weakness of these quantitative and qualitative factors that determines if a selected bond issue needs the added sweetener of convertibility.

Convertibility is the unique feature of these bonds. The owner of a bond can convert it at his option into the common stock of the issuing corporation. For example, the Phillips Petroleum $4\frac{1}{2}$ percent bond, maturing in 1987, is convertible into 20 shares of common stock for each $1,000 of the bond; the United Aircraft $5\frac{3}{8}$ percent bond, due 1991, is convertible into 1.185 shares of common stock for each $1,000 of the bond.

The number of shares of common into which the bond is convertible is fixed or is varied by a sliding conversion ratio that makes conversion less attractive as time goes on. For instance, the $4\frac{1}{2}$ percent subordinated debenture of the American Machine and Foundry Company, due 1981, is convertible into common stock at $60 until 1971 and thereafter at $65 until maturity.

Every convertible bond has a conversion price; for example, the $4\frac{1}{2}$ percent Phillips Petroleum issue would have a conversion price of the common of $1,000/20, or $50 per share. In addition, each convertible bond has a "conversion value." This value can be computed by multiplying the number of shares into which the bond is convertible by the current market value of the common stock. There may be a "conversion premium." This is the amount the common stock has to rise before a profit is made on the conversion rights. As an example, assume a $990 bond is convertible into 18 shares of common stock. The conversion price is $55. If the common is selling for $50, the conversion premium is $5, and the common will have to rise 10 percent to $55 before the $990 bond equals its value in stock.

When the common stock sells above the conversion price, the convertible bond value will increase with the common. When the common stock sells below the conversion price, the bond will remain at its investment value as a bond, without reference to the conversion feature.

Normally, the investor makes the conversion at his discretion by turning in the bond to the transfer agent. However, the company may take certain steps to force conversion. This may be necessary to eliminate the overhanging threat of nonconversion, which may jeopardize future equity financing because of potential dilution. The company may put a deadline on the conversion right, or it may reserve the privilege of changing the "conversion ratio." Many convertibles are "callable," and the company may redeem the bonds before maturity, usually at a small 3 or 4 percent premium above market value.

Warrants

A warrant is an option to buy securities, generally common stock at a given price for a stated period of time. They are occasionally issued in connection with a reorganization. At other times they are offered to help "sweeten" the sale to investors of otherwise unattractive bonds and common stock, or are sold to underwriters as part of their compensation for arranging financing.

When warrants have been issued as part of a senior security, they are either immediately detachable or detachable only after a certain period. Detachable warrants may be traded separately from the senior security.

When warrants are made detachable from the related senior issue, they assume existence and characteristics of their own. They develop into an independent form of security and a major vehicle for investment, since their prices usually swing more widely than the underlying stock. For example, Sperry Rand warrants, which allowed the holder to buy 1.08 shares of Sperry Rand common stock for $28 through Sept. 15, 1967, climbed nearly 44 percent in the rally that started early in June 1967, while the company's common moved up a more modest 15 percent.

Generally speaking, for every one-point gain or loss in the stock price, there is usually a corresponding one-point move in the price of the warrant; however, the warrant is always priced below the common stock and thus its one-point move represents a greater percentage move. Thus, if a person were convinced that a company's stock will rise and would be willing to risk an extra large decline if it falls, he would prefer the warrant to the stock.

Differences Between Warrants and Convertibles

There are several differences between warrants and the convertible security. The convertible feature is an undetachable part of the security and cannot be sold separately. Warrants, on the other hand, are detachable from the security and therefore have a different impact than the convertible upon the financial structure of the corporation when they are traded. When the convertible security is exchanged for common stock, the bond or preferred stock no longer appears on the balance sheet of the corporation. In other words, it ceases to exist. However, when the warrant is exercised, new capital flows into the corporation, and the bond or preferred stock that was the parent of the warrant still exists.

Since convertible bonds offer such unique advantages to both investor and issuer, one might expect that their use would increase. This, however, is not the case. The amount of convertible bonds newly issued each year has not displayed a fairly constant rate of growth.

Warrants, on the other hand, do not seem to offer such unique advantages to the issuer because they can be created out of "thin air" and can just as easily disappear into "thin air." Yet, this type of security seems to excite the imagination of many investors, and even though warrants do not maintain a steady level of popularity, at least they create widespread interest.

USES OF CONVERTIBLES

Convertible senior securities are issued for two main reasons: (1) indirectly to raise common equity capital, or (2) to increase the marketability of a security issue by using the convertible feature as a sweetener.[1]

Indirectly Raising Equity Capital

Convertible securities may be utilized indirectly to raise common stock, for the following reasons:

1. To sell common stock at a higher price per share than the current price of the common when the issuing corporation feels that the common stock is underpriced. This normally happens in the case of new securities.
2. To sell common stock on a delayed basis in order to allow the new funds time to generate additional earnings. This will minimize dilution.
3. To incur a lower cost of raising capital.

[1] C. J. Pilcher, *Raising Capital with Convertible Securities* (Ann Arbor: University of Michigan, 1955).

4. To appeal to segments of the capital market typically uninterested in common stock.
5. To assure the issuer that a definite amount of funds will be raised.

A corporation wishing to offer a new issue of common stock may be discouraged because the stock is underpriced in the market. Rather than issue stock at the undervalued price, the corporation may issue a convertible security, optioning the common stock at a price the corporation feels to be adequate. In addition, when a corporation issues new common stock, the offering price is usually a few points below the market price. This underpricing is necessary to keep the market price from falling below the subscription price as a result of the increased supply of stock on the market. Subscriptions to the stock will take place only as long as the subscription price is below the market price. If a $1,000 bond convertible into 20 shares is sold when the stock is selling at $40 a share, with a probable subscription price of $35 a share, it will raise the same amount of capital as the issuance of shares at $50 a share.

The lower the amount per share received, the larger the number of shares that must be sold to raise the capital required. This will have important consequences for a company that is committed to a stable dividend policy. The underpricing of new common stock means that more shares will have to be sold; thus, the dividend obligation will be higher than if new common shares were offered at or above the market price. The sales of convertible bonds with a conversion price set at or above the market price of the common, if and when converted, would result in fewer shares outstanding than if the same amount of capital had been raised through the sale of the common at the subscription price.

For example, a company desires to raise $4 million of equity capital. The common stock, selling at $46, has an annual dividend of $3 per share. Two plans are considered. Plan A is to offer 95,239 shares at a subscription price of $42 a share. Plan B provides for issuance of 4,000 bonds convertible at $50, with an interest rate of 7 percent.

The first plan would add 95,239 new shares to equity. At $3 per share, the common dividend would increase by $285,717. Issuance of the convertible bonds, assuming conversion, would result in 80,000 additional shares, with a dividend requirement of $240,000. Cash outflow would be lower by $45,717 after conversion. Up to the point of conversion, interest cost would be $280,000, or $140,000 after tax. Cash outflow would be lower by $145,717 before conversion.

If a company needs to raise $10 million for expansion, it can sell either 10,000 convertible bonds (convertible into 200,000 shares), or

250,000 shares immediately. Obviously, dilution is less with convertibles. Once the investment has begun to produce a return greater than the rate paid on the convertible security, common-stock prices will probably rise. Conversion will ensue and the company will have common capital at a time when earnings will support the additional shares.

If conversion does not occur, the delayed earning dilution will not continue indefinitely. The Accounting Principles Board of the American Institute of Certified Public Accountants (AICPA) issued two important rulings for companies with outstanding convertibles. First, whenever a convertible bond or preferred stock is selling for more than twice its estimated income value, the earnings-per-share calculation should be made on the basis of the securities being fully converted. Second, whenever the potential dilution from one or more convertible issues selling at less than twice the straight value is "material," a second calculation should be shown directly below the figure.

Convertible securities may result in a lower cost of raising equity capital. These savings result from two elements. First, investment banking charges for underwriting a bond or preferred-stock issue are usually smaller than for a common stock. Second, a larger volume of senior securities can be issued more successfully at one time, spreading the fixed costs over a larger base. The Securities and Exchange Commission found that the average cost of flotation for securities from 1965 to 1970 was $1.49 for bonds, $4.34 for preferred stock, and $10.28 for common stock.

A convertible bond appeals to those segments of the capital market that show very little interest in common shares, principally because some buyers of senior securities view the convertible as a hedge against inflation. The convertible will appreciate with the stock after conversion price is reached but, conversely, will not fall below its intrinsic worth as a bond if the stock depreciates. The result is a broader capital market for a corporation. A broad capital market is desirable if a large amount of capital is to be raised at some point in time.

Convertibles may also appeal to institutions that are restricted from buying common stock. Insurance companies, banking institutions, and pension funds all have some legal restrictions prohibiting the investment in common stocks. These firms can, however, enjoy the benefits of the price appreciation of common stock through high-quality convertible senior securities.

A considerable time period elapses between the decision to raise a certain amount of capital and the actual marketing operation. During this period, changes in the market price of the stock may make it difficult for a company to raise a given sum of money through the issue of common stock. For example, assume that a company desires to raise $1 million of new capital. It authorizes 100,000 shares of common, planning to offer them at $10 a share. During the 20-day waiting period required by the Securities and Exchange Commission, the stock declines to a point where the issuing price can be no higher than $7 a share. At this point, the company can either withdraw the offering or issue the registered shares and net only $700,000, an amount considerably less than desired.

In a similar case, a company has 1,000 convertible bonds for sale. Initially, 7 percent interest is to be paid. Again, a market decline is experienced a few days before the planned issue. However, by amending its rate to 8 percent, the corporation can still raise the desired amount of capital.

Convertibility as a "Sweetener"

A second major motivation behind the offerings of many convertibles is the desire to improve or sweeten an issue that by itself lacks sufficient marketability. Style and fashion pervade the capital markets just as they do the clothing markets. Sinking funds, different maturities, and convertible options have more acceptance during some periods than at other times.

The interest rate on a straight bond is usually lower when the convertible feature is included. The greater the value of the conversion feature to investors, the lower the yield the company will have to pay in order to sell the issue. Companies with relatively low credit ratings, but with good prospects for growth, may find it difficult to sell a straight issue of bonds or preferred stock at a high interest cost. However, the market may regard a convertible issue in a favorable light, not because of its quality as a bond or a preferred stock, but because of its common-stock characteristic.

Rulings of the Accounting Principles Board of the AICPA will increase the reported interest expense. This ruling holds that the portion of the bond proceeds attributable to the conversion privilege should be charged to debt discount. The discount must then be amortized over the life of the bond and consequently increase the reported interest expense of the bond, but not the cash outflow.

What we have said so far can be summarized in one word, leverage. The company is able to lever between senior and subordinated investors, between liened and unliened assets, between better capital structures in the future by managing the *debt* to *equity* ratio, and (probably most important) between the timing and use of funds made available to it through the issuance of the bonds.

We should not end the explanation of the characteristics of a convertible bond without discussing some of the limitations that it places on the issuing company. If the stock of the company remains dormant and the holders do not convert, then the company is handicapped by a debt issue. Consequently, the company will be faced with interest payments for a greater period of time than it had planned. Earnings projections might not have taken this into account and the corporation may be financially strained. Finally, if conversion occurs too quickly or in too great an amount, the equity base may be diluted by the extra shares.

Mechanics of Convertible Bonds

Figure 7-1 illustrates certain important relationships. The first relationship to deal with is the one expressed by the conversion line CON–D. This line represents the conversion value of the bond at any given time in the future, where D is the maturity date. The conversion value may be represented in one of two ways. One way is through a conversion parity price. This is the current market price of bond divided

FIGURE 7–1   Mechanics of convertible bonds.

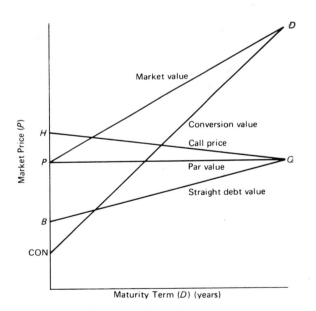

Source: Eugene F. Brigham, "Analysis of Convertible Bonds," *Journal of Finance* (March 1966), p. 37. Used by permission.

by the number of shares for which each $1,000 bond is exchangeable. From this formula we get the breakeven point in terms of a common-stock market price. In other words, if a $1,000 bond were convertible into 20 shares of stock and the current market price of the bond was $1,020, then the breakeven point (conversion parity price) would be $51 per share. If the stock were valued above this in the market, one would then obviously realize a gain.

A second way of looking at the conversion value is to judge it from a bond-value standpoint. Here the number of shares into which a $1,000 bond is convertible is multiplied by the current market price of the common stock. One can then estimate the breakeven point by measuring the percentage increase in the stock price that would equate the market price of the bond with its conversion value.

Also important is that the CON–D line and the market price line (P–D) meet at some point in the future. This point is the maturity date where the bonds are to be redeemed by the company or converted by the holders. Or simply, we might say that D is the expiration point of the security as a fixed-income obligation. The difference P–D minus CON–D along the vertical axis is one of the most critical factors in convertible bond management.

The call policy (H–Q) of a convertible bond (or for that matter, any bond) is merely a technique of trading off one type of capital for capital of another type. However, the implications of the call policy for a convertible bond are more complex than for straight debt because the company is trading one type of investor for another. This trade-off of the *debt* to *equity* makeup of the capital structure is very important. In order to regulate this to the company's best advantage, a workable call policy must be established. The crucial question here is how far up the conversion line (CON) should the holders' ride be allowed to go? If conversion is made too soon, the company will not be able to put the funds to use and thereby avoid dilution of the existing equity base. If the call is never enforced, the conversion will take place when the dividend-interest differential forces holders to convert. In the latter case, the company might not receive the funds from conversion at the time it needs them most. So the financial manager, in order to solve the problem of conversion timing, will prepare a bond-call schedule. However, this is no easy matter.

The first aspect that the finance man must contend with when preparing this call schedule is the investor cash-out preferences. From the investor's point of view, how far is he willing to ride the CON–D line? Probably the most important factor here is the *interest* to *dividend* relationship. Usually, the investor will not convert until the dividend payout on the number of shares convertible per bond is at least equal to, but probably in excess of, the dollar return from the interest payments on the bond.[2]

A second important aspect of the investor cash-out policy is the risk factor. The investor will usually have an aversion to accepting risk, so one should not expect conversion until the conversion rate and market price are nearly equal. In other words, the conversion parity price will be quite close to the market price of the stock. But no matter how it is stated, the conversion will never take place below the line connecting the B and D points.

However, even if we do fully understand the investor cash-out policy, the construction of a conversion timing schedule is still quite difficult because a projection of future earnings must be made. This is quite complicated, since the financial manager must take into account the reduction in the future interest payments, as the bonds are converted, and the increase in shares outstanding at given times in the future. The best way to handle this is to try to project the percentage of shares at different target dates in the future, and try to budget most capital expenditures around these target dates.

Usually, if the market price is high enough above the conversion parity price so that the convertible bond is about 40 percent above its straight-debt bond value, conversion will occur.[3]

Other external factors are present to complicate the bond-conversion schedule. The first factor is the margin requirement. If it is high, conversion will go slower because investors are in a better leverage position if they invest in the fixed-income security. Also, if the premium on the convertible bond is high enough to cover the tax and commission charges of trading rather than converting, studies have shown that the bondholders will not convert.[4] If the issuing company has another convertible bond outstanding with a lower conversion parity price and lower coupon rate, the financial manager would have to expect the older convertible to be exchanged first.

The second factor is the call provision. This provision, while of vital importance to the issuing company, is by no means an easy tool to handle. Yet it is essential for the needed flexibility if the capital structure is to

[2] Eugene F. Brigham, "Analysis of Convertible Bonds," *Journal of Finance* (March 1966), p. 39.

[3] Ashby Bladen, *Techniques for Investing in Convertible Bonds* (New York: Salomon Brothers, 1966), p. 20.

[4] Ibid., p. 28.

adjust to changing business conditions and needs. It is through the proper implementation of a sound call program and bond-timing schedule that dilution can be avoided. If the timing of the conversion is handled properly, the funds will already have been put to use to produce a profit that will increase earnings commensurate with the increasing shares from conversion, and the earnings per share will hold quite stable.

Other advantages the call provision affords the issuing company are, first, investor preferences. The call has certain effects on this; by forcing conversion, it will eliminate those investors who seek the protection of a fixed-income security and will attract those who desire more capital appreciation. Second, the tax structure of the firm will be affected by the interest-dividend relationship of a hybrid security. And last, the market price of the stock may be artificially affected by a threatened call by the issuing company.[5]

A third factor in managing the mechanics of a convertible bond is the premium. In Figure 7-1, the premium paid for a convertible bond is the area between B, D, and P, or the difference between the conversion value and the straight bond value, that is, CON–D minus B–L. Most, if not all, convertible bonds fall between the B, D, and P points because investors in this security are paying a privilege for the right to hold a hybrid security and to benefit from the reduction of risk such a security provides. In fact, as mentioned previously, the investor's risk will be protected by the B–D floor line. The greatest loss one might incur would be the difference between B–D and CON–D, at any given time that investment was made along these lines. This loss can be best explained in a theoretical sense. In other words, an investor will always be open to an exposure risk, which is the premium of the straight-bond value over what its intrinsic straight-bond value should be. Thus, the loss is the actual difference between the market straight-bond value and the intrinsic-bond value.[6]

The last point to be considered is the straight-debt value of a convertible debenture. The line B–Q is merely the price the bond would command if it were to sell without the hybrid feature attached to it. This is a weak measure because it is determined by external factors, one of which is the interest rate. If we say that the price of the bond is equal to the interest rate over the coupon rate, then a lower coupon-rate bond (which is a class that convertible bonds always fall into) will fluctuate much more violently than will the higher coupon-rate but equal-grade

[5] W. J. Winn and A. Hess, "The Value of the Call Privilege," *Journal of Finance* (May 1959), p. 183.
[6] Brigham, op. cit.

issue. For example, a 5 percent coupon-rate bond with a 1 percent change of interest rate will cause a 20 percent change in price (0.01/0.05), whereas a 3 percent coupon-rate bond with the same 1 percent change of interest rate will cause a 33 percent change in price (0.01/0.03).

Another external factor that affects bond-conversion scheduling is the grade rating. A new growth company may decide to issue a hybrid security to enhance its capital structure because straight-debt financing would not be feasible. In doing so, the company will usually not be able to command the rating grade of a more stable company. This will unduly hinder what might be a wise undertaking.

Hybrid bonds are convertible into stock, par for par, and companies that decide to use them should anticipate subsequent capitalization changes and provide for antidilution clauses to maintain equality with the original basis of conversion. On the other hand, a "sliding scale" arrangement and call provision are used to reduce the value of the conversion privilege, as time goes on, by accelerating conversion and curtailing the effective duration and the real value of the conversion privilege.

USES OF WARRANTS

Warrants are usually attached to bonds or preferred stock to obtain a lower interest or dividend cost. This practice is especially prevalent during periods of tight money and rising interest rates.

If the finance manager has certain hesitancies about the use of convertible bonds and their effects upon his leverage, then he will certainly love warrants because of the flexibility they provide. When the bonds and warrants are issued, the corporation receives cash; if the warrants are converted, there is an additional inflow of cash. However, earnings per share are less than those from convertibles because the debentures are still outstanding.

Warrants in Mergers and Reorganizations

As a result of a corporate merger, reorganization, or financial readjustment, a corporation may decide to issue warrants to streamline a top-heavy capital structure and to clear up arrears in interest or dividend payments on cumulative securities.

In the case of the reorganization or financial readjustment, the warrants often serve as an inexpensive bargaining tool or catalyst to obtain from reluctant security holders their agreement to the refinancing plan. For example, the warrant may be issued to a certain class of stockholder in exchange for his giving up the right to an accumulation of back dividends accrued on a cumulative preferred stock. One such instance was the Alleghany Corporation issue of 1952. In this reorganization plan, holders of preferred stock to whom $113 of dividends had accrued were persuaded to exchange each preferred stock for a tenth of a 5 percent debenture bond plus 20 perpetual warrants to buy Alleghany common stock at $3.75 per share. The warrant issue aided Alleghany Corporation in eliminating $11,300,000 in accumulated back dividends.

Mergers can also create warrants. An example of a warrant being used to smooth the path of a corporate merger is the Symington Gould Corporation and Wayne Pump Company merger in 1968. To make the merger more attractive to Wayne Pump stockholders, but to avoid penalizing Symington Gould stockholders, each share of Wayne Pump received $2\frac{1}{2}$ shares of Symington Gould common plus one warrant good for purchase of one share of the new stock at $10 until June 1968. The merger produced 263,973 warrants.

Why Investors Buy Warrants

In exploring the merits of privileged issues as a class, it has been pointed out that convertible bonds sometimes offer a very attractive combination of security and chance for profit. Many investors see in convertible bonds the possibility of "having their cake and eating it too." As debentures they offer stable income as opposed to the variable income of common stock. This stable income appears to make them relatively less vulnerable to price decline during a stock-market downturn. At the same time, the conversion privilege appears to offer most of the prospects for capital gain which are offered by common stock.

Investors buy warrants because of the volatile speculative powers that they possess. The speculation stems from the very difficult task of assigning value to the warrants. They may be valued either before or after the date of record. The value of a warrant depends on its terms (that is, the option price and duration), on the current price of the stock, on the number of warrants outstanding relative to the common-stock issue, and on the presumed speculative possibilities of the related common. Some implications of these criteria of value are obvious. If the stock is selling above the option price, the warrant has "current value" equal to the difference. If the stock is selling below the option price, the warrant still has market value because the stock has a future possibility of rising above the option price at some time during the life of the warrant. This future possibility sustains current market value.

Certain speculative maneuvers with warrants appeal to some selected investors. One of the more intriguing involves warrants that are due to expire within the next 18 months or earlier. If the stock is selling considerably below the exercise price, the warrant is a likely candidate for a short sale. The speculation can be made almost foolproof if the investor simultaneously buys the stock of the same company.

The best picture of the specific performance of warrants can be seen in the following two extremes. The first example is the American and Foreign Power Company warrants issued in 1911 in conjunction with an issue of notes by that company. By the year 1929 they obtained their peak price of $175 and had an indicated market value of over a billion dollars. In the recapitalization in 1952 when the company was still solvent, the warrants were declared worthless and they disappeared completely from the market.

The second example is reflected in an advertisement that begins: "$500 to $104,000 in 4 years." This ad tells the amazing but true story of the RKO warrant. In 1940, RKO reorganized after some years of bad fortune. The old common-stock holders seemed to fare badly. For each share, they received only one-sixth of a share of new common stock plus one warrant good for buying one share of new common stock from the company at $15 per share. In 1942, RKO common was selling at a low of $2\frac{1}{2}$, but with general pessimism rife, the chance was slim that RKO common would ever sell above $15, at which point the warrants would begin to have some actual value. As a result, RKO warrants were selling at only 1/16, or $6\frac{1}{4}$ cents, per warrant. But this picture changed in four years. The RKO common stock advanced to a high of $28\frac{1}{8}$. The right to buy RKO common at $15 per share from the company when it was selling on the market at $28 per share was worth $13, and the warrants did sell at exactly $13. Thus, $500 invested in these warrants in 1942 was worth $104,000 by 1946. The greater volatility of the warrant is apparent: Between 1942 and 1946, RKO common went from $2\frac{1}{2}$ to 28. Therefore, a $500 investment in the stock appreciated to $5,625. But the warrant went from $6\frac{1}{4}$ cents to $13. Therefore, a $500 investment rose to $104,000.

In the past, most warrants have behaved in the market like low-priced common stocks of the sort that lack immediate earning power and are essentially a call on the company's future. They offered opportunities for spectacular percentage gains when purchased at the low levels produced by a depressed stock market.

PART II
Controller Strategies

CHAPTER 8

Financial Analysis
and Return
on Investment

One of management's functions is to determine the present position of the firm and plan its future needs. Financial statements provide data of the company's performance. Financial analysis, by calculating strategic relationships, indicates the firm's strengths and weaknesses. From the present situation, plans can be determined for the future. This chapter deals with financial statements and with the techniques of their analysis.

We shall discuss some of the ratios most commonly used to compare, evaluate, and plan corporate performance. They have been grouped under three headings: liquidity, return on investment (or profitability), and common-stock ratios. Liquidity and profitability ratios are the defining criteria for judging management's performance because the company may cease to exist if it is either illiquid or unprofitable. Common-stock ratios are the market's valuation of the firm.

The company must maintain itself in a financial condition favorable to the criteria of present and potential suppliers of funds. If monies are to be raised from creditors, the financial position of the corporation must be related to their standard of protection. Investors of equity funds will be more interested in long-term profitability. Since monies will be raised from both sources, the degree of importance attached to their respective needs must be weighed.

FIGURE 8–1 XYZ Company, balance sheet, December 31, 1971 (with comparative figures for 1970).

ASSETS

	1971	1970
Current assets		
Cash	$ 5,000	$ 60,000
Marketable securities, at cost (quoted market, Dec. 31, 1971, $6,000)	5,000	5,000
Accounts receivable, trade	410,000	300,000
Less allowance for doubtful accounts	(10,000)	(5,000)
Net accounts receivable	$ 400,000	$ 295,000
Inventories, at lower cost (FIFO) or market (LIFO)		
Finished products	300,000	250,000
Work in process	90,000	65,000
Raw materials	200,000	150,000
Total inventories	590,000	465,000
Total current assets	1,000,000	825,000
Property, plant, and equipment, at cost		
Land	300,000	300,000
Buildings	750,000	550,000
Machinery and equipment	250,000	175,000
	1,300,000	1,075,000
Less accumulated depreciation	400,000	250,000
Net property, plant, and equipment	900,000	775,000
Total assets	$1,900,000	$1,600,000

LIABILITIES AND STOCKHOLDERS' EQUITY

	1971	1970
Current liabilities		
Current installments of long-term debt	$ 150,000	$ 75,000
Accounts payable	200,000	175,000
Accrued expenses	75,000	100,000
Federal income taxes	75,000	75,000
Total current liabilities	500,000	425,000
Long-term debt (excluding current installments)		
9% first mortgage payable in annual installments of $75,000	300,000	375,000
10% second mortgage payable in annual installments of $75,000	300,000	—
Total long-term debt	600,000	375,000
Total liabilities	$1,100,000	$ 800,000
Stockholders' equity		
Common stock without par value. Authorized 250,000 shares; issued 100,000 shares at stated value of $5	$ 500,000	$ 500,000
Retained earnings	300,000	300,000
Total stockholders' equity	800,000	800,000
Total liabilities and stockholders' equity	$1,900,000	$1,600,000

FINANCIAL STATEMENTS

Financial statements provide information needed for analysis. They summarize company transactions over a period of time and serve as a report on management's effectiveness. They may reveal shortcomings in control or indicate major areas for changes in corporate policy.

The balance sheet (Figure 8-1) is a statement of financial condition, at a certain point in time. It lists the resources (assets) owned, together with the amounts owed to individuals having an ownership interest in these assets, both creditors (liabilities) and owners (equity). The balance sheet is a cumulative record of all recorded accounting transactions since the inception of the corporation. Assets, when acquired, are listed on the balance sheet, and held in one form or another until they are used up or sold. The equities of both creditors and owners are continually changing as a result of changes in either debt structure or income.

The income statement (Figure 8-2) tells us how the company has progressed during the fiscal period. Assets flow in from the sale of products or rendering of services. These are shown in the revenue accounts. The expense accounts match assets used with revenue earned.

At the end of the fiscal period the net earnings or losses are transferred to the retained earnings portion of the stockholders' equity section on the

FIGURE 8–2 XYZ Company, income statement, year ending December 31, 1971 (with comparative figures for 1970).

	1971	1970	Increase (Decrease)
Net sales	$2,500,000	$2,500,000	—
Cost of sales	1,650,000	1,650,000	—
Gross profit	850,000	850,000	—
Selling expenses	270,000	350,000	(80,000)
General and administrative expenses	370,000	320,000	50,000
	640,000	670,000	(30,000)
Operating income	210,000	180,000	(30,000)
Other deductions			
Interest	60,000	30,000	30,000
Earnings before federal income tax	150,000	150,000	—
Federal income taxes	75,000	75,000	—
Net earnings	$ 75,000	$ 75,000	—

balance sheet. Figure 8-3 shows the changes in the components of stockholders' equity. Income increases equity, and either increases assets or, conversely, decreases liabilities. A loss decreases owners' equity, and either increases liabilities or, conversely, decreases assets. The creditors' share of revenue is shown as interest expense. This is deducted from the revenues before the owners' share is calculated, and reemphasizes the primary claim on assets of the creditors. The assets, of course, are the means used to repay the creditor.

It is important to note that identical companies may report different incomes because of varying accounting methods. Expansion-minded companies will try to keep their earnings and stock prices high by stretching out depreciation and capitalizing items that in other circumstances might be classed as expenses.

They may also try to record acquisitions as poolings rather than purchases, if the acquired company has a lower book value than its acquisition price. In a purchase, the assets are shown at purchase price, but in a pooling they are shown at their old book value. This avoids showing the intangible asset "goodwill" on the balance sheet, of which a write-off to profit is not allowable for tax purposes, and also avoids higher future depreciation expense that will negatively affect future earnings. In a purchase, earnings are part of the buyer's earnings from the date of acquisition. In poolings, however, earnings are treated as if they were part of the buyer's earnings for the whole year, even if the acquisition was made in the last month of the year. Poolings may create an appearance of earnings and growth when they are not really there.

Statement of Source and Application of Funds

A logical adjunct to the balance sheet and income statement is the statement of source and application of funds (Figure 8-4).

The term "funds" means net working capital, or current assets minus current liabilities. To sustain and increase earnings, a company must have adequate working capital and also a margin of protection for creditors. Figure 8-4 reflects movement and change as a result of management

FIGURE 8–3   XYZ Company, statement of stockholders' equity, December 31, 1971.

Balance, Jan. 1, 1971	$800,000
Net earnings for the year	75,000
Cash dividends $0.75 per share (1970, $0.75 per share)	(75,000)
Balance, Dec. 31, 1971	$800,000

decisions. It shows how resources enter the company (profitable operations, borrowing, asset disposition, stockholder investment) and the uses made of these funds (unprofitable operations, asset acquisition, dividends, retirement of debt). The statement answers questions such as: What happened to profits? Where did funds come from? What is the dividend policy in relation to profit and investment in new plant? What became of the proceeds of bond or stock issues? Projection of future fund flows helps determine the long-range outlook for dividends and new financing.

The Opinion

The certified public accountant, as an independent auditor, examines the financial statements prepared by management, and the records and data supporting them, in order to render an opinion (Figure 8-5) as to their fairness, their compliance with generally accepted accounting principles, and the consistency of their application. Although paid by the company, the auditor is giving the opinion and his primary responsibility is to third parties (investors, creditors, and the public). Consistency, of course, assures meaningful comparability of financial statements between periods within the same company. This opinion is very important in evaluating the financial statements.

An unqualified opinion means that the financial statements have been prepared in accordance with generally accepted accounting principles. If

FIGURE 8-4   XYZ Company, statement of source and application of funds, year ending December 31, 1971 (with comparative figures for 1970).

	1971	1970
Funds provided		
Net earnings	$ 75,000	$ 75,000
Add charges against earnings not requiring funds:		
Depreciation	150,000	100,000
Funds derived from operations	225,000	175,000
Proceeds from issue of second mortgage	375,000	—
	$600,000	$175,000
Funds used		
Dividends	$ 75,000	$ 75,000
Addition to plant and equipment	275,000	—
Reduction of long-term debt	150,000	75,000
Increase working capital	100,000	25,000
	$600,000	$175,000

there are qualifications because of a departure from these principles or because the scope of application was inadequate, a qualified opinion is given. If the departures are material, a negative opinion may be given.

Notes are an integral part of the financial statements and should be read with great care. They provide information such as restrictions and liens on dividend payments due to debt or preferred-stock agreements; commitments of an unusual nature, such as bonus and stock-option plans; contingencies such as lawsuits; changes in application of accounting principles, and their effect; and explanatory notes needed to understand the statements more fully. In some cases they may help in the comparison of the financial statements of two or more companies.

Ratios. In-depth analysis finds logical causal relationships among various items on the balance sheet and income statement. The income statement causes changes on the balance sheet, and the balance sheet reflects accounts that are used to earn income. Ratios reflect these interrelationships.

Once the ratio has been determined, how do we know what it should be? For example, is a current ratio of 3:1 too high or too low? To make meaningful decisions, we need standards. The comparison of ratios over a period of years may hide consistent mismanagement over the same period. Likewise, the nature of the company will change with variation in

FIGURE 8–5   XYZ Company, auditor's opinion.

SCOPE

We have examined the balance sheet of XYZ Company as of December 31, 1971, and the related statements of income, stockholders' equity, and source and application of funds for the year then ended. Our examination was made in accordance with generally accepted auditing standards, and accordingly included such tests of the accounting records and such other auditing procedures as we considered necessary in the circumstances.

OPINION

In our opinion, the accompanying balance sheet and statement of income and stockholders' equity and source and application of funds present fairly the financial position of XYZ Company at December 31, 1971, and the results of its operations for the year then ended, in conformity with generally accepted accounting principles applied on a basis consistent with that of the preceding year.

plant and warehouse location, corporate size, and stage in the product life cycle.

We should compare the company's ratios with those of similar concerns in the same industry. It is important to choose the proper industry. A heavy-equipment manufacturer will have a higher investment in fixed assets than will a company in a service industry. Even ratios of companies in the same industry vary. Dun & Bradstreet shows large variations between cash-and-carry discount stores and retail stores offering a full line of services. (Table 8-1 gives a partial list of these ratios.) Diversification in recent years has made the classification of a company by industry more difficult.

The large number of variables emphasizes the danger in using universal rules of thumb to evaluate a company. However, standards do provide a framework within which variations from the ideal may be isolated and investigated. There are many sources of industry standards.

Dun & Bradstreet has 14 ratios for 72 lines of business activity, available in booklet form. The ratios represent a large sample of companies and are classified as upper quartile, median, and lower quartile.

Federal government agencies, especially the Small Business Administration of the U.S. Department of Commerce, and some state departments of commerce, publish business statistics. Many of these studies include standard financial ratios.

Other sources, including banks, publish ratios for particular industries. *Fortune* magazine publishes a list of 500 largest companies in June of each year, which includes financial ratios. *Forbes'* first issue of the year also provides financial evaluation and data.

The nature of competition and economic factors must also be considered. Companies in highly competitive industries will earn lower profit margins than those in less competitive industries. Recessions will slow the collection of receivables and lower profit margins. All these factors only reemphasize that passive dependence on a mass of ratios is not a substitute for good judgment.

LIQUIDITY RATIOS

Assets are listed on the balance sheet in the order of their nearness to cash, whereas liabilities are itemized in the order in which they will be paid, since the assets are the only source of meeting the company's obligations to its creditors. The ratios showing the ability of the company to meet its obligation are those relating assets to liabilities. Turnover ratios, by showing the speed with which inventory and accounts receivable

TABLE 8-1 Selected ratios* of retail stores.

Line of Business (and number of concerns reporting)	Current assets to current debt (Times)	Net profits on net sales (Per cent)	Net profits on tangible net worth (Per cent)	Net profits on net working capital (Per cent)	Net sales to tangible net worth (Times)	Net sales to net working capital (Times)	Collection period (Days)	Net sales to inventory (Times)	Fixed assets to tangible net worth (Per cent)	Current debt to tangible net worth (Per cent)	Total debt to tangible net worth (Per cent)	Inventory to net working capital (Per cent)	Current debt to inventory (Per cent)	Funded debts to net working capital (Per cent)
5641 Children's & Infants' Wear Stores (43)	3.98	3.38	16.09	19.33	4.78	7.49	*	7.1	4.0	29.7	83.6	78.0	43.1	27.9
	2.61	2.25	9.12	13.50	4.21	5.18	*	4.8	12.8	51.9	97.3	105.5	64.6	35.2
	1.88	0.73	2.88	4.35	3.20	3.84	*	3.9	28.6	77.9	146.6	146.8	88.9	61.5
5611 Clothing & Furnishings, Men's & Boys' (221)	4.46	4.01	13.31	15.29	4.53	5.19	*	5.3	5.4	26.0	66.8	73.1	38.8	9.0
	2.71	2.40	7.88	8.89	3.33	3.74	*	4.0	10.1	49.2	106.0	97.2	63.4	22.7
	1.85	1.30	3.80	4.64	2.29	2.71	*	2.9	20.1	102.5	190.1	136.4	95.1	46.4
5311 Department Stores (264)	4.28	3.27	10.71	13.78	4.59	5.84	*	6.8	10.7	23.4	46.1	60.9	48.8	13.5
	2.76	2.12	6.46	8.06	3.15	4.16	*	5.5	24.7	41.9	75.7	76.9	72.1	33.4
	2.07	1.19	3.49	4.46	2.44	3.07	*	4.2	46.5	69.4	130.1	106.3	100.0	57.9
Discount Stores (215)	2.41	3.07	18.94	27.76	8.69	11.82	*	7.3	12.9	53.9	82.4	107.1	57.2	12.6
	1.82	2.00	13.19	17.29	6.30	7.68	*	5.2	27.9	90.3	131.6	153.7	78.7	32.5
	1.44	1.25	7.49	9.26	4.52	5.56	*	4.0	48.5	146.7	211.3	220.1	99.8	63.7
Discount Stores, Leased Departments (45)	2.12	2.97	18.94	26.43	9.40	11.11	*	6.4	18.8	83.0	87.2	117.3	63.2	8.4
	1.73	1.79	13.19	16.88	7.10	7.73	*	4.7	28.5	128.4	139.6	182.4	77.6	25.2
	1.37	0.84	5.66	6.93	5.57	5.85	*	3.5	43.3	232.7	222.6	235.8	108.7	41.6
5651 Family Clothing Stores (92)	5.60	4.88	12.35	14.89	4.45	5.47	*	5.8	4.1	15.3	53.0	59.3	30.6	11.3
	3.20	2.61	8.38	10.32	3.11	3.41	*	4.3	11.4	36.9	72.7	82.5	51.4	23.9
	2.22	1.53	5.16	5.58	2.10	2.54	*	3.2	23.0	66.9	129.8	126.2	83.7	40.8
5252 Farm Equipment Dealers (91)	2.57	3.32	15.64	19.50	7.46	8.42	16	4.8	8.1	59.1	126.9	98.9	60.4	16.5
	1.74	1.74	8.75	11.19	5.21	5.82	22	3.4	17.2	121.3	221.9	148.5	82.0	32.1
	1.36	0.56	3.56	4.07	2.72	3.45	46	2.5	27.7	236.1	357.1	283.1	101.0	52.8
5969 Farm & Garden Supply Stores (74)	4.75	4.62	13.25	23.06	4.87	8.06	*	13.3	17.9	16.2	57.0	43.6	50.0	16.5
	2.48	2.46	7.43	13.55	2.92	5.36	*	9.1	38.2	37.4	81.6	67.9	95.3	49.3
	1.68	0.83	2.70	5.53	2.20	4.00	*	5.8	57.7	63.1	121.5	104.3	170.7	127.8
5712 Furniture Stores (188)	5.34	4.52	10.11	11.50	4.18	5.20	54	6.5	4.3	23.2	61.0	30.5	58.6	11.3
	2.87	2.13	6.32	6.85	2.58	2.74	109	5.0	10.3	52.7	104.2	59.4	94.4	20.1
	1.92	0.87	2.11	2.43	1.67	1.75	212	3.7	22.0	98.1	178.6	100.7	146.6	40.0
5541 Gasoline Service Stations (63)	3.27	4.44	11.60	34.23	6.04	13.19	*	27.4	22.8	20.8	46.9	40.0	74.8	11.5
	2.08	2.06	7.50	16.37	3.84	6.83	*	12.0	47.4	38.1	67.5	63.2	159.7	47.2
	1.58	1.11	4.36	6.99	2.31	4.86	*	6.7	69.4	81.4	122.5	99.4	243.2	74.5

* Listed in order as upper, median, and lower quartiles.

Source: Reprinted by special permission from Dun's, September 1970. Copyright, 1970, Dun & Bradstreet Publications Corporation.

will be turned into cash, give a causal insight into the changes in these relationships.

Lenders are concerned with the amount of risk they bear in proportion to the owners' risk. This is reflected in the percentage of total assets that they have financed. The smaller that proportion, the more the value of assets can decrease before the creditors' interests are threatened, and the less they will lose if the firm becomes insolvent. Owners should provide the majority of the assets and bear the majority of the risk because, unlike the creditors, they have no upper limit on their share of future income. Their primary interest, however, is earnings, for it is the long-run ability of the company to operate profitably that determines its ultimate ability to repay the debt and its interest. Whereas short-term loans are self-liquidating, long-term debt is repaid either through accumulated earnings or by the issuance of new debt or equity. The success of any new issue of securities is primarily dependent upon the company's earning record. We shall now examine some liquidity ratios.

Current ratio. The current ratio of *total current assets* to *total current liabilities* indicates the company's ability to meet its obligations. A low ratio may suggest that the company is unable to pay its bills. A high ratio may point to poor management, if it reflects an excessive amount of cash or too large investment in accounts receivable and inventory.

The XYZ Company has a current ratio of $1,000,000/$500,000, or 2:1. Based on past history and on management standards, this ratio and the level of current assets are acceptable.

Quick ratio. The current ratio, however, has some shortcomings. It assumes that all components of the numerator have the same liquidity. However, although accounts receivable are only one step from cash, inventory is two steps away. The acid test, or quick ratio,

$$\frac{\text{Cash} + \text{marketable securities} + \text{net accounts receivable}}{\text{Total current liabilities}}$$

measures the extent to which cash and near-cash items cover the current liabilities.

Inventories are excluded at this point because of the time required to convert raw materials to finished goods and the ensuing uncertainty of selling the merchandise. Accounts receivable, on the other hand, represent completed sales. The quick ratio is $410,000/$500,000, or 0.8:1. This may suggest that the company is not liquid enough to meet its immediate obligations. To remain solvent, it should have a quick-asset ratio close to 1:1. Let us assume that the company has decided that its standard is 0.9:1. Total current assets will remain the same, but their components will change.

If X equals the required amount of quick assets, then

$$0.9 = \frac{X}{\$500,000}$$

$$X = \$450,000$$

Thus, it appears that the deficiency in quick assets will be $450,000 − $410,000, or $40,000.

Accounts receivable turnover. The ratio of *annual credit sales* to *average accounts receivable* measures the liquidity of the accounts receivable. If the turnover is twelve times, receivables are collected in the same month that the goods are sold; if three times, receivables are collected in the fourth month following the date of sale.

The use of average accounts receivable eliminates seasonalities. For example, if sales have increased rapidly in the months immediately preceding the fiscal year end, the accounts receivable will reflect the amount of these sales, lowering the turnover. Thus, it would appear that the receivables are more difficult to collect, although they would have increased only because of their timing.

A low turnover may indicate an inability to collect from customers. A high turnover may reflect an unnecessarily stringent credit policy that discourages slow-paying customers. It may also reflect too liberal cash discounts offered on sales.

Let us assume that the average month-end balance of $500,000 is higher than the year-end closing balance and that all sales are on credit. Turnover is 5:1 = $2,500,000/$500,000. Turnover of 5:1 is a standard acceptable to the company. However, taking into account the cyclical nature of sales, it determines that its year-end investment in accounts receivable should be $416,800 (see Table 8-2). The company arrives at this figure by annualizing the last quarter's sales of $521,000 ($2,084,000) and dividing by the turnover standard of 5.

TABLE 8-2   Statement of current assets.

	Actual	Standard	Difference
Cash	$ 5,000	$ 28,200	$(23,200)
Marketable securities	5,000	5,000	—
Accounts receivable	400,000	416,800	(16,800)
Inventories	590,000	458,667	131,333
Total current assets	$1,000,000	$908,667	$ 91,333

The underinvestment in accounts receivable is $400,000 − $416,800, or $16,800. Quick assets should be $450,000; accounts receivable, $416,800. Therefore, cash and marketable securities should be $450,000 − $416,800, or $33,200. The deficiency in quick assets of $40,000 consists of an underinvestment in accounts receivable of $16,800 and an underinvestment in cash and marketable securities of $23,200, or $33,200 − $5,000 cash − $5,000 marketable securities. The underinvestment of $23,200 is entirely in cash.

Inventory turnover. The ratio of *cost of goods sold* to *average inventory* shows how rapidly goods are being sold and whether the inventory is deficient or excessive in proportion to sales. Inventory is shown at cost, and since sales are computed by multiplying the quantity sold by the selling price, and cost of goods sold is determined by multiplying units sold by cost per unit, the cost of goods sold is used as the numerator in the ratio in order to compare like amounts. Again, use of average inventory eliminates seasonal fluctuations.

The method of inventory pricing affects the usefulness of this ratio. The last-in, first-out method (LIFO) assumes that goods are sold from the latest purchases, and therefore inventory is shown at old costs. Thus, it may be meaningless to compare the current prices of cost of goods sold with inventory valued at decade-old prices. The first-in, first-out method (FIFO) reflects inventory at current costs. However, the advantage of LIFO is that it shows income more accurately in periods of changing prices.

A manager must compromise between being out of stock and overinvesting in inventory. A low or declining turnover may indicate that the company is overstocked or that there are obsolete or slow-moving items on hand. A very high turnover is not necessarily favorable. If the inventory turns over too rapidly, there is danger that the firm may run out of stock. If the company is a manufacturer, this may cause a temporary shutdown of the production line; if a distributor, it may lose sales.

Turnover is usually computed for each class of inventory: raw materials, work in process, and finished goods. Excessive supplies of finished goods are the responsibility of the sales department; work in process, of production; and raw materials, of both sales and production. The level of inventory depends on many factors, among which are production, length of production run, efficiency, and storage capacity.

Let us assume that the average month-end inventory during the year is $650,000 and that the last quarter's cost of sales is $344,000. The turnover is $1,650,000/$650,000 = 2.5 times a year. Management sets a turnover standard of three times a year, or once every 122 days. However, taking into account the cyclical nature of sales, management estimates that year-end inventories should be $458,667. This is computed by annualizing the last quarter's cost of sales as $344,000 ($1,376,000) and dividing by the turnover standard of 3. The overinvestment in inventory is $131,333. These figures are tabulated in Table 8-2 and compared with the current-asset portion of the balance sheet, which is given in Figure 8-1.

The crucial problem is the $131,333 difference in inventories.

An examination of the inventory disclosed that no items were obsolete. The sales manager said that in order to support projected sales of $3,000,000, he maintained an average inventory of $650,000. When we examine the ratios, we find that an average inventory of $650,000 should result in a cost of sales of $1,950,000 (in contrast to that shown in Figure 8-2):

$$\frac{3}{1} = \frac{X}{\$650,000}$$

If we add the markup of $850,000/$1,650,000, or 51.5 percent, we find enough inventory to support $1,950,000 + $975,000, or $2,925,000 of sales. In this case, excessive buildup in inventory resulted from a failure to meet sales projections. The drop in inventories at the year's end reflected an attempt to adjust inventories downward.

Accounts payable turnover. Some firms use the ratio of *annual purchases* to *average accounts payable* to determine the firm's reliance on trade credit. If the average day's accounts payable outstanding are compared with available credit terms, the firm can determine whether or not it is taking advantage of these terms and can estimate the cost of this financing when it is unable to do so. If we assume that $650,000 of the $1,650,000 cost of sales represents material purchases and that average accounts payable during the year are $187,500, the accounts payable turnover is $650,000/$187,500, or 3.5 times a year. This is once every 120 days, quite in excess of normal credit offerings, and negatively affects the cost of financing.

Debt to net worth. The ratio of *debt* to *tangible net worth* is a safety measure relating the creditors' investment to that of the owners. Refer to Figure 8-1. Total long-term debt ($600,000) and short-term debt ($500,000) is compared with the net worth of assets capable of producing income (tangible net worth). Net worth is computed by taking the sum of outstanding stock ($500,000) and retained earnings ($300,000). Tangible net worth excludes intangible assets such as goodwill, trademarks, and organization expense. The XYZ Company's ratio of *debt* to *net worth* is therefore $1,100,000/$800,000, or 1.4:1. This shows that the creditors' investment in the company's assets is greater than that of the owners. A ratio this high suggests that the opportunities for additional borrowing are limited. Even if funds could be obtained, the high interest rates and loan restrictions (such as limiting dividends) would make such borrowing undesirable. If the ratio is too low, credit may not be properly utilized and an available source of cash will remain untapped.

Earnings coverage. Each investor is concerned with that portion of the earnings (the ratio of *operating income* to *interest earned*) to which he is entitled. A creditor especially wants to know if his interest return is covered adequately by the available earnings.

The interest coverage for holders of the first-mortgage bonds is $210,000/$30,000 = 7.0 times. The second-mortgage bonds have available only those funds remaining after first-mortgage interest has been paid. In this case (Figure 8-2), the earnings coverage for all bonds is $210,000/$60,000, or 3.5 times. Income from operations may thus decline up to one-third without endangering the creditors.

RETURN ON INVESTMENT

Owners and long-term creditors measure the success of a firm by its ability to earn profits. Creditors have an upper limit on the amount they can earn, as a result of restrictions on the interest-rate level. Owners, however, have no constraint placed on their share of corporate earnings. If profits are low in proportion to investment, they will either withdraw their funds and place them where they can earn more, or replace present management with new executives capable of providing a satisfactory return. We shall now discuss some measures of profitability.

Profit margin. The firm's profit margin is a common measure of profitability. The margin is expressed as the ratio of *operating income* to *net sales.*

The profit margin of the XYZ Company is $210,000/$2,500,000 = 8.4 percent. Operating income is computed before interest and taxes. Operating management is not responsible for financial costs. High profit margins, especially if combined with a small investment in fixed assets, may invite increased competition. Income varies because of changes in price or volume, or both. Due to the importance of this topic a major portion of the next chapter will be devoted to it.

Asset turnover. One measure of the energies spent by the company is the total assets it has used to sell its products. The asset turnover (the ratio of *net sales* to *operating assets*) reflects the amount of assets the company employed to sell its goods. The XYZ Company has an asset turnover of $2,500,000/$1,900,000 = 1.30 times. This turnover, however, does not tell us the income earned by employing these assets. Individually, these ratios have specific weaknesses. Combined, they are a powerful analytical tool.

The two ratios that determine profit ratio and asset turnover have certain shortcomings. Profit margin fails to consider the investment made by the company to earn the profit, since if the profit margin is low, it does not matter if the company had to invest very little money to earn that income. Asset turnover, on the other hand, provides a clue to the amount of the investment made by the company for its sales.

Return on investment. The manager of a company must be concerned about the earnings the company receives from investment of its limited funds. ROI, the return on investment (the ratio of *operating income* to *operating assets*), provides that measure. Capital has value because of its scarcity, and management is judged on its efficiency in using rationed capital within the firm. To arrive at ROI, the following formula is used:

$$ROI = (\text{profit margin} \times \text{asset turnover})$$

$$= \left(\frac{\text{operating income}}{\text{net sales}} \times \frac{\text{net sales}}{\text{operating assets}} \right)$$

By canceling out net sales and computing,

$$ROI = \frac{210,000}{1,900,000} = 11.1\%$$

The relationship of ROI to the XYZ Company's balance sheet and income statement (Figures 8-1 and 8-2) is portrayed graphically in Figure 8-6. ROI recognizes the importance of both operating expenses and the level of capital employed in relation to sales volume. ROI can be improved by increasing sales revenue through high prices (and probably lower volume) or higher volume (at probably lower prices). This may increase both profit margin and turnover. Costs can be reduced up to the point where they do not affect quality, and profit margin can be widened through improved control. The amount of capital employed can be reduced by increasing the turnover of inventory and accounts receivable, and by utilizing the fixed assets more efficiently.

In analyzing ROI as depicted in Figure 8-6, fixed assets are shown at original cost and are not depreciated, for if they were depreciated and not replaced, return on investment (investment turnover) would continually rise even during periods of stable earnings, thus hiding actual management performance. Actually, return would be rising as a result of this inflation, and profits would be shown at inflated values compared with the cost of fixed assets. Return should be increasing to account for the cost of replacing old assets. Using original cost also facilitates comparison of divisions within the same company, assuming the company has uniform accounting policies. If one division has old equipment that is fully depreciated, and another has a new plant, the division with the depreciated assets would have to earn very little to generate a high ROI. Additionally, although ROI varies with the riskiness of a venture, it is absolute and ignores the riskiness in the nature of the assets. Earnings are shown net of depreciation, since earnings must allow for the recovery of fixed-asset investment.

Overreliance on ROI may cause a manager to overemphasize the current year's return at the expense of research and training programs

FIGURE 8–6   Relationship of factors affecting return on investment.

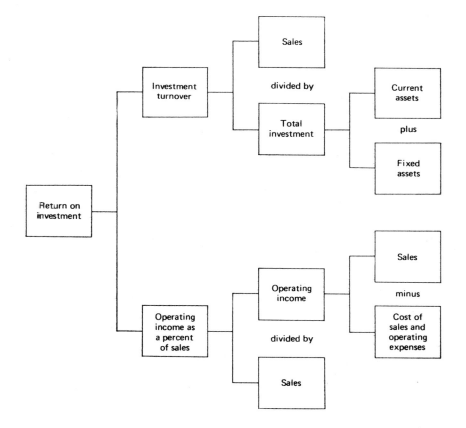

that may pay off in future years. The taking of risks is discouraged. Overall corporate interests may be ignored. Emphasis is placed on the improvement of ratios rather than dollar profits, which may affect the stockholder's ability to maximize his returns. One example would be that of a company using composite depreciation. In this method, when an asset is scrapped, fixed assets are reduced by the asset scrapped, but no loss is recognized because all assets are part of the same pool. An astute manager could scrap perfectly useful assets in order to increase ROI, and yet not show the loss in income. This would not be the case if assets were shown at net book value. Fixed assets include capitalized leases to avoid units' improving their returns over other units by leasing rather than buying.

Changes in ROI can be determined by examining its components. For example, assume that in the prior year, sales and earnings were constant. During the past year, however, the company acquired plant and equipment for $275,000, and also increased its working capital by $100,000. Total assets in the past year were $1,850,000, and ROI was $210,000/$1,850,000 = 11 percent. In order to achieve in the current year the same return with the same profit margin, the operating income would have to be

$$11\% = \frac{X}{\$2,300,000}$$

$$X = \$253,000$$

Sales would have to be

$$8.4\% = \frac{\$253,000}{X}$$

$$X = \$3,000,000$$

This is the estimate of the sales manager, but it would appear that the company had acquired assets to obtain more sales, which never materialized. As a consequence, the company is overinvested in inventory, and has a lower ROI than in the past year. Table 8-3 shows target ROIs for certain companies.

Return on equity. The XYZ Company has a return on equity, *r*, of 9.3 percent (see Figure 8-3):

$$\frac{\text{Earnings available to common stockholders}}{\text{(after payment of preferred dividends)}} = \frac{\$\,75,000}{\$800,000} = 9.3\%$$

Common stockholders' equity is the book value of common stock

TABLE 8-3   Target returns on investment.

Company	Target Return on Investment
Alcoa	20% (after taxes); higher on new products
General Electric	20% (after taxes)
General Motors	20% (after taxes)
International Harvester	10% (after taxes)
Johns-Manville	Return on investment greater than past 15-year average (about 15% after taxes); higher target for new products
Kroger	20% (before taxes)
Sears Roebuck	10–15% (after taxes)
U.S. Steel	8% (after taxes)

Source: R. F. Lanzilotti, "Pricing Objective in Large Companies," *American Economic Review* (September 1958), pp. 921–940.

plus retained earnings. Return on equity is closely related to ROI:

$$\text{ROI} = \frac{\text{operating income}}{\text{operating assets}}$$

If this ratio is revised by subtracting the following items, we have

$$\frac{\text{Operating income} - \text{interest} - \text{federal income tax} - \text{preferred dividends}}{\text{Operating assets} - \text{total liabilities}}$$

$$= \frac{\text{earnings available to common stockholders}}{\text{common stockholders' equity}}$$

This ratio represents *r*, which measures management's ability to effectively utilize the owners' investment. The ratio varies because of changes in the turnover of operating assets, operating margin, and financial leverage. For example, if ROI is multiplied by an operating ratio of *net profit after interest, taxes, and preferred dividends* to *operating income* and a leverage ratio of *operating assets* to *common stockholders' equity*, then

$$(9.1\%) \left(\frac{\$\,75,000}{\$210,000}\right)\left(\frac{\$2,300,000}{\$\,\,800,000}\right) = 9.3\% = r$$

or

$$r = \left(\frac{\text{Operating income}}{\text{Operating assets}}\right)\left(\frac{\text{net profit after interest, taxes, and preferred dividends}}{\text{operating income}}\right)$$

$$\times \left(\frac{\text{operating assets}}{\text{common stockholders' equity}}\right)$$

After canceling like terms,

$$r = \frac{\text{net profit after interest, taxes, and preferred dividends}}{\text{common stockholders' equity}}$$

The ten highest r of the 500 largest U.S. corporations, and for certain industries, are shown in Table 8-4.

TABLE 8-4   Return on stockholders' equity.

THE INDUSTRY MEDIANS

	Returns		THE TEN HIGHEST		
	1970	1969		Sales Rank	Returns
Pharmaceuticals	19.3%	16.3%	Smithfield Foods	789	64.2%
Petroleum refining	17.5	8.9	Tampax	823	36.8
Tobacco	16.1	14.9	Clorox	704	32.2
Office machinery (includes computers)	12.7	11.8	Inspiration Consolidated Copper	755	27.1
Publishing and printing	11.5	14.0	Telex	978	26.6
Soaps, cosmetics	11.2	12.7	Fleetwood Enterprises	638	26.4
Motor vehicles and parts	10.3	11.8	Dr. Pepper	973	25.8
Metal products	9.8	10.9	Aileen	950	25.0
Food and beverages	9.5	9.1	Champion Home Builders	743	24.7
Rubber	9.0	8.6	Dow Jones	577	24.1
Metal manufacturing	8.7	9.3			
Chemicals	8.6	12.1			
Apparel	8.5	10.6			
Glass, cement, gypsum, concrete	8.3	8.6			
Paper and wood products	8.2	11.2			
Farm and industrial machinery	7.0	10.1			
Textiles	7.0	8.8			
Mining	6.8	14.9			
Appliances, electronics	6.1	9.7			
Measuring, scientific, and photographic equipment	6.1	9.6			
Shipbuilding, railroad equipment, mobile homes	4.5	18.3			
Aircraft and parts	NA	12.4			
All industries	8.6	10.7			

Source: Reprinted from the 1971 Fortune Directory by permission.

COMMON-STOCK RATIOS

The value of the ownership interest is the amount a buyer is willing to pay for it. For companies listed on stock exchanges, this is market price. Many factors enter into this price. If the market is interested in income, it will examine the company's dividend policy; if in growth, the market is interested in future earnings.

Dividend payout. The common stockholders are interested in the proportion of earnings they receive. The payout ratio is $0.75/$0.075, or 100 percent. The company may be paying out all its earnings because of a lack of investment opportunities within the firm.

Book value per share. For the XYZ Company, $800,000/100,000 = $8. The usefulness of this ratio of *common stockholders' equity* to *number of common shares outstanding* is highly questionable. There is no relationship between book value (based on historical balance-sheet cost) and market value (based on future earnings and dividends). It may have some pertinence if the company is highly invested in liquid assets and is considering liquidation. In this case, book value is greater than market value. This may reinforce the lack of investment opportunities within the firm and account for the high dividend-payout ratio. The high dividend-payout ratio and the additional borrowing increases the *debt* to *net worth* ratio and the risk posture of the firm. Preferred stockholders would have a claim on surplus if, under a cumulative dividend provision, an arrears exists or if a premium over the par value of the stock was paid at the time of subscription.

Earnings per share. The ratio of *earnings after tax and preferred dividends* to *number of shares outstanding* reflects management's ability to earn profits for the owners. The common stockholder is interested in the amount available to him after the payment of all senior charges and taxes. The earnings per share are

$$\frac{\$75,000}{100,000} = \$0.75$$

Earnings per share increase by improving ROI. This can be shown by multiplying ROI (the ratio of *operating income* to *operating assets*) by book value (which is the ratio of *common stockholders' equity = operating assets* to *shares outstanding*) and adjusting for interest, tax, and preferred dividends.

Price-earnings ratio. The *P/E* (or ratio of *average market price per share* to *earnings per share*) reflects how much the investing public is willing to pay for the company's prospective earnings. The XYZ Company has an average market price of $6. The price-earnings ratio is $6/$0.75 = 8 times earnings. If the market has assigned a price earnings of 12 to the industry, it does not have much confidence in XYZ's future earning prospects. Examination of this ratio shows chances for financial leverage. ABC Company, with a high P/E ratio, could immediately increase its earnings per share by acquiring a company with a low P/E. This analysis assumes that the acquisition of B does not adversely affect ABC's P/E. For example, let us look at companies ABC and DEF, using the data in Table 8-5.

TABLE 8-5   Comparison of ABC and DEF companies.

	ABC	DEF
P/E	60	20
Earnings	$2,000,000	$2,000,000
Shares outstanding	1,000,000	1,000,000
$(E/P)_S$	$2.00	$2.00
Market price	$120.00	$40.00

Company ABC offers Company DEF $40 per share, or one share of ABC for three shares of DEF. Then, the E of ABC becomes $4,000,000/1,333,333, or $3, an increase of $1; and if ABC's earnings remain the same, market price will increase to $180. The shareholders of DEF have their earnings valued at three times their old rate. Although ABC has increased its outstanding shares by $33\frac{1}{3}$ percent, its earnings have increased 50 percent. If, however, the shareholders of DEF should want a premium, ABC could offer them $60 per share or one share of ABC for two shares of DEF. Then E of ABC becomes $4,000,000/1,500,000 = $2.67, an increase of $0.67; and if ABC's P/E remains the same, market price will increase to $160.20. In this case, outstanding shares would have increased by 50 percent and E by only $33\frac{1}{3}$ percent. In order to avoid dilution, companies should not acquire other companies unless the percentage increase in earnings plus the contemplated change in share price exceeds the percentage increase in shares outstanding. The price to pay in this example should be between $40 and $60 per share.

Capitalization rate. This is the rate of return that the market demands for the XYZ Company. It is the reciprocal (the ratio of *earnings per share* to *average market price per share*) of the price-earnings ratio. As the price-earnings ratio increases, the capitalization rate decreases. The E/P ratio for XYZ is $0.75/$6 = 1/8, or 12.5 percent.

Dividend yield. For XYZ, $0.75/$6 = 12.5 percent. The ratio of *dividends per share* to *average market price per share* is of particular importance to investors primarily seeking current return rather than future growth. Growth companies have conservative dividend policies because they are using their income for expansion.

Let us return for a moment to the statement (Figure 8-4) of source and application of funds. Although working capital increased, the management of the corporation was inefficient. Assets were acquired in anticipation of increased sales that did not materialize. ROI declined because assets increased more than sales and earnings. The payment of dividends equal to earnings reduced the chance for favorable borrowings. Assets were financed with debt, not equity, because all earnings were paid out. The *debt* to *net worth* ratio increased to the danger point. This is reflected in the onerous terms the company had to accept on its second mortgage. Now we see how ratios can be an incisive tool of analysis, not only of current performance but also for future planning.

CHAPTER 9

Cost-Volume-
Profit Analysis

It is very important for management to plan effectively for changes in the level of business activity. This demands an understanding of the inter-action of costs and volume on corporate profits and is obtained through breakeven and cost-volume-profit analysis. A knowledge of these operating relationships is essential to the preparation of cost estimates, setting of selling prices, and analysis of the effect of changes in volume on costs and profits. In Chapter 4, "Cost of Capital," we computed the financial breakeven point; this chapter deals with the operating breakeven point.

THE CONCEPT

Operating costs follow certain patterns of behavior. Although the greater the volume, the greater the costs incurred, changes in total cost are not necessarily proportionate to the change in volume. Plant, equip-ment, and administrative personnel tend to be inflexible to and unaffected by changes in volume. Physical equipment cannot be disposed of during periods of low volume, and key personnel cannot be laid off. Those costs that do not change with the level of output are fixed costs. These sunk costs remain constant within the normal time range of operations.

Companies with a greater degree of cost flexibility, such as those with a high direct-labor content, have costs more proportional to their volume. Personnel can be hired or laid off as conditions warrant. Those costs varying in direct proportion to changes in the volume of production are variable costs. Variable costs are shown as a constant percentage of sales.

Figure 9-1 is a graphic presentation of these costs. Dollars are shown on the vertical axis and unit volume on the horizontal. At any level of volume, fixed costs remain constant, but variable costs are assumed to have a linear relationship to volume. Total cost, of course, is fixed plus variable costs.

The conventional income statement presents a reasonably accurate picture of the company's performance after the fact. It shows the company's profit for a given period at a given volume. However, it ignores dynamic factors. It does not indicate what will happen to profits if there are variations in the volume of items sold.

The most important factor in profit planning is its relation to volume. If all costs varied directly with volume, profits would bear a constant relationship to sales. For example, if each unit sold for $1.50 had a variable cost of $1 the company would earn $0.50, or $33\frac{1}{3}$ percent, on all units sold. If one unit were sold, earnings would be $0.50. For 1 million units of sales, earnings would be $500,000. This relationship is shown in Figure 9-2.

If all costs were fixed, profits would increase disproportionately with volume. For example, if fixed costs were $150,000 and each unit sold for $1.50, losses would be incurred until 100,000 units were sold. After this point was reached, the first unit over 100,000 would produce earnings of $1.50 on sales or $1.50/$150,001.50, an extremely small percent, while the 200,000th unit would produce earnings of $150,000 on sales, or $150,000/$300,000 = 50 percent. In this case, the rate of profit per unit varies with the number of units sold. This is illustrated in Figure 9-3.

BREAKEVEN ANALYSIS

Total cost contains both variable and fixed elements. It is for this reason that we use breakeven analysis. Breakeven analysis is an approach

FIGURE 9–1   Illustration of fixed, variable, and total costs.

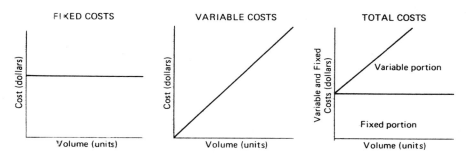

toward profit planning based on the relationships among cost, volume, and profit. The breakeven point is that sales volume where sales revenue equals the cost to make and sell the product. Neither a profit is earned nor a loss incurred.

Breakeven analysis assumes that sales will equal production, which over a long period is correct. Over a short period, sales and production volume will differ, accounted for by changes in inventories. Breakeven analysis also assumes that selling prices will remain uniform and one of three pricing programs is in effect:

A single product is sold either at a fixed unit price or at a range of prices always averaging a fixed price; or

A variety of products are sold at a fixed price always averaging a fixed unit price; or

A variety of products are sold at a variety of unit prices, but always averaging a fixed percentage over variable costs.

If the spread between selling price and variable cost is not uniform between products, then two or more computations are required. Finally, this analysis assumes that costs can be rigidly defined as either fixed or variable. These underlying assumptions must be considered when using breakeven analysis.

We may compute the breakeven point by a trial-and-error method as in Table 9-1, where the breakeven point is 300,000 units on sales revenue of $450,000. This point can be easily calculated by algebra.

FIGURE 9–2   Illustration of companies with all costs variable.   FIGURE 9–3   Illustration of companies with all costs fixed.

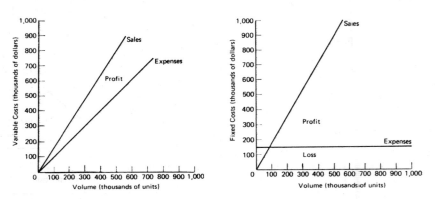

TABLE 9-1   Relationships among units produced, variable costs, fixed costs, and income (in thousands).

| Units Sold | Total Revenue | Operating Cost | | Total Operating Cost | Operating Income (Loss) |
		Fixed Cost	Variable Cost		
—	—	$150	—	$150	($150)
100	$150	150	$100	250	(100)
150	225	150	150	300	(75)
200	300	150	200	350	(50)
250	375	150	250	400	(25)
300	450	150	300	450	—
350	525	150	350	500	25
400	600	150	400	550	50
450	675	150	450	600	75
500	750	150	500	650	100

Let R = sales at breakeven point

F = fixed operating costs (in our example, fixed costs are $150,000)

V = variable operating costs (since variable costs vary directly with sales, variable costs may be expressed as a percent of sales; in our example, variable costs are $66\frac{2}{3}$ percent)

Since there is neither profit nor loss, our formula for the calculation of the breakeven point is

$$\text{Sales} - \text{fixed costs} - \text{variable costs} = \text{profit (or loss)}$$

or

$$R - F - V = 0$$

therefore

$$R = F + V$$
$$= F + (66\tfrac{2}{3})R$$
$$= \$150,000 + (66\tfrac{2}{3})R$$

The breakeven point is a sales level of $450,000.

The breakeven point is converted to units by dividing sales revenue by the unit selling price of $1.50 to arrive at 300,000 units. This is illustrated in the breakeven chart, Figure 9-4, where volume produced is shown on the horizontal axis. The vertical axis shows dollars, both revenue and cost. Fixed costs are shown as a horizontal line. Variable costs cause the total cost line to increase with production. Income is a linear function, and its slope is greater than the total cost line because, for every unit sold, the firm gains $0.75 while incurring an additional cost of only $0.50.

The breakeven chart is an easy visual aid to the comprehension of the cost-volume-profit relationship. It indicates not only the volume required to break even but also the profit or loss that can be expected at any particular sales volume. Because the volume of sales does not remain constant, neither do profits. This relationship between profits and volume is very important. Management is interested in many factors affecting profit fluctuations. What increase in sales volume is required to cover additional fixed expenses? What sales volume is required to produce a desired profit?

Let us assume that the LMN Company is considering an investment in new equipment, which will have an annual depreciation of $100,000. The present level of fixed costs is $150,000. If the company makes the investment, the breakeven point is

$$R = \$250,000 + 0.66\tfrac{2}{3}R = \$750,000$$

Therefore, if the expansion is carried out, sales must increase by $750,000 − $450,000, or $300,000, for the company to break even. Let

FIGURE 9–4 Breakeven chart.

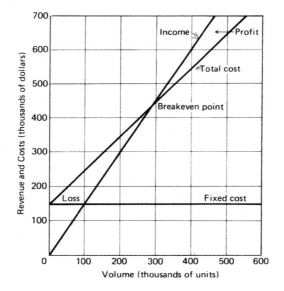

us assume that to provide an adequate ROI after the expansion, operating income should be $300,000. Then

$$R = \$250,000 + 0.66\tfrac{2}{3}R + \$300,000$$

Thus, sales would have to be $1,650,000.

The breakeven point can be lowered by decreasing both fixed and variable costs and changing product mix. This effect is explained further in a later section of this chapter. The first and last alternatives will also be discussed. Cost control is not within the scope of this book.

PROFIT TO VOLUME RATIO

We can revise the format of the income statement to a marginal contribution statement by reclassifying all expenses between that portion which meets variable costs and the remainder, or marginal portion, which contributes both to fixed costs and profit. This is sometimes referred to as direct costing.

Let us use four examples from Table 9-1 and also assume borrowings of $200,000 at $7\tfrac{1}{2}$ percent and a tax rate of 50 percent. Table 9-2 shows data for these four *profit* to *volume* ratios. Variable costs are shown as a percent of sales. Once the variable costs have been covered, the remaining portion of the sales dollar is used to meet fixed costs and provide an operating profit. Since variable costs are a direct function of revenue, the marginal contribution to fixed costs and operating profit must also be a constant percent of revenue. A change in sales revenue of $150,000 will change operating profit by $150,000 times the marginal contribution of $33\tfrac{1}{3}$ percent, or $50,000.

The *profit* to *volume* ratio is the same as marginal contribution and is that portion of the sales dollar remaining after variable costs have been

TABLE 9-2   Effects of cost and volume on profit.

Costing Factor	Case 1	Case 2	Case 3	Case 4
Sales revenue	$300,000	$450,000	$600,000	$750,000
Variable costs, $66\tfrac{2}{3}$%	200,000	300,000	400,000	500,000
Marginal contribution, $33\tfrac{1}{3}$%	100 000	150,000	200,000	250,000
Fixed costs	150,000	150,000	150,000	150,000
Operating income (loss)	(50,000)	0	50,000	100,000
Interest	15,000	15,000	15,000	15,000
Earnings (loss) before tax	(65,000)	(15,000)	35,000	85,000
Tax	0	0	17,500	42,500
Earnings (loss) after tax	$ (65,000)	$ (15,000)	$ 17,500	$ 42,500

FIGURE 9–5   Profit-volume chart (in thousands of dollars).

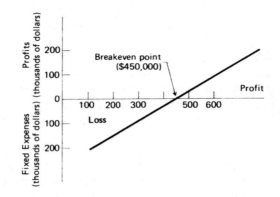

met. This ratio shows the rate at which fixed costs are recovered, and also shows the rate of profit accumulation once the breakeven point has been reached. We can calculate this ratio by expanding our breakeven formula:

$$R = F + vR$$

where v is the portion of the sales dollar that covers variable costs, and $(1 - v)R = F$. Therefore, $R = F/(1 - v)$, where $1 - v$ is the *profit* to *volume* ratio and is equal to fixed costs plus profit at a point above the breakeven point. The *profit* to *volume* relationship is illustrated in Figure 9-5. We can use this relationship to calculate the breakeven point:

$$R = \frac{\$150,000}{1 - 0.66\frac{2}{3}} = \$450,000$$

We can also determine the sales volume required to meet fixed costs and provide a profit of $50,000:

$$R = \frac{\$200,000}{0.33\frac{1}{3}} = \$600,000$$

And we can also determine the loss suffered if sales are $300,000:

$$\$300,000 = \frac{F}{0.33\frac{1}{3}}$$

$$F = \$100,000$$

We know that our fixed costs are $150,000. Since sales are contributing only $100,000 to these costs, our loss is $100,000 − $150,000 = $50,000.

Two factors determine profit patterns. One is the alternative cost structure and the other is the amount of fixed costs that must be recovered before profits are earned. The amount of fixed costs that must be recovered sets the distance to be traveled before we reach the breakeven point. The *profit* to *volume* ratio determines the rate at which these costs are recovered. In our example, every dollar of sales contributes $33\frac{1}{3}$ cents to fixed costs. Once the breakeven point is reached, each sales dollar adds $33\frac{1}{3}$ cents to profit. If our variable costs were $33\frac{1}{3}$ percent, then $(1 − v)$ would be $66\frac{2}{3}$ percent, and we would earn profit at twice the present rate. Ideally, the *profit* to *volume* ratio should be high. This means low variable costs.

If fixed costs were negligible, we would earn profits with the first dollar of sales. However, a combination of low variable and low fixed costs is unrealistic because variable costs are inversely dependent upon the amount of capital employed. The best alternative depends upon the nature of the company. Large-volume producers need large-capital investments and have high fixed costs, which tend to lower variable costs and raise the *profit* to *volume* ratio. Although more sales are needed to reach the breakeven point, once it is reached, profits will accumulate rapidly. If the company is a low-volume producer, fixed costs tend to be small, variable costs high, and the $(1 − v)$ low.

Let us examine companies ABC, DEF, UVW, and XYZ. Table 9-3 lists the pertinent data. The profits of DEF and XYZ will increase faster than those of ABC and UVW. DEF will have greater profits than XYZ because it covers its fixed costs earlier and will be earning profits while XYZ is still trying to cover fixed costs. UVW has both high fixed costs and a low $(1 − v)$. This accounts for its high breakeven point.

The profits (losses) of each company at varying sales levels are shown in Table 9-4. This is shown graphically in Figure 9-6. The slope is the *profit* to *volume* ratio.

TABLE 9-3   Effects of cost and volume on breakeven point.

	ABC	DEF	UVW	XYZ
Fixed costs	$100,000	$100,000	$ 250,000	$250,000
Variable cost as a percent of sales	75	25	75	25
$(1 − v)$ percent	25	75	25	75
Breakeven point	$400,000	$133,333	$1,000,000	$333,333

TABLE 9-4   Profits of ABC, DEF, UVW, XYZ at varying sales levels.

	Profit (Loss)			
	ABC	DEF	UVW	XYZ
$ 0	$(100,000)	$ (100,000)	$(250,000)	$ (250,000)
500,000	(25,000)	275,000	125,000	125,000
1,000,000	150,000	650,000	0	500,000
1,500,000	275,000	1,025,000	125,000	875,000
2,000,000	400,000	1,400,000	250,000	1,250,000
2,500,000	525,000	1,775,000	375,000	1,625,000
3,000,000	650,000	2,150,000	500,000	2,000,000
3,500,000	775,000	2,525,000	625,000	2,375,000
4,000,000	900,000	2,900,000	750,000	2,750,000

COST-VOLUME-PROFIT APPLICATIONS

Cost-profit-volume analysis can determine the effect of a change in the selling price on both volume and profit. This in turn will indicate which product should be emphasized by sales personnel. If price is reduced to sell more products, what will be the effect on profits? Will the increased volume make up for the lower unit price received? If the *profit* to *volume* ratio is low, the increase in volume required to offset a decrease in selling price may be stupendous. Let us assume that ABC Company sells its product at $2 per unit. The sales manager proposes to cut the selling price by 20 percent, to $1.60. Variable costs will not change because of a change in selling price. In turn, he believes that demand will

FIGURE 9–6   Comparative profitability of companies ABC, DEF, UVW, XYZ.

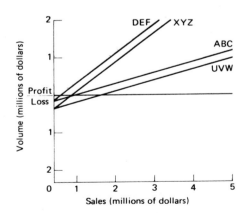

increase by 50 percent. Let us examine the implication of a price reduction.

	Present	Proposed
Selling price per unit	$2.00	$1.60
Variable cost per unit	1.50	1.50
Contribution per unit	$0.50	$0.10
Decrease in contribution per unit		$0.40

In actuality, to offset the proposed decrease in price, unit sales must increase:

$$\frac{\text{Decrease in unit contribution}}{\text{Proposed contribution per unit}} = \frac{\$0.40}{\$0.10} = 400\%$$

Conversely, ABC may consider increasing its price:

	Present	Proposed
Selling price per unit	$2.00	$3.00
Variable cost per unit	1.50	1.50
Contribution per unit	$0.50	$1.50
Increase in contribution per unit	$1.00	

If the price was increased by 50 percent to $3, sales volume could decrease by

$$\frac{\text{Increase in cost per unit}}{\text{Proposed contribution per unit}} = \frac{\$1.00}{\$1.50} = 66\tfrac{2}{3}\%$$
without affecting profits

Up to this point we have assumed that only one product was manufactured and sold. If more than one product is involved, the *profit* to *volume* ratio must be determined for each. This is no different from determining $(1 - v)$ for two different companies, each making a single product. The breakeven points, *profit* to *volume* ratios, and consequent profit patterns are affected by the proportion of each of the products manufactured and sold, that is, the mix of products.

POR Company sells a total of 300,000 units of two products, A and B:

	Product A	Product B
Selling price per unit	$10	$5
Variable cost per unit	8	1
Contribution per unit	$ 2	$4
$(1 - v)$	20%	80%

If the company sells 100,000 units of A and 200,000 units of B, the *profit* to *volume* ratio is

Sales	$2,000,000
Variable cost	1,000,000
Contribution	$1,000,000
$(1 - v)$	50%

This can also be calculated by the following tabulation, where the weighted *profit* to *volume* ratio is $180\%/3 = 60\%$.

	$(1 - v)$	*Mix*	$(1 - v)$ weighted by *mix*
A	20%	1	20%
B	80	2	160
		3	180%

If the proportion of dollar sales shifts to A, and 200,000 units of A and 100,000 units of B are sold, the *profit* to *volume* ratio for the company is computed in the following table, where the weighted *profit* to *volume* ratio decreases to $120\%/3 = 40\%$. Therefore, the breakeven point increases. This type of analysis shows that the salesmen should emphasize product B. This could be encouraged by paying larger commissions on B.

	$(1 - v)$	*Mix*	$(1 - v)$ weighted by *mix*
A	20%	2	40%
B	80	1	80
		3	120%

LEVERAGE

Leverage is the utilization of fixed costs to effect disproportionate changes in income. The return exceeds the cost. There are operating and financial leverages as well as leverage that is a combination of the two.

Operating Leverage

Operating leverage results when fluctuations in revenue produce a wider fluctuation in operating income. Breakeven analysis shows the degree of a firm's operating leverage. Since the degree of operating leverage depends upon the amount of fixed elements in the cost structure, operating leverage is akin to financial leverage because the use of senior securities with fixed payments provides a firm with greater earnings than the fixed charges (that is, debt earns more than its interest cost). A greater utilization of capital will lower fixed costs per unit. Letting R = sales, F = fixed costs, V = variable costs, the degree of operating leverage at any level of sales is

$$\frac{R - V}{R - V - F} = \frac{\text{marginal contribution}}{\text{operating income}}$$

From Table 9-1 we can calculate operating leverage at 400,000 units to be

$$\frac{\$600,000 - \$400,000}{\$600,000 - \$400,000 - \$150,000} = \frac{\$200,000}{\$50,000}, \quad \text{or 4 times}$$

Thus, a 100 percent increase in output will produce a 400 percent increase in operating income. The leverage varies at each level of production because of the changing weight the fixed costs have to total costs. Operating leverage decreases as the firm's sales increase. Operating leverage here is 4.0.

Financial Leverage

Leverage results from the use of borrowed funds to earn for equity holders a greater return than the fixed interest payment. The degree of financial leverage, at any level of operating income (where I = amount of interest), is

$$\frac{R - V - F}{R - V - F - I} = \frac{\text{operating income}}{\text{earnings before interest and tax}}$$

Using the same figures as in the preceding example, we calculate financial leverage at an operating income of $50,000 to be

$$\frac{\$600,000 - \$400,000 - \$150,000}{\$600,000 - \$400,000 - \$150,000 - \$15,000} = \frac{\$50,000}{\$35,000} = 1.42 \text{ times}$$

A 100 percent increase in operating income causes a 142 percent increase in earnings before tax. The greater the degree of interest-cost coverage, the lower the degree of financial leverage. Thus, an increase in interest relative to operating income will increase financial leverage; equally, the greater the proportion of debt to equity, or the greater the trading on equity, the greater the financial leverage.

Financial leverage is the firm's capital structure risk. The leverage ratio in this alternative is the ratio of the firm's capital structure to the equity of common-stock holders. It does not show how the earnings of common-stock holders will be affected. Rather, it is an indication of financial risk and the ability of the firm to meet the fixed charges (F in the preceding formula). The breakeven technique can be used to show at what level of earnings the leverage is appropriate. For example if a firm is to raise $1,500,000 and management cannot decide between equity or debt with an interest cost of $4\frac{2}{3}$ percent, the minimum earnings before interest and tax (EBIT) can be calculated. Having determined the EBIT, the breakeven point can be found from the following formula:

$$\frac{(\text{EBIT} - I)(1 - t) - \text{PSD}}{\text{CS}_1} = \frac{\text{EBIT}(1 - t)}{\text{CS}_2}$$

where EBIT = operating income (income before interest and income tax) at the breakeven point
$\quad\quad I$ = interest charges for the levered firm
$\quad$ PSD = preferred dividends for the levered firm
$\quad\quad t$ = tax rate on income
$\quad$ CS$_1$ = common-stock holders' equity if the firm were levered
$\quad$ CS$_2$ = common-stock holders' equity if the firm were nonlevered

Given the values

$$I = \$70,000$$
$$\text{PSD} = \$30,000$$
$$\text{CS}_1 = \$1,500,000$$
$$\text{CS}_2 = \$3,000,000$$
$$t = 50\%$$

$$\frac{0.5(\text{EBIT} - \$70,000) - \$30,000}{\$1,500,000} = \frac{0.5\ \text{EBIT}}{\$3,000,000}$$

$$\text{EBIT} = \$200,000$$

Leverage should thus be considered, once EBIT exceeds $200,000. Financial leverage here would be 1.42.

Combined Leverage

Combined leverage measures the interaction on the firm of both operating and financial leverages. The utilization of both leverages magnifies profits or losses. The degree of combined leverage is calculated by multiplying the financial leverage by the operating leverage.

$$\left(\frac{R - V}{R - V - F}\right)\left(\frac{R - V - F}{R - V - F - I}\right) = \frac{R - V}{R - V - F - I}$$

$$= \frac{\text{marginal contribution}}{\text{earnings before tax}}$$

Using the same figures as those for computing operating leverage, we can calculate combined leverage at an operating income of $50,000 to be

$$\frac{\$600,000 - \$400,000}{\$600,000 - \$400,000 - \$150,000 - \$15,000} = \frac{\$200,000}{\$35,000} = 5.7 \text{ times}$$

A simpler calculation would multiply operating leverage (4.0) by financial leverage (1.42), yielding the same result of 5.7. An increase in revenue of 100 percent will increase earnings before tax by 570 percent.

CHAPTER 10

Financial Planning and Budgeting

Management must make effective use of the capital at its command. The essence of effective management is good forecasting because decisions depend upon our expectation of the future. The effectiveness of the decision depends upon the accuracy of the prediction.

FINANCIAL PLANNING

Planning interprets the objectives of the company and describes the means of achieving them. It is advanced decision making in a nonpanic atmosphere. Planning is based upon an appraisal of the external environment and any opportunities or constraints imposed by present corporate strengths or weaknesses. Therefore, it identifies future company needs in light of company objectives. Since there are usually alternatives for each course of action, planning requires a search for the best alternative in light of the objective. Plans may change as expectations do not coincide with realization and as objectives change with social changes.

Planning Criteria

Without profits, the company could not sustain operation; consequently, it would be unable to meet other goals such as maximum market share or the support of various community efforts, and would cease to exist. Return on investment, ROI, is the prime index of profitability. Initially, planning revolves around maximizing ROI, since this is the means to improve profitability.

Once an ROI has been established, consistent with sound continued growth and competitive conditions, the company must choose the products that will best maximize profits. Demand considerations, competitive factors, and social and government constraints must be considered. Market potentials (what, how much, and under what conditions the market will buy) must be determined. This is the basis for sales projections and subsequent production planning.

Once the products have been chosen, we must determine the resources needed to support the plan logistically. Certain levels and varieties of inventory are required to support sales. Fixed assets are needed to produce and handle the goods. Production must be scheduled and controlled. This interrelationship is shown in Figure 10-1.

Sales estimates depend upon external and internal factors. The outlook for the economy as a whole—its effect on each industry and on the market in particular—determines the level of industrial activity. The firm's competitive position will determine its share of the market. Some of these factors are external and beyond the control of the individual company. Others can be influenced by the company. Logistic factors such as delivery time and inventory levels, as well as quality-control strategies, determine the firm's ability to satisfy customers' needs and to maintain or expand its share of the market. The sales-planning cycle is similar to the planning cycle for new products, shown in Figure 10-2.

Advantages of Planning

Planning, by forcing all levels of management to think ahead, gives the corporation flexibility. If additional cash is needed six months from now, the corporation has half a year to investigate sources and revise operations to fit the requirements of its lenders. If it fails to plan, it may be putting itself at the mercy of the suppliers of external funds. Lenders like to plan their commitments in advance and to keep their funds constantly working. The shorter the notice given, the fewer the suppliers who have not made other commitments. In the eyes of the few remaining suppliers, a corporation's lack of financial planning questions the competence of its management. This may increase the price it has to pay for its funds.

Almost every policy decision affects more than one function. Planning makes heads of various departments—such as production, marketing, and

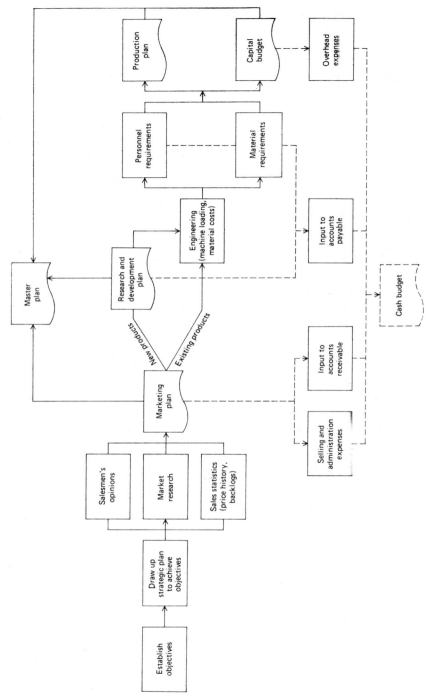

FIGURE 10–1   Interfunctional relationships in planning (solid line) and budgeting (dashed line).

finance—aware of the impact their decisions will have on the rest of the company, and encourages them to unite as a team to meet the common objective. Coordinated effort results if employees identify their jobs with the overall goals. Planning accomplishes this. If department goals rather than company objectives are more important to management, the company will become "factionalized." This can destroy initiative and stultify overall objectives.

Plans provide standards with which to measure management performance and control operations, by measuring and isolating deviations of actual performance from budgetary projections. The continuous cycle of planning leads to management by exception, with its inherent efficiency. Plans provide a more accurate measure than an indiscriminate reliance on historical performance because they consider the future and those external factors that affect corporate health.

Effective Planning

To plan effectively, a company must have a clear understanding of its corporate objectives. There must also be policies that spell out the means for achieving these ends. The interrelationship of many functional areas in planning necessitates a planning organization that includes all the diverse elements affecting the future performance of the firm. The company must also concentrate its limited resources by assigning priorities to those projects that will maximize ROI. This may necessitate cutbacks in certain areas, but the result must be increased profits. Finally, plans should be built around timetables, since each phase of the plan depends upon the success of a prior phase. In this way, plans can be changed as actual performance deviates from preset goals.

BUDGETING

The budget is nothing more than the plan expressed in specific goals and dollars. Plans have nebulous goals and serve as guides. Plans deal in

FIGURE 10–2   Planning cycle for new products.

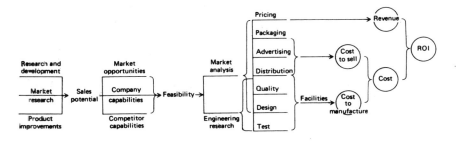

opportunity costs, whereas budgets deal in real dollars. Budgets serve three purposes. First, they provide management with a measure of the expected results of the various proposed operating plans. This helps management decide which plan to accept. Second, they serve as operating guides to lower-level management and department heads. Although the budgets delegate authority and responsibility, this does not result in any loss of control; for third, they measure performance. Variations reflect either the failure of management to achieve the planned goals or its ability to better them.

Budgets are either fixed or variable. Fixed budgets ignore the effect of volume changes on unit costs; variable budgets account for different costs at different volumes. The variable budget is a better control device, since all possible levels of volume are considered and may more easily be compared with actual results. Budgets should have their cost components broken down between fixed and variable costs so that management will know, when comparing budgeted with actual costs, the causes of variances from budget.

The budgetary system is interdependent. Estimates of cash flows and profits are based on sales forecasts. Profits depend upon the income-producing ability of the sales, and sales are dependent upon the availability of cash to carry accounts receivable and inventories. A final estimate of revenues cannot be reached until their effect has been tested on cash flows and profits.

The period covered by the budget will vary from company to company. Trading-type companies rely on short-term capital. Therefore, planning is short term. A retailer of high-style ladies' dresses may budget from one season to the next. Manufacturers employ long-term capital and must plan through the longer cycle of capital availability and demand changes. A manufacturer of locomotives may budget for two years. The longer the period covered, the less accurate the budget will be because factors such as economic conditions, cost, and competition are more likely to change. The shorter the period, the greater the probability that certain inter-relationships will be ignored. If we plan cash and sales only for the first quarter, we may ignore bank loans that have to be paid in the following quarter or may avoid an inventory buildup required for a second-quarter spurt in sales.

Cash Budget

The statement of source and application of funds concentrates on the reasons for changes in working capital. The cash budget is similar to the statement of source and application of funds but differs in that it emphasizes the change in the cash portion of funds. It provides information on the timing of cash receipts and disbursements. This is essential for planning cash flow.

The cash budget attempts to predict both how much and when cash will come into the firm and when and in what amounts it will flow out. The cash budget is an essential tool for managing liquidity. Proper use of the budget will reveal when there will be insufficient funds on hand over the operating cycle. Likewise, it will reveal when there is excess cash on hand for additional investment. The cash budget also guides the timing of dividend, tax, and fixed asset payments, and enables management to work as closely as possible to a minimal cash balance without jeopardizing liquidity or credit rating.

Preparation

The period of the budget depends upon the information needed by the financial manager to maintain liquidity. If the flows are constant and level, the budget may cover a period as long as six months. Erratic cash flows indicate either that shortages will arise or that surplus cash may not be properly utilized. In this case, budgets should be prepared for a short period, such as monthly or weekly if the firm is in financial difficulty.

The sales estimate is an integral part of the cash budget. The sales department examines external factors and modifies these by internal considerations, such as the opinions of the salesmen in the field. Supplementing the sales budget is the production budget. This gives the volume and cost for each item to be sold. From this the material, labor, and overhead budgets are prepared. The level of activity is indicated by cash receipts from accounts receivable and by disbursements on accounts payable and wages. Only those items affecting cash are considered. Noncash expenses, such as depreciation, are not considered because they represent a charge for which an expenditure has already been made.

The XYZ Company manufactures four products: A, B, C, and D. The data are given in Table 10-1. The sales manager foresees a tremendous market for product D in the next year. However, a further investment of $150,000 is needed to capture these sales. Assume the company is unable to raise external funds, but has general-purpose equipment that can be adapted to product D. The only way to increase production is to use the facilities now being used to produce other products. The problem revolves around two questions: Should the sales of product D be emphasized at the expense of another? If so, what product?

The two criteria that management uses to make its decision are ROI and the *profit* to *volume* relationship. Since product B has both the lowest ROI and $1 - v$, the company's operation would be more profitable if product D were produced instead. Therefore, the $150,000 in equipment

TABLE 10-1 XYZ Company data for manufactured products.

| | Revenue | | | Cost | | | Operating Income | Operating Assets | ROI | 1 – v |
Product	Selling Price	Volume (Units)	Total	Variable	Fixed	Total				
A	$10.00	40,000	$ 400,000	60%	$150,000	$ 390,000	$10,000	$100,000	10%	40
B	8.00	50,000	400,000	65	135,000	395,000	5,000	150,000	3	35
C	7.50	60,000	450,000	30	275,000	410,000	40,000	500,000	8	70
D	4.00	40,000	160,000	25	100,000	140,000	20,000	200,000	10	75
Total			$1,410,000		$660,000	$1,335,000	$75,000	$950,000	8%	

TABLE 10-2 XYZ Company sales projection.

| | | Cost | | | Operating Income | Operating Assets | ROI |
Product	Revenue	Variable	Fixed, Excluding Depreciation	Total			
A	$ 400,000	$240,000	$150,000	$ 390,000	$ 10,000	$100,000	10 %
C	450,000	135,000	275,000	410,000	40,000	500,000	8
D	400,000	100,000	200,000	300,000	100,000	350,000	28.5
Total	$1,250,000	$475,000	$625,000	$1,100,000	$150,000	$950,000	15.5%

presently used for B is to be adapted for D. The sales projection for the coming year is given in Table 10-2.

Let us assume that the financial officer of XYZ is preparing a monthly cash budget for the first six months of the year. Of the total year's sales, 10 percent will occur in each of the months January, February, and March, and 5 percent of the year's sales will occur in April, May, and June, as shown in the tabulation below.

Product Sales	January	February	March	April	May	June
A	$40,000	$40,000	$40,000	$20,000	$20,000	$20,000
C	45,000	45,000	45,000	22,500	22,500	22,500
D	40,000	40,000	40,000	20,000	20,000	20,000

Of the sales made, 20 percent are to be for cash and 80 percent on credit. On the basis of past performance the company estimates that the receivables arising from the credit sales will be collected approximately one month after sale. At December 31, the accounts receivable were $100,000. The sales forecast is converted into an analysis of cash receipts, as given in Table 10-3.

The sales forecast provides the information needed for the manufacturing schedule, which establishes material needs and serves as a guide for purchasing.

Variable costs are directly related to sales volume, and fixed costs are incurred evenly throughout the year. XYZ's variable costs consist of material and labor, and their percentages of selling price are 60 percent for product A, 30 percent for product C, and 25 percent for product D. Of the variable costs for each of the products, 50 percent represents material. The remaining 50 percent is labor. Material is bought one month preceding the date of sale, and payment is made within 30 days of purchase. Wages are paid weekly, and the incurrence of expense and date of payment coincide. Fixed costs of $625,000 (excluding annual depreciation of $20,000) occur evenly throughout the year at the rate of $52,083 per month. The cash disbursements, by product, are listed in Table 10-4.

We can now construct an analysis of cash disbursements, as in Table 10-5.

Now let us consolidate into a cash budget the computations of cash receipts and cash disbursements. The change in cash is total receipts less total payments. This is added to the cash at the beginning of the month to determine the amount of cash surplus or deficiency. The cash on hand at December 31 was $50,000, and the cash budget looks like Table 10-6.

TABLE 10-3 XYZ Company analysis of cash receipts.

Cash Receipts	January	February	March	April	May	June	Total
Total sales	$125,000	$125,000	$125,000	$ 62,500	$62,500	$ 62,500	$562,500
Credit sales	100,000	100,000	100,000	50,000	50,000	50,000	450,000
Cash sales	25,000	25,000	25,000	12,500	12,500	12,500	112,500
Accounts receivable	100,000	100,000	100,000	100,000	50,000	50,000	500,000
Repayment of note	—	—	—	—	—	300,000	300,000
Total	$125,000	$125,000	$125,000	$112,500	$62,500	$362,500	$912,500

TABLE 10-4 XYZ Company cash disbursements.

Distribution	January	February	March	April	May	June
Wages						
A	$12,000	$12,000	$12,000	$ 6,000	$ 6,000	$ 6,000
C	6,750	6,750	6,750	3,375	3,375	3,375
D	5,000	5,000	5,000	2,500	2,500	2,500
	$23,750	$23,750	$23,750	$11,875	$11,875	$11,875
Materials						
A	$12,000	$12,000	$12,000	$ 6,000	$ 6,000	$ 6,000
C	6,750	6,750	6,750	3,375	3,375	3,375
D	5,000	5,000	5,000	2,500	2,500	2,500
	$23,750	$23,750	$23,750	$11,875	$11,875	$11,875
Total variable costs						
A	$24,000	$24,000	$24,000	$12,000	$12,000	$12,000
C	13,500	13,500	13,500	6,750	6,750	6,750
D	10,000	10,000	10,000	5,000	5,000	5,000
Total	$47,500	$47,500	$47,500	$23,750	$23,750	$23,750

TABLE 10-5 XYZ Company analysis of cash disbursements.

Payments	January	February	March	April	May	June	Total
Purchases	$23,750	$23,750	$ 23,750	$11,875	$11,875	$ 11,875	$106,875
Wages	23,750	23,750	23,750	11,875	11,875	11,875	106,875
Fixed costs	52,083	52,083	52,083	52,083	52,083	52,085	312,500
Dividends and bank loan payments	—	—	200,000	—	—	200,000	400,000
Total	$99,583	$99,583	$299,583	$75,833	$75,833	$275,835	$926,250

TABLE 10-6 XYZ Company cash budget.

Cash	January	February	March	April	May	June
On hand at beginning of month	$ 50,000	$ 75,417	$100,834	$ 0	$36,667	$ 23,334
Receipts	125,000	125,000	125,000	112,500	62,500	362,500
Available	$175,000	$200,417	$225,834	$112,500	$99,167	$385,834
Borrowing (repayment)	—	—	73,749	—	—	(73,749)
Disbursements	(99,583)	(99,583)	(299,583)	(75,833)	(75,833)	(275,835)
On hand at end of month	$ 75,417	$100,834	$ 0	$ 36,667	$23,334	$ 36,250

PROJECTED FINANCIAL STATEMENTS

The projected balance-sheet method is an easier and quicker way to forecast the cash position. Information for this statement is obtained from a projected income statement and from historical and projected financial ratios. However, this method assumes 100 percent variability and ignores constant factors. This is acceptable in the long run where no factors are fixed, but not in the short run, where costs have a fixed incidence.

Expenses, both variable and fixed, are matched against revenues to arrive at projected net income. An alternative method would be to determine operating income by multiplying projected sales by the anticipated profit margin. Interest and taxes are deducted from operating income to arrive at projected net income.

As shown in Figure 10-3, the cash forecast is made by adding depreciation of $10,000 to the net income and adjusting for other expenses that do not require cash outlay during this period: interest ($1,250), taxes ($12,500), and adjusting for June credit sales, which will not be received until July ($50,000), and December credit sales paid for in January ($100,000). The cash change from operations would then be $12,500 + $10,000 + $1,250 + $12,500 − $50,000 + $100,000 = $86,250.

To arrive at the budgeted figure of $36,250, we must adjust cash from operations of $86,250 for dividends paid ($200,000), reduction of notes

FIGURE 10–3 *Pro forma* income statement, January 1 to June 30.

Sales		$562,500
Cost of sales		
Material	$106,875	
Labor	106,875	
Overhead (including depreciation of $10,000)	122,500	336,250
Gross profit		226,250
Operating expenses		
Selling	125,000	
Administrative expense	75,000	200,000
Operating profit		26,250
Interest expense	1,250	
Taxes	12,500	13,750
Net profit		$ 12,500

payable ($200,000), the collection of the note receivable ($300,000), and the opening balance of $50,000. The budget figure would be

$$\$86,250 - \$200,000 - \$200,000 + \$300,000 + \$50,000 = \$36,250$$

This type of thinking parallels the projection of source and application of funds. (See Figure 10-4.)

Once the cash portion of the projected balance sheet has been determined, accounts receivable and inventory can be calculated by using financial ratios. For example, XYZ, with projected credit sales for the first six months of $450,000, has an accounts receivable turnover of 9 times and inventory turnover of 3.3 times. The level of accounts receivable at June 30 would be

$$\frac{\text{Credit sales}}{9} \quad \text{or} \quad \frac{\$450,000}{9} = \$50,000$$

XYZ has a cost of goods sold for the first six months of $326,250. The inventory level at June 30 would be

$$\frac{\text{Cost of goods sold}}{3.3} \quad \text{or} \quad \frac{\$326,250}{3.3} = \$100,000 \text{ (approximately)}$$

Fixed assets would increase by any investment made, and depreciation would accumulate at its normal rate. Retained earnings are affected by profits and dividends.

Once a cash budget has been developed, it is simple to prepare a *pro forma* balance sheet. (See Figure 10-5.)

FIGURE 10–4   *Pro forma* statement of source and application of funds, June 30.

Funds provided		
Net earnings		$ 12,500
Charges against earnings not requiring funds		
Depreciation		10,000
Decrease in working capital:		
Working capital, Dec. 31	$350,000	
Working capital, June 30	172,500	177,500
		$200,000
Funds used		
Pay dividends		$200,000

BUDGET VARIANCE

The key to budgetary control is in comparing actual results with budget projections and in determining the causes of variance. This is particularly important with fixed budgets, but applies equally to variable budgets. The basic analysis centers around gross profit variance. Although selling and several administrative cost variances must be analyzed, this analysis is simple, since fixed-cost variances are the differences between actual and budgeted costs. When dealing with gross profit, however, there are also volume and product mix factors to consider. The total variance of actual profit less budgeted profit is caused by price versus cost variances and volume versus mix variances.

Total variance = actual profit − budgeted profit
= [(actual selling price − actual cost)(actual volume in units)]
− [(budgeted selling price − budgeted cost)(budgeted volume in units)]

FIGURE 10–5   XYZ Company balance sheet, December 31, and *pro forma* balance sheet, June 30.

Distribution	*December 31*	*June 30*
ASSETS		
Cash	$ 50,000	$ 36,250
Accounts receivable	100,000	50,000
Inventories	100,000	100,000
Note receivable	300,000	
Total current assets	550,000	186,250
Machinery and equipment, cost	950,000	950,000
Less depreciation	100,000	110,000
Net book value	850,000	840,000
Total	$1,400,000	$1,026,250
LIABILITIES		
Accounts payable	$ —	$ —
Bank loan	200,000	—
Interest payable	—	1,250
Taxes payable	—	12,500
Total current liabilities	200,000	13,750
Capital stock	500,000	500,000
Retained earnings	700,000	512,500
Total	$1,400,000	$1,026,250

The price versus cost and volume versus mix variances are made up of components of the total variance calculation.

Price versus Cost Variance

Selling price variance is the difference in budgeted versus actual selling price, multiplied by the units sold:

Sales price variance = (actual selling price − budgeted selling price)(actual volume)

Cost variance is the difference in budgeted versus actual cost, multiplied by the units sold:

Cost variance = (actual cost − budgeted cost)(actual volume)

The total effect of price and cost variance on gross profit is equal to

Price versus cost variance = [(actual selling price − budgeted selling price) + (actual cost − budgeted cost)](actual volume)

Volume versus Mix Variance

Sales volume variance is the difference between the budgeted and actual volume, multiplied by the budgeted selling price:

Sales volume variance = (actual volume − budgeted volume)(budgeted selling price)

Cost volume variance is the difference between the budgeted and actual volume, multiplied by the budgeted cost:

Cost volume variance = (actual volume − budgeted volume)(budgeted cost)

and

Total volume variance on gross profit = (actual volume − budgeted volume)(budgeted selling price − budgeted cost)

As an example, we return to the XYZ Company and its operational data listed earlier in the chapter for manufacture of products A, B, C, and D (Table 10-1). The budget and actual results are given in Table 10-7, showing how a favorable total profit variance of $13,232 was derived. Table 10-8 shows how this total profit variance is related to cost and volume variances. Then, in Tables 10-9 and 10-10, the effect of mix of product units is shown to be negligible. Finally in Table 10-11, after determining the cause and effect of these variances, we analyze and summarize the reasons for the variance between actual and budget performance.

STATISTICAL AIDS

Forecasting Through Correlation

Correlation is the relationship of two items. The behavior of one affects the behavior of the second. We can call the unknown item a dependent variable and assign to it the symbol Y; we can call the given item an independent variable and assign to it the symbol X.

The concept. Correlation analysis refers to the closeness of the relationship of Y to X, and vice versa. This relationship may be a straight line, and the formula for a straight line is $Y = a + bx$. Whether the relationship be linear or curvilinear, we can calculate the line of best fit by regression analysis.

Regression analysis. Regression analysis describes the average relationships between the two variables, not only by estimating the

TABLE 10-7   XYZ Company budget versus actual.

	Budget	Actual	Difference: Favorable (Unfavorable)
Sales			
A	$ 400,000	$ 510,000	$110,000
C	450,000	495,000	45,000
D	400,000	300,000	(100,000)
	1,250,000	1,305,000	55,000
Variable cost of sales			
A	240,000	269,688	(29,688)
C	135,000	157,080	(22,080)
D	100,000	75,000	25,000
	475,000	501,768	(26,768)
Fixed cost of sales			
A	150,000	160,000	(10,000)
C	275,000	275,000	0
D	200,000	205,000	(5,000)
	625,000	640,000	(15,000)
Operating income			
A	10,000	80,312	70,312
C	40,000	62,920	22,920
D	100,000	20,000	(80,000)
	$ 150,000	$ 163,232	$ 13,232

TABLE 10-8   XYZ Company, effect of price and volume variances on profit variance.

Sales price variance

A	($12.50 − $10.00)(40,800)	=	$102,000
C	($7.50 − $7.50)(66,000)	=	0
D	($3.00 − $4.00)(100,000)	=	(100,000)
			$ 2,000

Sales volume variance

A	(40,800 − 40,000)($10.00)	=	8,000
C	(66,000 − 60,000)($7.50)	=	45,000
D	(100,000 − 100,000)($4.00)	=	0
			53,000
	Total favorable sales variance		55,000

Cost price variance

A	($6.61 − $6.00)(40,800)	=	(24,888)
C	($2.38 − $2.25)(66,000)	=	(8,580)
D	($0.75 − $1.00)(100,000)	=	25,000
			(8,468)

Cost volume variance

A	(40,800 − 40,000)($6.00)	=	(4,800)
C	(66,000 − 60,000)($2.25)	=	(13,500)
D	(100,000 − 100,000)($1.00)	=	0
			(18,300)
	Total unfavorable variable cost variance		(26,768)
	Total price−cost−volume variance		28,232
	Total unfavorable fixed-cost variance		(15,000)
	Total favorable profit variance		$13,232

TABLE 10-9   XYZ Company, budget versus actual units.

Product	1 − v	Budget Units	Actual Units	Difference Units
A	40%	40,000	40,800	800
C	70	60,000	66,000	6,000
D	75	100,000	100,000	0
Total		200,000	206,800	6,800

TABLE 10-10   XYZ Company, effect of budget versus actual units on profit variance.

Product	1 − v	Budget		Actual	
		Mix	1 − v	Mix	1 − v
A	40%	1.0	40%	1.0	40%
C	70	1.5	105	1.4	98
D	75	2.5	188	2.6	195
Total		5.0	333%	5.0	333%

TABLE 10-11   Causes of variance between actual and budget.

Product A		
The price was increased (sales price)	$102,000	
In addition, the volume increased (sales volume)	8,000	
However, because of increased labor costs, the variable costs increased		
Due to cost	(24,888)	
Due to volume	(4,800)	
Fixed costs increased because of additional personnel	(10,000)	
A's contribution to increased profits		$70,312
Product C		
The price did not change (sales price)	—	
But because of higher commissions, volume increased (sales volume)	45,000	
However, these higher commissions increased variable cost (cost variance)	(8,530)	
This was more than offset by increased volume	(13,500)	
C's contribution to increased profits		22,920
Product D		
The price was decreased because of competitors' pricing policy (sales price)	(100,000)	
Volume did not increase above budget (sales volume)	—	
The decrease in price was partly offset by the use of cheaper materials and less quality control (cost price)	25,000	
Fixed costs increased because of improved machines	(5,000)	
D's contribution to increased profits		(80,000)
Total product contribution to increase in income		$13,232

dependent variable from the independent variable, but also by evaluating the reliability of the estimate by calculating the standard error of the estimate. The standard error shows how the average amount of the estimated values varies from the actual amount. The standard error of estimate is

$$\sqrt{\frac{\sum Y^2 - a\sum Y - b\sum XY}{n}}$$

This value is then compared with the standard error of estimate of a normal distribution in order to determine the reliability of the estimated values. This type of analysis enables us to use the estimate of one item in order to forecast a second. This forecasting, of course, is only as good as the relationship between the two variables. There must be both a logical and a mathematically proven relationship between the independent and dependent variables. For example, sales may be related to disposable income, or gasoline sales to registered automobiles. The independent variable may also have to be forecast. It is important to know the time relationship between the variables, whether they rise and fall simultaneously or whether one leads the other. If the independent variable leads the dependent variable, then the dependent variable can be determined by the trend of the independent variable. If they rise simultaneously, then the independent variable must also be forecast.

It is not necessary to go through all the mathematical calculations in order to do correlation analysis. We can use visual examination, by means of a scatter diagram, to determine whether the relationship forms a straight line.

Scatter Diagram

A scatter diagram is a graph showing a visual plotting of two logically related variables. The dependent, or Y, variable is plotted on the vertical axis, and the independent, or X, variable is plotted on the horizontal axis. Visual examination tells us that the scatter diagram in Figure 10-6(a) closely resembles a straight line, whereas Figure 10-6(b) does not. We can use this diagram to forecast future behavior by fitting a line to Figure 10-6(a) so that we obtain the straight-line relationship shown in Figure 10-6(c). The closer the dots lie to the straight line, the more confidence we have in our forecast, that is, the less is the standard error of estimate.

If we want greater accuracy, we can determine the mathematical relationship of the two variables by solving for a and b in the formula for a straight line:

$$Y = a + bX$$

where $a = \dfrac{\sum X^2 \sum Y - \sum X \sum Y}{n \sum X^2 - \sum X^2}$ and $b = \dfrac{n \sum XY - \sum X \sum Y}{n \sum X^2 - \sum X^2}$

FIGURE 10–6   Scatter diagrams of two related variables.

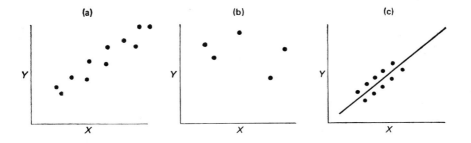

The symbol *a* represents the level of the regression line (value of *Y* when *X* is zero), and *b* its slope or rate of change. Our reliance upon this line depends upon the standard error of estimate. For example, if we have a logical cause-effect relationship between disposable income (independent) and the sales of our product (dependent), then we could plot the historical interrelationship. In Figure 10-7(a), each dot represents a year. Visually, it appears as if we have a straight line. We can determine the mathematical formula and our reliability in any forecast by calculating the standard error of estimate. It is beyond the scope of this book to expand upon the calculation of the formula for the straight line and the standard error of estimate, so let us assume that the fit is reliable. The regression line would be drawn (with *actual* solid and *forecast* dotted) as in Figure 10-7(b).

Therefore, if we had the federal government's estimate that disposable income next year would be $800,000,000 (Figure 10-7(a)), we could forecast our sales at $690,000, and if we had confidence that disposable income two years from now would be $950,000,000 (Figure 10-7(b)), our sales would be $810,000. This may necessitate some capital expenditures or other cash outlays with a two-year lead time. This is the advantage of forecasting in general and of correlation analysis in particular.

PERT Analysis

PERT (program evaluation and review technique) is a method of planning and controlling the time it takes to perform a project. The steps required to perform a task are defined and then laid out graphically in a

FIGURE 10–7   Cause-effect relationship between disposable income and sales.

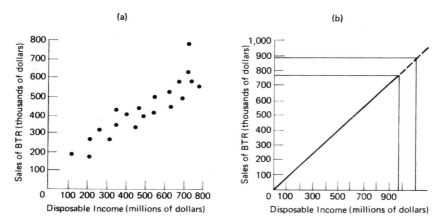

FIGURE 10–8   PERT network.

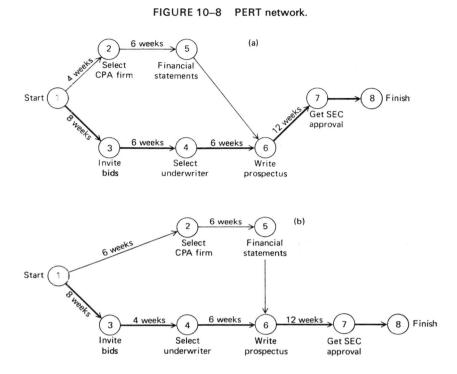

network. Together with the steps, the required times are also plotted. The planning task is enhanced by the ability to shift the steps in order to shorten the time. Control is exercised by comparing the plan to actual performance.

CPM (critical path method) involves identifying the sequence of events that must be accomplished to achieve a desired objective in a minimum of time. This path, however, will require the greatest elapsed time. The difference in elapsed time on the critical path and the other paths representing events to be accomplished to achieve the objective is the slack time on the other paths. Often, by reassigning manpower, time can be taken from a noncritical path (that is, this path will now take longer to accomplish than before) and assigned to the critical path, shortening it. Obviously, if this is carried too far, the "other path" may become the critical path.

The applications are numerous, from installing and debugging a computer system to making a public stock offering, from building a plant to planning and introducing a new product.

The Technique

Each job is defined, together with preceding and succeeding tasks. Then the network is graphed, showing the accomplishment (PERT) or activity (CPM), or both. Once this is graphed, the critical path is computed. This is the sequence that will take the greatest time to complete and is the minimum time needed to complete the project. The time to complete the whole project can be reduced only if the jobs along the critical path can be shortened.

The activities not along the critical path have slack time. Their completion can be delayed to some degree without negatively affecting the success of the entire project. Therefore, resources can be shifted from them to critical activities.

As an illustration, let us construct a simple network of a public offering. Figure 10-8(a) shows the critical path (heavy line) along the 1, 3, 4, 6, 7, and 8 path (32 weeks). Manpower can be shifted from the 1, 2, 5 path (10 weeks) if manpower is interchangeable; if it is not interchangeable, the 1, 2, 5 path start may be delayed; Figure 10-8(b) shows the network after manpower has been reassigned. The critical path (1, 3, 4, 6, 7, and 8) now requires only 30 weeks, a reduction of 2 weeks. The time saving results from putting greater emphasis on the selection of an underwriter. Path 1, 2, 5, and 6 has been lengthened, however, from 10 weeks to 12.

CHAPTER 11

Capital
Budgeting

A major task of the financial manager is to plan capital expenditures and determine whether to increase his investment in, or to replace, existing fixed assets. Substantial sums of money are involved, and investments are made for a considerable period of time. Poor decisions with regard to these critical investments can bring about adverse results that may burden the company for years. On the other hand, good decisions are responsible for successful performance.

THE CONCEPT

Capital budgeting is the decision-making process involved in formally planning the investment of capital. A capital expenditure is a strategic investment of material magnitude and nonroutine nature, whose economic life and benefits continue over a series of years; for example, acquisition of plant and equipment.

Every firm must make those expenditures necessary to sustain modern production, distribution, and service capacity as well as maintain market share. Dynamic firms will attempt to develop new products and processes, and thereby increase their market share. Thus, they tend to expend greater amounts in these areas. What, then, makes up capital expenditures?

1 Expansions of a new product or product line, or of a new production, distribution, or service facility

2. Replacements or renovation of worn or obsolete production, distribution, or service facilities with more efficient facilities

3. Other, including research and development, improved working conditions or investments required by government regulations to improve the health and welfare of the community; for example, control of air and water pollution

Capital expenditures differ from an operating expenditure of a current, routine, and repetitive nature, whose economic benefits are forthcoming immediately upon the sale of the product. Capital expenditures are more difficult to manage and control because of the alternatives available and the administrative problems of coordination and implementation. Despite the difficulties involved, sound procedures for capital expenditures are important to the overall success of a company.

A large number of alternatives must be examined, for there may be different assumptions with regard to start-up dates and capacities, selling prices, sales volume, and operating costs. In some projects there may be a score of possible combinations. Sometimes, as assumptions change, these combinations may have to be recalculated before a project can be ultimately accepted or rejected. The problem of quickly processing many combinations of information is ideally suited to a computer because most capital projects are of a similar type and subject to the same factors. Similarly, the constantly recurring problems of determining the optimal replacement policy for any given type of asset, optimal asset life, and annual depreciation are all adaptable to computer programs.

The fundamental theory in capital budgeting is that a dollar received today has a greater present value than a dollar to be received tomorrow; likewise, a dollar to be received next week has a greater present value than a dollar to be received a month or a year from now (by the amount of interest earned during a deferred period). The cost of forgoing those earnings is an opportunity cost. Moreover, the closer to the present, the more a firm is able to defend itself against various risks such as purchasing power, obsolescence, and uncertainty.

Planning for Capital Expenditures

Many opportunities for profitable investment are constantly uncovered and recommended to management. These suggestions must fit within the formulation of long-range goals, and in turn there must be a suitable framework within which relevant information can be assembled to achieve these goals. This requires a set of evaluation tools to select from among those alternatives that will meet the firm's objectives.

The fundamental investment decision is how deeply the company wishes to be involved in a given line of business and whether it wishes to expand or contract that commitment. This analysis must deal with the whole system over long periods of time. If the added investment is not made, then the business may be noncompetitive and ultimately unprofitable.

EVALUATION USING NET PRESENT VALUE

This section deals with the net-present-value method of evaluating capital investment alternatives. The decision whether or not to undertake a proposed capital project involves five steps:

1. Determining the net cash outlays for the project and when the cash will be expended
2. Determining the net differential cash inflows from the project and how long and when the cash will be received
3. Determining the net present value of the project
4. Appraisal of project risk
5. Evaluating the nonmonetary aspects of the proposed project

Note that we have used cash outlay and inflow. The evaluation of capital projects is based upon cash flows because, in order to compare inflows with cash outlay, cash rather than accounting income must be used. Accrual accounting may make different allocations from the same item, which reduces comparability. In some instances, cash flow may exceed reported income, and in other instances it may be less. The components of these flows are shown in Figure 11-1. Since the economic life of a capital expenditure is generally longer than one year, the opportunity cost, which is the cost of capital, must be also considered.

Determination of Net Cash Outlay

The ABC Company is considering the purchase of an improved machine costing $120,000. The economic life of the machine is estimated to be four years, with a $20,000 salvage value. Therefore, the depreciable cost is $100,000, and annual depreciation is $25,000. The present tax book value of the old machine is $40,000 and it has a remaining life of four years. Four years from now the salvage value will be zero, but today it is $20,000.

The proposed machine will perform the operation so much more efficiently that ABC engineers estimate that installation of the new machine will reduce labor, materials, and other direct costs (excluding depreciation) of the operation by $45,000 per year for four years.

ABC employs straight-line depreciation and pays income taxes at the rate of 50 percent. Tax depreciation, and not book depreciation, is used in capital budgeting.

The company has two alternatives: keep the old machine or buy the new one. First, management must determine the net cash outlay necessary to produce the enlarged stream of cash inflows. All cash receipts and expenditures associated with the acquisition of the new machine must be included. Included as part of the net cash outlay are any outlays for working capital, such as inventory.

FIGURE 11–1   Components of cash inflow and outflow affecting method of evaluating capital investment alternatives.

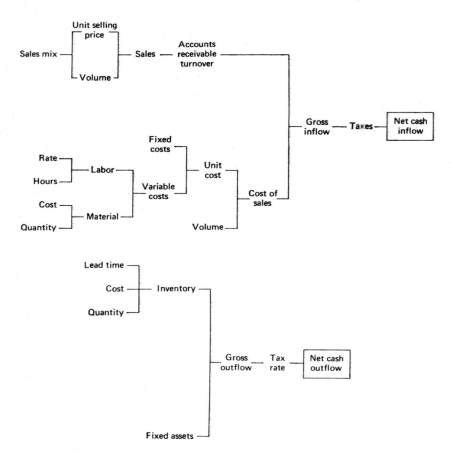

Were there no old machine involved, total cost would equal the net cash outlay. When a new machine replaces an existing piece of machinery, further adjustments must be made before determining net cash outlay. If the old machine is sold today, a book loss of $20,000 ($40,000 tax book value less $20,000 salvage value) must be recognized. This will reduce taxes and cash outlay by $10,000, which is computed as ($20,000 tax book loss) × (50 percent tax rate). If the new machine is bought, the cash return realized from the sale is $20,000 plus a lower tax bill of $10,000. If the old machine is kept, no immediate return from its sale is realized. However, the annual tax shield afforded by its depreciation of $10,000 ($40,000 tax book value ÷ 4 years) will be preserved. Consequently, the net cash outlay associated with the proposal (namely, buy the new and sell the old) is computed as shown in Table 11-1.

TABLE 11-1   ABC Company, computation of net cash flow.

	Outlay	Inflow
Cost	$120,000	
Salvage (old)		$20,000
Tax savings on book loss		10,000
	$120,000	$30,000
Net cash outflow	$ 90,000	

If the old machine is sold at a loss, this loss is not a cost of the new machine because the old machine is a sunk cost and its loss reflects decisions made in the past. Possibly the old equipment should have been depreciated at a faster rate; or an unwise purchase may have been made. Past errors of judgment should not burden the new equipment. The decision on the new machine must be made in terms of changes in future cash flows, not sunk costs.

Differential Cash Inflows

The second step in evaluating capital investment alternatives is to calculate the future net changes in cash inflows resulting from the purchase of the new machine, which will allow the company to reduce direct labor costs, use cheaper materials, and reduce repairs, lowering its cash outlay by $45,000 per year for four years. If a plant expansion or new-product decision were being considered, the effect of changing demand on cash inflow would be taken into account. In determining differential cash flows, the company must consider the effect of differential payments of income taxes under each alternative.

The proposed net cash outlay of $90,000 brings about a savings before depreciation and taxes of $45,000 annually. Therefore, these recurring savings are converted into the net cash inflows given in Table 11-2.

TABLE 11-2   Net cash flow before adjusting for salvage value for each of four years.

Source	Cash Flows for Each of Four Years		
	New	Old	Differential
Savings in labor and material costs	$125,000	$80,000	$45,000
Less depreciation expense	25,000	10,000	15,000
Taxable income	100,000	70,000	30,000
Less income tax, 50%	50,000	35,000	15,000
Income after tax	50,000	35,000	15,000
Plus depreciation expense	25,000	10,000	15,000
Net annual cash inflow after tax	$ 75,000	$45,000	$30,000

To summarize, the company has calculated the net cash outlay and the annual net cash inflow, both after tax, for each of the four years. However, the new machine has a $20,000 salvage value that was not depreciated. This represented a net cash outlay in year zero, already taken into account, and a $20,000 cash inflow in year 4, which was not considered. Therefore, the net cash inflows in the fourth year must be increased by $20,000, as shown by Table 11-3.

TABLE 11-3   Adjustment for salvage value.

Year	Net Cash Outlay	Net Cash Inflow
0	$90,000	0
1	—	$30,000
2	—	30,000
3	—	30,000
4	—	50,000

If working capital had been required for the project, it would be considered as an outlay in year zero and an inflow in the last year of the economic life of the project.

Also to be considered are the total cash benefits of $140,000 received over the four years. Suppose another proposal had the same cash outlay but returned $20,000 in year 1, $20,000 in year 2, $20,000 in year 3, and $80,000 in year 4. Would this project be as attractive as the purchase of the new machine? Although both have the same total cash inflows and outlays, one is more attractive than the other. The cost of capital must be taken into account when evaluating investment proposals that generate cash inflows in different periods.

Net Present Value and Profitability Index

Two basic tables are used in capital budgeting. The first table (see Appendix, Table A-1) is the present value of $1. It deals with a single lump sum of cash inflow or outflow at a given instant of time, the end of the period in question. The second table (see Appendix, Table A-2) is also the present value of $1. It deals with a series of equal cash flows to take place at the end of successive periods of equal length. The derivation of the tables and the explanation of the theory underlying them are given at the end of this chapter.

In net present value, we calculate the present value of the net cash inflows discounted at the after-tax cost of capital. The present value of the net cash inflows is then compared with the present value of the net cash outlays. If the present value of the net cash inflows is greater than the present value of the net cash outlays, then the rate of return is greater than the cost of capital, and net monetary benefits are realized by undertaking the project. In contrast, if the present value of the net cash inflows is less than the present value of the net cash outlays (net present value is negative), then rate of return is less than cost of capital, and the investment cannot be undertaken without suffering a monetary loss. Thus, if the net present value is positive (present value of net cash inflows greater than present value of net cash outlays), the investment should be considered.

The after-tax cost of capital for the ABC Company is 8 percent. The present value of the net cash outlays in year zero is $90,000. The present value of the net cash inflows is computed by using Tables A-1 and A-2 in the Appendix.

Where n equals the number of periods and K_C equals the after-tax cost of capital,

Present value of
$$
\begin{aligned}
\text{net cash inflows} &= [(\$30,000)(A_{\overline{n}|K_C})] \; + \; [(\$50,000)(S_{\overline{n}|K_C})] \\
&= [(\$30,000)(A_{\overline{3}|0.08})] + [(\$50,000)(S_{\overline{4}|0.08})] \\
&= [(\$30,000)(2.5771)] \; + \; [(\$50,000)(0.73503)] \\
&= \$77,313 \; + \; \$36,752 \\
&= \$114,065
\end{aligned}
$$

Present value of net cash inflows	$114,065
Less present value of net cash outlays	90,000
Excess of inflows over outlays	$ 24,065

Note that $114,065 represents the top price the financial manager of ABC should pay for the machine.

The present value is often converted into a profitability index by dividing the present value of the net cash inflows by the present value of the net cash outlays. For the ABC Company machine the profitability index is

$$\frac{\text{Present value of net cash inflows}}{\text{Present value of net cash outlays}} = \frac{\$114,065}{\$90,000} = 1.27$$

The decision rules would be as follows:

1. If the profitability index is greater than 1, then rate of return is greater than cost of capital, and the project is worthy of further consideration.
2. If the profitability index is equal to 1, then the rate of return is equal to the cost of capital.
3. If the profitability index is less than 1, then rate of return is less than cost of capital and shareholders would be worse off if management accepted such a project.

For the ABC Company, the profitability index is greater than 1. Therefore, the rate of return is greater than cost of capital and the investment is worthwhile from a monetary point of view.

Appraisal of Project Risk

Up to this point we have assumed that the cash flows associated with the ABC Company proposal are known with certainty. If we could always be certain of cash flows it would be possible to establish relatively simple and straightforward rules for making capital-budgeting decisions.

Each estimate of cash flows requires certain assumptions about the level of business activity, actions of competitors, cost of the factors of production, future sales, market size, selling prices, and market growth rate. Since there is a large amount of uncertainty connected with each of these factors, our computations to date were indications rather than numbers with 100 percent accuracy. We know that there are future events that will affect the cash flows, but we do not know in advance which of these events will occur and to what extent. Our fourth step, then, is to subjectively assign a chance of occurrence to our cash flows. If we believe that an event (expected flows under certain conditions, such as optimistic, most likely, and pessimistic) is certain to occur (where there are several probable outcomes), then we can say its probability (expressed with a certainty of X) of occurring is 1. However, if we believe that an event is certain not to occur, then we say that its probability of occurring is zero. We are concerned with events whose probabilities of occurrence are somewhere between zero and 1. In our case they are 0.25, 0.50, and 0.25. Using the formula

$$\text{Probability} \times \text{conditional value} = \text{expected value} \qquad (1)$$

let us assume that the computation of expected net cash inflows will be

Optimistic:	$0.25 \times \$40,000 =$	$10,000
Most likely:	$0.50 \times 30,000 =$	15,000
Pessimistic:	$0.25 \times 20,000 =$	5,000
	1.00	$30,000

This method represents an attempt at a systematic, rational approach to the difficult problem of forecasting. The preceding formula is the result of rigorous balanced analysis on the part of those who know most about the problem. In our example, the company's engineers agreed that $30,000 (the mean, median, and mode) was the best single-figure estimate of probable cash inflows, but they realized their forecast was subject to error. The subjective measure of that probable error may be portrayed graphically as a symmetrical distribution about the $30,000 best guess.

Let us consider another example. Assume that the financial manager has a choice between two projects that require the same net cash outlay, but that one affords a cash inflow of $150,000 while the other returns $100,000. For simplicity, assume that each project has a one-year life. We are told that the probability of achieving the $150,000 cash inflow is 0.5 and the probability of obtaining zero cash flows (the only two possible outcomes) is 0.5. Moreover, the probability of obtaining $100,000 of cash inflows is 0.8 and the probability of zero cash flows is 0.2. Now we can compute the expected value of each project, using Formula 1.

For project A:

$$0.5 \times \$150,000 = \$75,000$$
$$0.5 \times 0 = \underline{0}$$
$$\$75,000$$

For project B:

$$0.8 \times \$100,000 = \$80,000$$
$$0.2 \times 0 = \underline{0}$$
$$\$80,000$$

Armed with the expected values, the financial manager might be inclined to reverse his initial decision in favor of the higher-income project.

Finally, let us consider a more comprehensive example. The financial manager of XYZ Corporation is considering a proposed investment in a new product. The project requires a net cash outlay of $150,000. It has an economic life of two years. At the end of year 1 the probability of receiving a $300,000 net cash inflow after taxes is 0.5 and the probability of receiving a zero cash inflow is 0.5. In the second year the project can also generate net cash inflows after taxes of $300,000 or zero, with probabilities of 0.8 and 0.2. The amount received the second year is statistically independent[1] of the amount received the first year. The after-tax cost of capital to XYZ is 10 percent. Should the financial manager recommend the acceptance of the proposal?

The tree diagram in Table 11-4 shows the possible outcomes. Actual figures have been rounded off; the figures shown are approximate.

TABLE 11-4   Tree diagram of possible outcomes.

Year 0	Year 1	Year 2	Net Present Value of Path 2*	Probability of Path 3†
		0.8 $300,000	$370,500	0.4
	$300,000	0.2 0	122,700	0.1
−$150,000 0.5				
−0.5	0 −0.8 300,000		97,800	0.4
	−0.2 0		−150,000	0.1

* Net present value of path equals cash flows $\times$ $S_{\overline{n}|K}$.

		Path 1	Path 2	Path 3	Path 4
(+ $30,000)(0.826)	=	+ $24,780		$24,780	
(+ $30,000)(0.909)	=	+ 27,270	$27,270		
(− $15,000)(1.0)	=	− 15,000	− 15,000	− 15,000	− $15,000
		+ $37,050	+ $12,270	+ $ 9,780	− $15,000

† Probability of path equals (probability year 1)(probability year 2).

Path 1	Path 2	Path 3	Path 4
[(0.5)(0.8) = 0.4] ×	[(0.5)(0.2) = 0.1] ×	[(0.5)(0.8) = 0.4] ×	[(0.5)(0.2) = 0.1]

[1] Statistical independence refers to the fact that the probabilities of all possible outcomes for each single decision are the same; regardless of what outcomes occur for the other decisions being averaged, and for individual decisions, the probabilities of extremely good or extremely bad outcomes are not too large. On the other hand, statistical dependence refers to the fact that the probabilities of all possible outcomes for each single decision are influenced by the outcomes of other decisions being averaged and for individual decisions; the probabilities of extremely good or extremely bad are very high. Thus, risk of a loss is much greater.

The expected net present value is $184,590, which is obtained by using Formula 1 and the probability outcome of path 2 from the preceding tabulation. The calculations are as follows:

$$
\begin{array}{rl}
0.4 \times \ \$370,500 = \ \$148,200 \\
0.1 \times \ \ \ \ \ 122,700 = \ \ \ \ 12,270 \\
0.4 \times \ \ \ \ \ \ \ 97,800 = \ \ \ \ 39,120 \\
0.1 \times \ -150,000 = \ -15,000 \\
\end{array}
$$

Expected net
present value = $184,590

Using the formula

(Net present value of path) − (expected net present value) = deviations (2)

and converting to the net present value of path 2 in the tree diagram, together with the expected net present value from the preceding tabulation, we have

$$
\begin{array}{rl}
\$370,500 - \$184,590 = \ \$185,910 \\
122,700 - \ 184,590 = - \ 61,890 \\
97,800 - \ 184,590 = - \ 86,790 \\
-150,000 - \ 184,590 = -334,590 \\
\end{array}
$$

Then, applying

(Deviations)^2(probability of path) = expected cash flows (3)

and converting to obtain the expected standard deviation σ, we have

$$
\begin{array}{rl}
\$ \ 34,562,528,100 \times 0.4 = \$13,825,011,240 \\
3,830,372,100 \times 0.1 = \ \ \ \ 383,037,210 \\
7,532,504,100 \times 0.4 = \ \ \ 3,013,001,640 \\
111,950,468,100 \times 0.1 = \ \ 11,195,046,810 \\
\end{array}
$$

$28,416,096,900

and

$$
\sigma = (\$28,416,096,900)^{1/2} = \$170,000
$$

The financial manager can recommend acceptance of the project because it has a positive expected net present value of $184,590. In addition, the project has an expected standard deviation of $170,000. Assuming that the present values are normally distributed, and since we know the expected net present value and its standard deviation, we can arrive at the probability distribution of present values. At 1 deviation the net present value is $184,590 − $170,000 = $14,590; at 2 deviations the net present value is $184,590 − $340,000 = −$155,410. The area under a normal curve between any two points represents the probability that the net present value will actually fall within the specified interval. (The probability distribution of a normal curve is shown in Table 11-5.) Hence, the probability that the actual realized present value will lie within $\pm 1\sigma$ of the expected net present value or within the range \$14,590 to \$354,590 is 68.2 percent. Two standard deviations account for 95.45 percent of the area and $\pm 3\sigma$ account for 99.8 percent of the area. The information on the probabilities associated with the indicated cash flows can best be expressed from a practical point of view in terms of probabilities of achieving expected net present values of at least some target amounts.

TABLE 11-5 Probability distribution of present values.

Expected Net Present Value of at Least:	Number of Standard Deviations from the Mean	Probability on Each Side of the Mean	Cumulative Probability (Approx.)
− \$325,410	− 3σ	49.9%	99.9%
− 155,410	− 2σ	47.7	97.7
14,590	− 1σ	34.1	84.1
184,590	0σ	0.0	50.0
354,590	+ 1σ	34.1	15.9
524,590	+ 2σ	47.7	2.3
694,590	+ 3σ	49.9	0.1

Our objective is to find the cumulative probabilities for expected net present values. The probability of a net present value of at least + \$14,590 is represented by the area under the normal curve for all of the area to the right of the mean (expected value = 0.50) plus all of the area to the left through − 1σ. This represents 50.0 percent + 34.1 percent = 84.1 percent. The probability of achieving a return of each indicated amount can be determined for other probability levels. The probability of achieving the mean or expected value of the project is 50.0 percent. Finally, note that the sum of the cumulative probability for (plus the deviations) must equal 100.0 percent. For example, + 3σ = 0.1 percent and − 3σ = approximately 99.9 percent for a total of 100.0 percent.

The last consideration is the probability of breaking even. The probability of breaking even may be expressed as

$$\frac{\text{Expected net present value (mean)}}{\text{Expected standard deviation}} = \frac{\$184,590}{\$170,000} = 1.08$$

The area under the right tail of the normal curve associated with 1.08 is 0.36, so 0.50 + 0.36 = 0.86, and the probability of at least breaking even is 86 percent. By inspection we can check on this in Table 11-5 and find that at − 1σ we determined a positive expected net present value of $14,590 which accounted for 84 percent of the area. It therefore seems reasonable to expect breakeven at about 86 percent.

Let us now assume that the amounts received the second year were statistically dependent on the amounts received the first year. In other words, if we "hit" with the new product, our returns are very large, and if the product is not accepted in the first year, it will certainly not be accepted in the second. The tree diagram in Table 11-6 shows the possible outcomes. Again, figures are only approximate.

TABLE 11-6   Tree diagram of possible outcomes.

Year 0	Year 1	Year 2	Net Present Value of Path	Probability of Path
		0.8 $300,000	$370,500	0.4
	$300,000 0.5	0.2 300,000	370,500	0.1
− $150,000 −0.5		−0.8 0	−150,000	0.4
	0	−0.2 0	−150,000	0.1

The expected net present value is $185,250. Using Formula 1,

$$0.5 \times \ \ \$370,500 = \$185,250$$
$$0.5 \times \ -150,000 = -75,000$$

Expected net
    present value $110,250

The expected standard deviation is approximately $261,200. Using Formula 2 and converting to values in the tree diagram and the preceding tabulation, we have

$$+\$370,500 - \$85,250 = +\$285,250$$
$$- \ 150,000 - \ \ 85,250 = - \ 235,250$$

Then, applying Formula 3 and converting to obtain the expected standard deviation σ, we have

$$\$81,111,040,000 \times 0.5 = \$40,555,520,000$$
$$55,342,562,500 \times 0.5 = \ \ 27,671,281,250$$
$$\$68,226,801,250$$

and

$$\sigma = (\$68,226,801,250)^{1/2} = \$261,200$$

The recommendation may be that the project should be accepted because it has a positive expected net present value of $85,250. However, the expected standard deviation is $261,200. Hence, the probability of breaking even is only 62.7 percent. This is a vital bit of information. If the company cannot afford a loss, then it should steer clear of the investment, even though it has a positive expected net present value. The reader is encouraged to scale the distribution and verify the breakeven probability.

Nonmonetary Considerations

Up to this point we have examined the monetary benefits of proposed capital expenditures. However, almost every capital expenditure has intangible attributes. This is the last factor to be considered in selecting capital projects. Some capital expenditures are approved on the basis of nonmonetary considerations even though they may be unprofitable. Some examples are research and development expenditures involving new products, processes, and services; expenditures for improved working conditions and employee morale; investments required by government regulations to improve the health and welfare of the community (for instance, air and water pollution control).

Many times we have no way of knowing the cash inflows associated with basic research. Such research is often vital to the growth and profitability of a company, and it is futile to attempt to compute an estimated rate of return on such projects. Some companies are primarily concerned with monitoring the expenditures. Others are more concerned with trying to determine whether they received at least some return rather than with trying to estimate the actual return. Product, process, and service development are all somewhat different. Here we often have some past experience to rely upon, but again it is difficult to estimate rate of return.

Capital expenditures for improved working conditions and employee morale involve considerable nonmonetary benefits. Sometimes we can compute a rate of return for proposed expenditures for improved working conditions, but it can be frustrating to attempt to quantify increases in employee morale as a result of establishing a health and recreation club for employees.

Expenditures for air and water pollution control often have detrimental monetary results, but are nevertheless required by governmental regulation. At one company, however, a project for air pollution control generated unexpected cash inflows. After installing air-purifying equipment, management was surprised to find a firm offering to buy the materials collected by it. The firm buying the matter treated it and then packaged it into briquets used for outdoor home barbecues. Thus, an investment made for purposes of the health and welfare of the community is now generating a small cash inflow. In this case, the cash inflows proved to be a pleasant surprise.

PAYBACK TECHNIQUE

The payback technique is another method for evaluating capital expenditures. The payback period is the length of time necessary for the annual net cash inflows to equal the net cash outlays. The payback period for the ABC Company was 3 years because its net cash outlay of $90,000 equaled the accumulated net cash inflows after taxes at the end of the third year ($30,000 per year for 3 years). The $50,000 net cash inflow received in the fourth year is not considered. This is a major deficiency of the payback concept, for it fails to consider any stream of cash inflows extending beyond the payback period. Hence, it indicates only how many years are required to recover the net cash outlay. Furthermore, it ignores the rate of return and overemphasizes liquidity. Few firms wish to make continual commitments merely to get their funds back. For example, assume we are considering two projects, P and Q, which have an initial net cash outlay of $250,000 and a uniform annual cash inflow of $50,000. However, project P has an economic life of 6 years and project Q an economic life of 10 years. The payback period is identical in both cases, namely, 5 years:

$$\frac{\text{Net cash outlay}}{\text{Annual net cash inflow}} = \frac{\$250,000}{\$50,000} = 5 \text{ years}$$

However, the excess of total cash inflows over total cash outlay for project P is $50,000 and $250,000 for project Q. Payback does not assist us in the correct evaluation of these projects.

Payback also ignores the timing of the realization of net cash inflows, as the following tabulation shows. In this case the sum of the first three years' cash flows is $250,000 for each project and the payback period is three years. However, the investments are not equally desirable because of the time value of money. Project P is more desirable than project Q because it has a greater rate of return. However, we can judge the length of time our funds will be tied up. This is important if we are in an industry characterized by high risk; in a period of cash shortage we may want to isolate projects having short paybacks. However, we must recognize that we are emphasizing liquidity rather than the rate of return.

Year	Project P	Project Q
1	$150,000	$ 50,000
2	50,000	50,000
3	50,000	150,000
4	50,000	50,000
5	50,000	50,000

POSTCOMPLETION AUDITS OF CAPITAL EXPENDITURES

A postcompletion audit is a review of a capital project for the purpose of comparing actual and estimated results. This improves future decisions by knowledge gained from the past. For instance, consistent biases in estimates may indicate that a different procedure or estimator should be used. Or if it is discovered that important factors have been overlooked, steps can be taken to ensure that they are considered in future evaluations.

Postcompletion audits contribute to successful decisions. Frequently a project that has failed was hampered by the omission of a vital component, such as an important accessory. Or the asset, although complete, is not being utilized effectively because operating personnel have not been adequately trained. In these cases, feedback is crucial and the post-completion audit is the information pipeline.

Audit Model

We can control the project throughout its life by using an r formula, whereby we determine the average annual time-valued rate of return on investment; r is the required rate of return or cost of capital. This formula differs from rate of return (operating income divided by operating assets). Here, the r represents cash and is dynamic because it deals with flows over time; in contrast, ROI deals with income at a given point and is static.

$$r \text{ (to date)} = \frac{[\text{NCI}(A_{\overline{n}|K_c})] - [\text{NCO}(n/x)]}{n(\text{NCO})} \tag{4}$$

where r = average time-valued rate of return on investment
  NCO = net cash outlay
  n = years expired in project
  x = life of project
$\text{NCI}(A_{\overline{n}|K_c})$ = present value of net cash inflow discounted by cost of capital (derived from Table A-1 in the Appendix)

This rate may be directly compared with the rate predicted prior to the investment. It may, of course, have a negative value.

To determine r for a single year of operation, only the cash flow for the year under consideration is time-valued to the project commencement date. Table 11-7 illustrates the results obtained when actual flows are as budgeted and weighted cost of capital remains constant at 6 percent. For example: Using Formula 4 for year 3 (y_3) in the table, the r to date is

$$r = \frac{[(2,000)(2.6730)] - [(8,000)(3/6)]}{(3)(8,000)} = \frac{5,346 - 4,000}{24,000}$$

$$= \frac{1,346}{24,000} = 5.6\%$$

and the r per year is

$$r = \frac{(2,000)(0.83962) - (8,000/6)}{8,000} = \frac{1,679 - 1,333}{8,000}$$

$$= \frac{346}{8,000} = 4.33\%$$

TABLE 11-7   Actual present rates.

		Present Rate to Date and per Year	
Year	Actual Cash Flow	r to Date	r per Year
0	− $8,000	—	—
1	+ 2,000	6.91%	6.91%
2	+ 2,000	6.25	5.59
3	+ 2,000	5.61	4.34
4	+ 2,000	4.99	3.14
5	+ 2,000	4.40	2.01
6 (or x)	+ 2,000	3.82	0.96
			22.95*

* Average $r = 22.95/6 = 3.82\%$.

If inflows continue to be generated after the originally expected project life, two alternatives are available. First, the project may be terminated, either immediately or upon the expiration of the originally expected project life, and the expected cash flows treated as a separate project, with the working capital and salvage value of the original project becoming the net cash outlay or original investment for the extended project. The r determined may be helpful in deciding whether or not to continue with the project or to terminate it.

In the second alternative, the original project may be continued and the r to date may be monitored until it appears desirable to actually terminate the project. If this method is followed, n in the numerator and n in the denominator of the model are not identical. In the numerator, n may not exceed x, resulting in a ratio of $n/x = 1$ when the originally expected project life is exceeded. In the denominator, n will equal the actual life in years of the project to date.

Illustrated below is the use of the latter alternative when a cash inflow of $2,000 occurs in the period immediately following the originally expected termination date. (The investment or project is the same as in the preceding tables, and the cost of capital remains at 6 percent.) For monitoring the present rate of return, the computations are as follows:

$$r \text{ (to date)} = \frac{11,165 - 8,000(1)}{8,000(7)} = 5.65\%$$

$$r \text{ (per year)} = \frac{1,330}{8,000} = 16.6\%$$

Also $\qquad r \text{ (to date)} = \dfrac{22.95 + 16.6}{7} = 5.65\%$

Note that Formula 4 is no longer applicable for the single-year rate because n has become zero, though in the denominator it remains equal to 1. Thus, beyond the originally expected project life, the model for a single-year rate becomes

$$r = \frac{NCI(A_{\bar{n}|Kc})}{NCO}$$

Implementing the Audit

Top management has many objectives that influence capital expenditure decisions. A comparison of actual and estimated results of a capital project must relate performance to corporate goals.

Capital expenditure decisions are not made by one individual or by a group acting alone; rather they are the result of coordinated activity in many parts of the organization. Therefore, before initiating an audit program, management must determine when the audit should be performed, who will be responsible for performance and review of the audit, and what projects and types of information should be audited.

Timing

Timing is a particularly difficult problem in the administration of an audit program. The optimum timing depends upon the purpose of the audit, as well as on a need to achieve a degree of balance between the costs of the audit and the benefits derived.

As a general rule, the first audit should take place as soon as the project has had an opportunity to "shake down." The length of the shakedown period will depend on the complexity and novelty of the project, the amount of "debugging" required, and the time necessary for operators to reach normal efficiency.

Premature audits are not a realistic basis for taking corrective action with respect to either project implementation or future capital-investment decisions. On the other hand, if too much time lapses, the opportunity cost of delayed corrective action may be substantial. Since the length of the shakedown period will vary from project to project, there is ample justification for a reasonably flexible timing policy.

Responsibility

Responsibility for preparation of postcompletion audits is normally assigned to personnel who have convenient access to the data required for the reviews. An accounting group, responsible either to the controller or to line management, is most frequently selected. If one of the management's purposes for the audit is to ensure realistic estimates for project evaluation, it is desirable to have an independent third party check the accuracy of the forecasts. This may result in placing audit responsibility with those people who made the original study. One obvious advantage is that the group doing the audit will know more about the project and the conditions surrounding the justification study. However, one may well wonder whether such a group can be objective enough to produce an unbiased evaluation. A solution to this dilemma is to appoint a post-audit team comprising both the people involved in the justification study and one or more "outsiders."

Selection of Projects for Audit

One approach to selecting projects is to audit all large ones and select a sampling of smaller ones. The sample should include (1) projects which are forerunners of possible large future investments, (2) projects having relatively large prospective savings or incremental profits, and (3) a random sampling of other projects, regardless of type. If a selective sampling approach is used in auditing smaller investments, the size of the sample should be adjusted to reach the point where the incremental costs of additional auditing equal its expected incremental benefits.

PRESENT-VALUE TABLES

Refer to Table A-2 in the Appendix and assume that a corporation is issuing a three-year, noninterest-bearing note that promises to pay a lump sum of $1,000 exactly three years from now. A rate of return of exactly 6 percent, compounded annually, is desired. How much would you be willing to pay now for the three-year note? The situation for years 0, 1, 2, and 3 is depicted as follows:

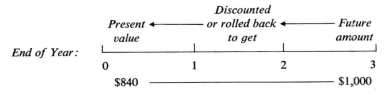

Let us examine the chart, *period by period*. First, assume that you are to purchase the $1,000 note at the end of year 2 instead of at time zero. How much would you be willing to pay? If you wish to earn 6 cents annually on every $1 invested, you would want to receive $1.06 in one year for every $1 you invest today. Therefore, at the end of year 2 you would be willing to pay ($1.00/$1.06)($1,000) for the right to receive $1,000 at the end of year 3, or ($0.943)($1,000) = $943. Second, assume that you purchase the $1,000 note at the end of year 1 instead of at time zero. How much would you be willing to pay? At the end of year 1 you are willing to pay [($1.00)($1.06)²][$1,000] for the right to receive $1,000 at the end of year 3, or ($0.890)($1,000) = $890. Finally, assume that you purchase the $1,000 at the end of year zero. How much would you be willing to pay? At the end of year zero you are willing to pay [($1.00)($1.06)³][$1,000] for the right to receive $1,000 at the end of year 3, or ($0.840)($1,000) = $840.

Note that we have a series of computations, which could be formulated as follows:

$$S_2 = \$1,000 \, \frac{1.00}{1.06} = \$943$$

$$S_1 = \$1,000 \, \frac{1.00}{(1.06)^2} = \$890$$

$$S_0 = \$1,000 \, \frac{1.00}{(1.06)^3} = \$840$$

This can be written as a formula for the present value of $1:

$$S = \frac{x}{(1 + i)^n}$$

where S = present value at time zero
   x = future amount
   i = interest rate
   n = number of periods

Check the answers in the tabulation by using Table A-1 in the Appendix. For example, the period 3 row and the 6 percent column show a factor of 0.83962. Multiply this factor by the future cash flow, $1,000, to obtain its present value, $839.62.

Assume that you buy a noninterest-bearing serial note from a corporation that promises to pay $1,000 at the end of each of three years. How much should you be willing to pay, if you desire a rate of return of 6 percent, compounded annually? The illustration below shows how the formula for A in Table A-2 of the Appendix, the present value of an ordinary annuity, is developed. Complete computation of the value of A is given following Table A-2 of the Appendix. Compound interest rates are listed in Table A-3.

	Present value			Future amount
End of Year:				
	0	1	2	3
First payment: 1,000/1.06	$ 943	$1,000		
Second payment: 1,000/(1.06)²	$ 890		$1,000	
Third payment: 1,000/(1.06)³	$ 840			$1,000
	$2,673			

CHAPTER 12

Leasing

The capital-budgeting decision requires that a choice be made among those alternatives earning rates of return in excess of the cutoff point for each particular risk class. The problem considered in this chapter goes one step beyond: The choice between alternatives has already been made, and therefore the problem is not to decide whether to commit but rather how to finance the acquisition. To arrive at a decision, management uses economic analysis as a tool in financial decision making.

THE CONCEPT

In leasing, the user (lessee) pays a rental charge to the owner of the property (lessor) for the right to utilize it. The lessee substitutes the rent charge for depreciation and other costs of ownership such as taxes, interest, and insurance, which are normally included in the rental. The lease payments also include the profit and risk of the lessor, and may be $\frac{1}{2}$ percent to 1 percent more than conventional financing. If the company does not have access to low-cost credit, because of tight money or undercapitalization, the choice may not be between lease or buy, but between lease or not expand.

If it chooses to lease the company does not have to raise capital, since the responsibility for financing is passed on to the lessor. The lessee can therefore preserve his borrowing capacity for other uses. However, leasing may positively affect future financing costs, since leases need not be shown on the balance sheet, and the balance sheet ratios that are important to lenders do not readily reflect the effects of leasing.

Although leasing has the advantage of capitalizing, and consequently of depreciating, land values, the accelerated depreciation and investment tax credit available by ownership may be lost unless the lease period is shorter than the depreciable life.

Leasing also tends to be inflexible. Use of the leased item may be restricted, and the annual charge is definite and fixed. Ownership, on the other hand, enables the firm to use the assets in whatever way it desires and to eliminate a commitment as a tax-allowable loss. Leasing does offer certain flexibility if the company is subject to an indenture that restricts future borrowings, or if it wishes to avoid the after-acquired clause. If there is a serious danger of obsolescence (for example, computers), or if the assets are provided for a period less than the life of the assets (for instance, government contracts), or if in government contracting the interest costs are not allowable but lease payments are, leasing may prove to be more flexible. If the assets have a low obsolescence factor, residuals that revert to the lessor may be involved. Leasing is more attractive than purchasing when internal rate of return exceeds the cost of leasing.

Sale Leaseback

Sale and leaseback is a variation of the lease or buy decision. This results in an increase in working capital, net of capital gains tax, greater than the amount realizable by normal debt financing. Suppose that a fully depreciated building, constructed in 1960 for $1 million, is now worth $2 million. The maximum loan normally obtainable is 50 percent of the value, or $1 million. If sale-leaseback were employed, the net proceeds available would be $2 million less the tax of $600,000 on the fully depreciated building (30 percent of $2 million), or $1,400,000. An additional $400,000 is available. This is relevant only if the firm can employ these funds to earn a return in excess of its cost. Additionally, the assets may be "redepreciated," since lease payments are allowable for tax purposes, while the building, being fully depreciated, can no longer be amortized. Assuming a tax rate of 50 percent, the cost is really only 50 percent of the rental fee. New buildings are also financed by this method because of the lower capital commitment.

THE MODEL

As a result of increased competition, companies have become more market-oriented in recent years. This necessitates a maneuverable sales force, and the automobile is one of the best methods to achieve this mobility. For this reason we shall now examine a route for fleet financing.

In addition to the normal analysis, we shall examine the profitability of paying mileage allowances to employees for use of their vehicles. The criterion for decision making is the lower after-tax net present value of cash flows, discounted at the cost of capital.

Financing Methods

The appropriate cutoff rate is the after-tax cost of borrowing, which is the opportunity cost of alternative financing ventures. The before-tax cost of borrowing is 10 percent and the tax rate is 50 percent. We assume that none of the financing methods affects the weighted average cost of capital. We also assume that the company has enough cash to purchase the automobiles outright, as well as an adequate credit rating to choose among other alternatives: direct purchase with borrowed funds, lease either with or without maintenance, or paying employees a mileage rate for the use of their private automobiles. The use of average mileage ignores the variation in miles driven by individual salesmen, and the profitability of paying mileage will fluctuate as the mileage driven varies from the mean. For this reason, we have calculated the breakeven point for each alternative.

Purchase with funds on hand. Refer to Table 12-1. Ownership requires a large initial capital investment. The delivered fleet price cost of each of the autos is $2,330 (which varies with optional equipment), and each car will be driven an average of 22,735 miles per year. In addition, extra personnel are required to arrange trade-ins and insurance and to keep detailed cost and assignment records. Some of these costs are eliminated if the autos are leased.

Purchase with borrowed funds. Refer to Table 12-2. Another method of obtaining use of a fleet is to negotiate a loan to buy the autos. In this way, the company can benefit from trading on equity as well as avoid a capital outlay at the time of purchase. However, the net cash flows under this alternative may prove to be the same as for ownership, assuming the corporation can borrow funds at the cost of capital.

Leasing plans. Refer to Tables 12-3 and 12-4. Leasing eliminates a certain amount of administrative work; for example, shifting to leasing eliminates the expense of negotiating the purchase and sale of cars, the processing of bids, invoices and payment for cars, maintaining vehicle records, and title files. A lessee only has to prepare a simple requisition for each car leased and pay the monthly invoice submitted by the leasing company for the entire leased fleet.

Finally, the lessor has certain cost advantages, which may be passed on to the lessee. The great size of their fleets allows lessors to spread their

TABLE 12-1   Costs of fleet automobile purchase with funds on hand.

Account	Year 0	Year 1	Year 2	Year 3	Total
Average purchase price	$2,330				
Operating costs					
Variable:					
Gas and oil		$ 477.44	$ 500.01	$ 522.91	
Repairs, maintenance		113.50	150.05	170.51	
Other (including tires)		39.50	77.50	65.00	
Total variable		630.44	727.56	758.42	
Fixed					
License		45.00	38.00	30.00	
Insurance		205.00	195.00	175.00	
Depreciation, straight line		776.67	776.66	776.66	
Total fixed		1,026.67	1,009.66	981.66	
Total operating costs		1,657.11	1,737.22	1,740.08	
After-tax cost at 50%		828.55	868.61	870.04	
Less depreciation		(776.67)	(776.66)	(776.66)	
Operating cash outflow		51.88	91.95	93.38	
Add proceeds from the sale of auto at end of year 3, after tax, as ordinary income				(300.00)	
Net cash flow	$2,330.00	$ 51.88	$ 91.95	$ (206.62)	
Time-adjusted factors at after-tax cost of borrowing (5%)	1.0	0.95238	0.90703	0.86384	
Net present value of cost of ownership	$2,330.00	$ 49.41	$ 83.40	$ (178.49)	$2,284.32

TABLE 12-2   Costs of fleet automobile purchase with borrowed funds.

Account	Year 1	Year 2	Year 3	Total
Net cash flow from Table 12-1	$ 51.88	$ 91.95	$ (206.62)	
After-tax interest (5%)	116.50	77.70	38.90	
Principal repayment	776.00	776.00	778.00	$2,330.00
Adjusted net cash flow	$944.38	945.65	610.28	
Time-adjusted factors at cost of borrowing (5%)	0.95238	0.90703	0.86384	
Net present value of cost of ownership with borrowed funds	$899.41	$857.73	$ 527.18	$2,284.43

TABLE 12-3   Cost of fleet automobile leasing—maintenance.

Account	Year 1	Year 2	Year 3	Total
Fuel	$ 477.44	$ 500.01	$ 522.91	
Lease payments at $98.50 mo.	1,182.00	1,182.00	1,182.00	
Total costs	1,659.44	1,682.01	1,704.91	
After-tax cost at 50%	$ 829.72	$ 841.00	$ 852.45	
Time-adjusted factors at cost of borrowing (5%)	0.95238	0.90703	0.86384	2.7232
Net present value of cost of maintenance lease	$ 790.21	$ 762.81	$ 736.38	$2,289.40

TABLE 12-4   Cost of fleet automobile leasing—finance.

Account	Year 1	Year 2	Year 3	Total
Fuel	$ 477.44	$ 500.01	$ 522.91	
Maintenance	113.50	150.05	170.51	
Other (including tires)	39.50	77.50	65.00	
Lease payments at $65 mo.	780.00	780.00	780.00	
Total costs	1,410.44	1,507.56	1,538.42	
After-tax cost at 50%	705.22	753.78	769.21	
Proceeds from sale of auto	—	—	300.00	
Total	$ 705.22	$ 753.78	$1,069.21	
Time-adjusted factors at cost of borrowing (5%)	0.95238	0.90703	0.86384	2.7232
Net present value of cost of finance lease	$ 671.64	$ 683.70	$ 923.62	$2,278.96

overhead over a far greater number of autos, thereby reducing unit costs. Their size allows greater discounts on volume purchases, and greater skill in selling their used autos enables them to get "top dollar" on disposal. The average lessee would not be of adequate size to enjoy these advantages of ownership.

Lease plans are of two general types: the maintenance lease and the nonmaintenance or finance lease. The terms of these leases are usually 24 months, but to provide a better comparison, a 36-month lease is used in developing the figures shown in the exhibits.

The maintenance lease (see Table 12-3) is the traditional arrangement where the lessor is responsible for maintenance, repairs, insurance (collision), license, and registration. The lessee is responsible for gas, oil, ard liability insurance. In the lease contract used in this example, the liability insurance is included in the monthly charge.

With the finance lease (Table 12-4), the lessee operates the car as if it were company owned and pays all operating costs. The rental charge includes depreciation plus a service charge. Once the lease has expired, any difference between the selling price of the used car and its book value is charged or refunded to the lessee.

Reimbursing mileage. The cost of mileage reimbursement to salesmen using their own automobiles, at 10 cents per mile, is the most costly of the available alternatives.

22,735 miles × $0.10 per mile	$2,273.50
After-tax cost at 50%	1,136.75
Present value factor at cost of borrowing (5%) for 3 years	2.7232
Net present value of cost of reimbursing	$3,095.60

The costs of the various alternatives are summarized as follows:

Method of Finance	Total Net Present Value
Ownership	$2,284.32
Borrowing to buy	2,284.43
Leasing	
Maintenance	2,289.40
Finance	2,278.96
Paying mileage	3,095.60

The difference between the alternatives is insignificant.

Breakeven Points

On cursory examination, paying mileage at the mean number of miles traveled (22,735 miles) should be rejected on the basis of cost. However, if the number of miles traveled per year is less than 11,640 (the standard deviation of the distribution was 11,275), reimbursing salesmen will prove to be the cheapest of any of the alternatives.

The total costs of operation comprise both variable (gas, oil, maintenance) and fixed (depreciation, insurance, and so on) elements. Fixed costs are not functionally related to miles driven; thus, up to a point, the more miles driven, the less the cost per mile. Average operating costs (Table 12-5) have been derived from the actual cost experience discussed under the third assumption. When average costs are combined with the mileage cost distribution indicated by Table 12-5, we have the costs of reimbursing mileage at various operating levels (Table 12-6). When average mileage falls in category A, the fixed costs of having cars available for company use are too great to be practical. On the other hand, reimbursing mileage when annual mileage falls in category C will cost the company more than the alternative of operating the vehicles. Thus, paying mileage may prove to be the best alternative for companies whose employees need cars only occasionally.

TABLE 12-5   Average annual operating costs.

Variable	
Gas and oil	2.25¢/mile
Maintenance and other	1.05¢/mile
Total variable costs	3.30¢/mile
Fixed	
License	$ 38.00
Insurance	195.00
Depreciation	776.00
Total fixed costs	$1,009.00

TABLE 12-6   Costs of reimbursing mileage.

	Category		
	A	B	C
Mileage	8,500	16,000	30,000
Annual payment at $0.10	$ 850.00	$1,600.00	$3,000.00
Cost of operation			
Variable at $0.033	280.50	528.00	990.00
Fixed	1,009.00	1,009.00	1,009.00
Total cost	$1,289.50	$1,537.00	$1,999.00
Net profit (loss) to company	$ 439.50	$ (63.00)	$(1,001.00)

It is feasible to set a cutoff point above which furnishing a car is more practical than paying mileage. This necessitates the computation of a breakeven point for each of our alternatives. The breakeven point in miles per year is that point where the costs of reimbursing (10 cents) equal the costs of furnishing an auto. We can determine the breakeven point for each of the alternatives, using the formula

$$\text{Annual fixed cost} + \text{variable cost} = \text{reimbursement} \times X$$

where X equals breakeven miles. Then, computing for alternatives, we have

Buy:	$1,009 + 0.033X$	$= $0.10X$	($X = 15,060$ miles/yr)
Lease-maintenance:	$1,182 + 0.0225X$	$= $0.10X$	($X = 15,251$ miles/yr)
Lease-finance:	$ 780 + 0.033X$	$= $0.10X$	($X = 11,640$ miles/yr)

These breakeven points again indicate that the finance lease is the preferable choice. Since the finance lease has the lowest breakeven point, gains accrue to the company at a lower mileage than in the other alternatives.

PART III
Merger
Strategies

CHAPTER 13

Legal, Tax, and Dilution Aspects of Mergers

This section of the book discusses mergers and acquisitions. An acquisition or merger occurs when one corporation acquires either controlling[1] stock or substantially all properties of another corporation. The acquiring corporation survives. Figuratively, BYR + SLR = BYR, where BYR and SLR represent buyer and seller, respectively. A consolidation, on the other hand, is the combination of two or more corporations through the transfer of their assets to a new corporation organized for the purpose. Neither of the original corporations survives. Figuratively, BYR + SLR = ABC, where ABC represents the new corporation.

This chapter first briefly examines the legal restraints that must be considered if a merger or acquisition is to be free of government challenge and can meet the Securities and Exchange Commission requirements. Finally, the complicated tax and dilution aspects are briefly discussed. Chapter 14 presents a method of determining price to be paid in an acquisition. This chapter presents, in logical sequence, the aspects of a merger, shown in Figure 13-1.

[1] Control for tax purposes means 80 percent (also a criterion for filing a consolidated return); for accounting purposes, 50.1 percent; for practical purposes, anywhere from 10 to 30 percent, the percentage depending on the number and distribution of the outstanding shares.

LEGAL ASPECTS

Before we discuss the legal problems inherent in a merger, let us mention some practical problems. The buyer should always beware, and in acquisitions he should especially beware, of buying problems. Although the seller may have been a hard-working owner-manager in the past, he may be selling in order to take life easier, and any management contracts signed may prove to be a burden to the buyer. The seller, historically, may not have been maintaining his plant or updating his production in order to show increased profits, or he may be heavily dependent on a few customers who are about to desert him. Things may change once the buyer has taken control. Non-union plants may face pressures to unionize, either from the buyer's union or from the workers who are now part of a larger company. And finally, the selling company may have an overly generous employee benefits program, some portions of which may have been unfunded.

A horizontal acquisition takes place at the same level of economic process, that is, a merger between competing manufacturers of the same products. A vertical acquisition is the integration of two or more successive stages in the economic process, from the production of the raw material to the sale of the finished good.

Federal Guidelines

The Department of Justice has released certain guidelines to apply to mergers and acquisitions under Section 7 of the Clayton Act. The objective of the Department is to maintain and encourage vigorous market competition. Market structure is the crucial factor because it influences the firm's conduct. The criteria for judging structure include

FIGURE 13–1   Sequence of mergers.

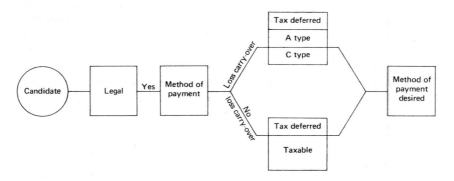

number of large firms, relative size of market share, and barriers to entry. Therefore, the Department opposes mergers and acquisitions that give the parties involved a substantial influence over a product in any specific market.

Horizontal mergers. Of primary significance in the merger of direct competitors is the size of market share held by both companies. In a market where the four largest firms account for 75 percent or more of the market, the Department will oppose mergers between firms accounting for the market share shown in the following tabulation.

Acquiring Company		Selling Company		New Company
4%	+	4%	=	8%
10%	+	2%	=	12%
15% or more	+	1% or more	=	16% or more

If the four largest firms account for less than 75 percent of the market, the Department will oppose mergers between firms accounting for the following market share:

Acquiring Company		Selling Company		New Company
5%	+	5% or more	=	10% or more
10%	+	4% or more	=	14% or more
15%	+	3% or more	=	18% or more
20%	+	2% or more	=	22% or more
25%	+	1% or more	=	26% or more

Even if the selling company has an insubstantial share of the market, but has an unusual competitive advantage, its acquisition by a substantial firm will be challenged.

Vertical mergers. Acquisitions backward into a supplying market or forward into a purchasing market will be challenged if they raise barriers to entry or if they bring about disadvantages to existing nonintegrated firms. The Department will oppose a merger when the company that supplies that market accounts for 10 percent of total sales in the market and the company that purchases from that market accounts for 6 percent of total purchases in that market.

Conglomerate mergers. These types of mergers are neither horizontal nor vertical. They include market extension mergers, involving firms selling the same product in different geographic markets. In this case the Department will challenge any potential entrant to a market if it has technological and financial advantages relative to the firms presently in the market. If a conglomerate buys a firm with 25 percent or more of a market, it will be challenged. It will also be challenged if it buys one of the four largest firms in a market if the firm has 10 percent of the market, or if it buys one of the eight largest firms in a market if the shares of this firm approximate 75 percent or more and if the company it is acquiring is a rapidly growing firm.

Securities Laws

Any interstate public offering of securities exceeding $300,000 must be registered with the Securities and Exchange Commission under provisions of the Securities Act of 1933. For securities less than $300,000, the SEC must be informed under Regulation A. Although this requires almost the same amount of paperwork as a full registration, the financial statements need not be certified and the expenses are therefore less. The 1933 Act is a disclosures act, and disclosure is accomplished by the Registration Statement (Form S-1). Part I of the S-1 is the prospectus. The prospectus includes audited financial statements for three fiscal years as well as historical and legal information requiring the services of certified public accountants, lawyers, and underwriters. These services are expensive: 15 to 18 percent of the issue price.

In addition to these federal laws, registration is required by each state within which the securities are to be sold. The state Blue-Sky laws may require forms additional to those filed with the SEC.

The Securities Exchange Act of 1934 extended the disclosure requirements of the 1933 Act to include all securities listed on stock exchanges. In order for securities to be sold publicly interstate, they must be registered under the 1933 Act. For securities to be traded on any stock exchange, they must be registered again under the 1934 Act. In order to keep information current, certain forms must be submitted periodically. Form 10-K, the updated registration statement, together with the complete financial statement, must be submitted annually, 120 days after the fiscal year end, both for companies registered under the 1934 Act and certain other companies registered by the 1933 Act. In addition, Form 8-K must be filed by a listed company within 10 days of the month end if it acquired a company with more than 15 percent of its preacquisition revenues or of its previously outstanding assets. Form 10-Q must be filed for the first three fiscal quarters, 45 days after the quarter ends. In addition, companies registered under the 1934 Act are subject to Section 14, on proxy statements, and Section 16, on insider trading by officers and controlling shareholders.

All these forms are a part of disclosure regulations. Information such as salaries, transactions with management, mode of operation, and material contracts might place the company at a competitive disadvantage if it were made public. The ability to act quickly may be lost if approval is required from shareholders or outside directors.

TAX ASPECTS

Each method of acquisition has certain tax implications. All transactions are taxable except those that qualify under special provisions of the Internal Revenue Code, 1954 (or the Code). These provisions generally are concerned with the tax position of the seller, since ordinarily no tax arises on the acquisition of property.

The term "tax free" does not mean that income tax is avoided forever; it simply means that the recognition of the capital gains tax is postponed until the property received in the exchange is finally disposed of. In a "taxable" transaction, the tax (which may be capital gains or ordinary income) is recognized in the year of sale. The importance of the tax status depends on two conditions: whether or not the selling shareholders want to postpone tax outlays, and the motives of the buyer.

In a "tax free" transaction, the assets bought have the same tax basis as they had in the hands of the seller; for example, tax depreciation is the same for the buyer as the amount recorded by the seller. In a "taxable" transaction, the buyer has a new tax base allocated on fair market value, and there is no carry-over of any tax factor of the selling corporation, such as loss.

Motives of Buyer and Seller

The motives of buyer and seller differ. The seller wants to sell stock so that he can claim a long-term capital gain, taxed at a maximum 35 percent and payable on a deferred basis. If he sells for cash or its equivalent, the gain will have to be paid immediately. On the other hand, the buyer may want to acquire assets to avoid future contingencies. When stock is bought, the new owners acquire its assets subject to its liabilities, known and unknown, including liabilities or federal income taxes, which may be assessed for prior years. However, the problem of contingent liabilities can be minimized by holding part of the purchase price in escrow, to be released after a long enough time has passed to resolve any problems.

The buyer may also wish to buy assets if the underlying basis of the assets is higher (but book value is lower) than the purchase price. This will increase the tax base of the assets, increasing amortization of the assets and, through lower taxes, cash inflow. However, although cash inflows may increase in the future, in a taxable transaction assets are bought with cash, resulting in a heavy outflow. Of course these reasons

are irrelevant if assets are bought tax free with stock in a C-type transaction.

Tax-Free Acquisitions

Section 368 (a) (1) of the Code describes three types of transactions
that are tax free or, more accurately, tax deferred. Generally, any
transaction made with stock is tax free. The three types are the statutory
merger or consolidation (A-type), stock for stock (B-type), and stock for
assets (C-type).

Statutory merger or consolidation (A-type). A statutory merger is
made in accordance with the statutory requirements of the state govern-
ments concerned. The acquiring company buys the entire selling company's stock, with voting stock, nonvoting stock, and cash. This use of
nonvoting stock and cash differentiates the A-type from the B- and
C-types. The selling stockholders must receive a continuing equity interest
(voting stock) that is substantial in relation to the stock sold. Theoretically,
50 percent of the purchase package may be made up of cash. Bonds or
other debt securities (but not short-term notes) are not treated as cash
only to the extent of the face amount of securities sold. Any amount in
excess of the face amount of these securities is treated as cash. Although
preferred stock may be issued, if it is redeemable, it may be treated as
cash. Common stock may be convertible into common or preferred
voting or nonvoting shares and not be considered cash. This method
offers greater flexibility in the design of the package offered to the selling
shareholders than do the other two tax-free methods, and is useful if the
selling shareholders want different types of securities.

Stock for stock (B-type). The controlling portion (80 percent) of all
the selling company's actual voting stock must be exchanged solely for
actual voting stock (common or preferred) of the buying company in a
single transaction or in a series of transactions within a short period of
time. The voting rights must be actual, not contingent. Stock rights and
warrants are not considered to be stock, but are treated as cash.[2] If any
cash or property other than voting stock is paid, the transaction is taxable.

This type of acquisition is the route taken if the buying corporation
plans to operate its acquisition as a subsidiary. It is also one of the easiest
ways to acquire another company, since only stock is exchanged. If there
are loss carry-overs, this method is not the best method unless the acquired
company can earn enough to offset these losses.

Stock for assets (C-type). In the C-type of transaction, the buyer
issues voting stock for substantially all assets of the selling corporation.

---

[2] Reg. 1354-1 (e): *Southwest Consolidated Corp.* 315 U.S. 194.

"Substantially" means at least 90 percent.[3] The voting stock issued must be at least 80 percent of the fair market value of the assets acquired, and the remaining 20 percent may be made up of cash or the assumption of liabilities.

In the case of an A or B acquisition, the stock and securities are paid directly to the shareholders of the selling corporation. In a C-type of transaction, the selling company holds the stock. The corporation may then distribute this stock to its shareholders, if it liquidates itself and if the original sales and liquidation are part of a unified plan. The shareholders treat any gain in excess of the value of the property exchanged as a capital gain, provided the stock is held for at least six months.

Taxable Acquisitions

Any acquisition not meeting the requirements of an A, B, or C transaction has its capital gains taxed immediately. Taxable acquisitions take one of two forms: the direct purchase of assets from the selling corporation, or the purchase of stock from selling stockholders.

Direct purchase of assets. Direct purchase is the least desirable, since it results in double taxation, a tax payable by the corporation on the gain realized on the sale of its assets (if the corporation has a gain) and the tax payable by the shareholder on the gain realized. The tax to the shareholder can be deferred until the corporation makes a distribution to its stockholders, but the double-taxation aspect remains.

The tax to the corporation can be eliminated in a purchase of assets by liquidation within 12 months, under Section 337. The liquidation must be conducted under a plan adopted before the assets are sold, and all assets must be distributed within this 12-month period. The shareholder, of course, will pay his capital gains tax within this 12 months and cannot defer it.

The purchase of stock from selling shareholders is less complex than the purchase of assets. No formal action has to be taken by the selling or buying shareholders. This may be burdensome and time consuming. Shareholders are paid cash or its equivalent and there is only one tax—to the shareholder.

Assets rather than stock would be purchased if the selling corporation had losses to offset any gains or if there were loss carry-backs that could not be utilized by the buying corporation. We shall now briefly examine the tax laws relevant to loss carry-overs.

[3] *First National Bank of Altoona* v. *U.S.* Court of Appeals 3.104 F2d 865C1939, and *Southland Ice Company,* 5 Tax Court 842C1949.

Loss Carry-overs

Loss carry-overs can be utilized only in a type A or C acquisition, but not in a type B acquisition. The opportunity to recover part of the purchase price through future tax reductions is an important reason that selling companies with loss carry-overs are acquired by an A- or C-type transaction. Although all of the acquired company's losses may be used, they cannot be carried back and can be carried forward for only five years from the date of acquisition. However, if the stockholders of the loss corporation do not own at least 20 percent of the successor corporation, the net operating loss available is scaled down. For each percentage point below 20 percent, the net operating loss carry-over is reduced by 5 percent.

Losses cannot be carried over if the principal purpose of the acquisition is to avoid tax, or if the company with the loss changes its trade or business before the end of the corporation's taxable year that follows the one in which the purchase occurs.

Due to the complexity of the tax laws, errors are possible. Therefore, advance rulings from the Treasury are important. If the Treasury issues a favorable ruling, the acquisition can be completed with the intended tax consequences.

DILUTION ASPECTS

Dilution is the uncompensated opportunity cost, which may be dilution in control book value or earnings, that results from the issuance of new common equity.

Dilution of control. Dilution of control occurs whenever new voting shares are issued to new stockholders. The amount of dilution is directly proportional to the number of new and old shares involved, or quantitatively NS_2/NS_2, where NS_2 is number of shares issued to new stockholders and NS_1 is number of shares held by old shareholders. This can be avoided by purchasing the new shares in proportion to the old number of shares held.

Dilution of book value. Dilution of book value depends upon the price of the shares sold in relation to the replacement value of the assets; dilution will not occur if, quantitatively,

$$P_2 > NCO_2$$

where P_2 = total price at which new shares are sold

NCO_2 = replacement value of assets after issuance of new shares

This may be rephrased and we may say that dilution of book value will not occur if $P_2 > NCI_1$, where NCI_1 is the book value of present shareholders. However, if the new assets have a greater earning power than the old, dilution has not taken place to the extent that

$$P_2(\text{ROI})_2 = (\text{NCO})_2 \text{ROI}_1$$

where ROI_2 = return on investment of new assets
ROI_1 = return on investment presently earned

Dilution of earnings. Dilution of earnings depends upon the earning power of the new shares, as related to the old shares, so there will be no dilution of

$$E_{1+2} = E_1$$

where E_2 = earnings per share after issuance of new shares
E_1 = earnings per share prior to issuance of new shares
E_{1+2} = earnings per share for all shares, old plus new

The return on investment after issue must at least be equal to the return on investment presently earned, or

$$\frac{E_2}{P_2} = \text{ROI}_1$$

This assumes that the rate of earnings growth for both old and new assets will be the same. If not, either positive or negative dilution will occur. Therefore, to mitigate dilution, all control, assets, and earnings must be investigated, both *pro forma* and after the issuance of new common equity.

CHAPTER 14

Valuing
Acquisitions

A corporation that has passed the legal constraints and determined the method of payment faces the problem of determining the value of the merger candidate. The potential returns from mergers are numerous. The multiproduct company is the most suitable form for responding to rapid technical change. It also has the greatest potential for diversifying into new areas at the lowest startup cost.

This is important when corporate objectives can no longer be accomplished within the present structure; that is, when there is excessive cash or borrowing power relative to present needs, and when diversification will provide a greater profit than the alternative of internal expansion. There may also be synergistic benefits such as sales (common channels of distribution, common warehousing, line completion or improvement, common promotion, and market accessibility), production (spreading of overhead, efficient purchasing, direct-cost scale economies, and sharing of research and development), and management (application of rare management resources if time is being bought). Primarily, the defining purpose of an acquisition is to maximize the return on equity, r, by maximizing the earnings per share at the minimal cost of capital while maximizing common-stock price. Therefore, in order to maximize total leverage, acquisitions should be made in order of preference, with cash, debt, preferred stock, convertible debt, warrants, common stock, or some combination of these. Of course the tax factors mentioned in Chapter 13 must be kept in mind.

The first portion of this chapter deals with evaluating publicly held, listed corporations, and the last portion deals with privately held, unlisted companies. Neither of these methods deals with asset valuation. Asset valuation is important only in large classic mergers of companies in industries, such as steel and cement, which require large initial and subsequent investments to produce sales and earnings.

PUBLICLY HELD COMPANIES—*P/E* APPROACH

Regardless of the motivation of corporations contemplating the merger or acquisition route of expansion, the problem of selection of the right candidate is the most difficult of the capital expenditure decisions it must make. Our objective is to develop a preliminary screening model.

Although there are numerous elements that affect common-stock prices, growth in earnings per share and the *price* to *earnings* ratio multiple (*P/E*) in growth industries are the critical factors. An acquisition of a "low" multiple company by a "high" multiple company at a favorable price may result in the "growth" of earnings per share (and an increase in *r*).

The *P/E* ratio as an element of acquisition strategy may have a decided impact on the range of purchasable companies. The relationship between the *P/E* ratio of the candidate and that of the prospective purchaser determines whether earnings dilution will result, and hence whether the common-stock exchange is desirable. The premerger *P/E* ratios are, of course, the single most important factor in the negotiation of agreeable exchange terms.

Smalter and Lancey[1] illustrate one method of employing *P/E* analysis as a screening criterion for acquisition candidates. They suggest in their article that adequate perspective on how *P/E* can affect selection and implementation of an acquisition strategy involves simultaneous consideration of the *P/E* multiplier and amount of earnings (Figure 14-1).

THE MODEL

In order to show the significant relationships among the major decision variables, it is first necessary to indicate the effect of increasing leverage on a firm's capital structure. Starting from an all-equity capital base, a firm can obtain a certain amount of debt at advantageous rates by effectively lowering its weighted average cost of capital. However, as the percentage of debt in the capital structure increases, a point will be

[1] Donald J. Smalter and Roderic C. Lancey, "P/E Analysis in Acquisition Strategy," *Harvard Business Review* (November–December 1966).

reached where the amount of risk to the firm's stockholders increases simultaneously. This point is called the firm's optimal capital structure.

When a firm's debt increases beyond that point suggested by the optimal capital structure, the stockholders will demand a higher return to compensate for this added risk. Specifically, a certain amount of debt will cause the firm's P/E ratio to fall at a slower rate than its earnings per share increase from trading on the equity. Conversely, at points beyond the optimal amount of debt, a firm's P/E ratio will fall faster than its earnings per share will rise. Consequently, a firm's optimal capital structure is that combination of debt and equity that will maximize the market value of its common stock. Moreover, at the point of optimal leverage, a firm's rising marginal cost of capital will equal its average cost of capital. When the marginal cost becomes greater than the average cost, additional debt will cause the average cost to increase sharply.

The shaded area in Figure 14-1 represents a "field of interest" defined by managers of the ABC Company. (In this example, decision rules are

FIGURE 14–1 Immediate per-share effects on earnings for prospective acquisition.

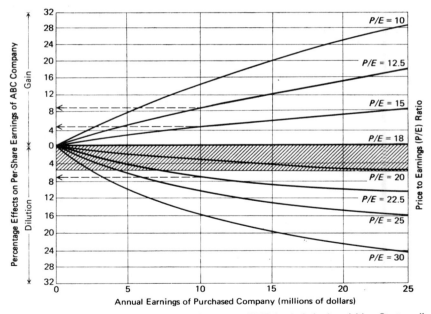

Source: Donald J. Smalter and Roderick C. Lancey, "P/E Analysis in Acquisition Strategy," *Harvard Business Review* (November–December 1966), p. 92. Used by permission.

that dilution must be less than 5 percent and the P/E of the candidate must be greater than 22.5.) To this point, however, only the immediate effects on the ABC Company's shareholders have been included in the analysis. The price effects over the long term have not been assessed. In order to properly consider long-term effects, management should give much attention to deriving the likely P/E multiplier that investors will apply to future composite earnings. If management is to do the best possible job of maximizing the common-stock price, the ability to accurately estimate the P/E ratio that will result from the acquisition of various candidates is critical.

What follows, then, is a development of a model that can be used to forecast the postmerger composite P/E multiple (hereafter called the adjusted P/E). The buyer's P/E multiple is adjusted as a result of the acquisition and is developed as a function of premerger P/E multiples of the buyer and candidate and of their respective earnings per share (E), expected growth rates, and number of shares of common stock outstanding.

A MODEL FOR SCREENING ACQUISITION CANDIDATES

The following simplified example will serve to introduce Z (to be discussed under "Model Development"), the adjusted P/E multiple approach to the analysis of acquisition candidates.

BUY Corporation, a large conglomerate, is negotiating to acquire SELL Corporation. BUY, aided by acquisitions, has been increasing earnings per share by 30 percent a year, and its stock currently sells at 30 times current earnings of $1. SELL is a fine old company that is currently increasing its earnings at a 10 percent rate and also is earning $1 per share. These data are summarized in the accompanying table.

	BUY	SELL
P/E	30	20
Growth rate	30%	10%
EPS	$ 1	$ 1
Number of shares	1	1
Market value	$30	$20

After lengthy negotiations, the management of BUY persuades the management of SELL that a purchase price equivalent to the market price of SELL is sufficient. SELL agrees, knowing that the expected future benefits (such as financial and technical know-how) to accrue to SELL as a result of the combination with BUY are substantial. The purchase price p that BUY must pay is determined as follows:

$$p = P_{sell}$$
$$= (P/E)(E)(NS)_{sell}$$
$$= (20)(\$1)(1)$$
$$= \$20$$

where P/E = price/earnings multiple of SELL
E = earnings per share of SELL
$(NS)_{sell}$ = number of shares of SELL common stocks outstanding

BUY Corporation will issue common stock in payment in order to enact a tax-free exchange. The common-share holders of SELL Corporation must each receive \$20 value ($= E(\$20) \div 1$, the number of shareholders) in terms of shares of BUY common stock:

$$P = (P/E)_{buy}(E_{buy})$$
$$= (30)(\$1) = \$30$$

Value promised each shareholder is

$$\$20 = x(P_{buy}) = 30x \quad \text{or} \quad x = \frac{20}{30} = \frac{2}{3}$$

where x = terms of exchange of BUY shares per SELL share. Therefore, the holder of one share of SELL receives $\frac{2}{3}$ share of BUY (an equivalent value of \$20).

The effect on postmerger (denoted by asterisk) earnings per share of BUY (E_{buy*}) is calculated as follows:

$$E_{buy*} = E_{sell} + E_{buy}$$
$$= \$1 + \$1 = \$2$$

Postmerger shares outstanding, $(NS)_{buy}$, are

$$(NS)_{buy*} = (NS)_{buy} + \text{(new stock issue of BUY in exchange for SELL)}$$
$$= (NS)_{buy} + (\tfrac{2}{3}NS)_{sell} = 1 = \tfrac{2}{3}(1) = 1\tfrac{2}{3}$$

and

$$E_{buy*} = \frac{E_{buy*}}{(NS)_{buy*}} = \frac{\$2}{1\tfrac{2}{3}} = \$1.20$$

Note that the leverage of BUY Corporation's higher P/E multiple resulted in favorable purchase ("growth") of earnings. BUY's earnings increased from \$1 per share to \$1.20 per share. The earnings per share accretion is due to a 100 percent increase in earnings achieved with only a $66\tfrac{2}{3}$ percent increase in shares outstanding.

The result of the combination on BUY's P/E is unknown until determined by the market. The P/E at which the market will value these earnings, however, is a critical factor. Prior to the merger, the total value of BUY and SELL equaled

$$P_{buy} + P_{sell} = [(P/E)_{buy}(E_{buy})] + [(P/E)_{sell}(E_{sell})]$$
$$= \$30 + \$20 = \$50$$

This value represents the minimum postmerger value of BUY necessary to avoid a dilution in the value held by all stockholders. Consider the following two cases:

Case 1. Postmerger earnings valued by market at SELL's P/E multiple (20):

$$P_{buy*} = (E_{buy*})(P/E)_{buy*}(NS)_{buy*}$$
$$= (\$1.20)(\$20)(1\tfrac{2}{3}) = \$40$$

Case 2. Postmerger earnings valued by market at BUY's P/E multiple (30):

$$P_{buy*} = (\$1.20)(\$30)(1\tfrac{2}{3}) = \$60$$

With SELL Corporation's P/E multiple applied to the postmerger earnings per share, the market value of the combination (\$40) is less than the premerger value of BUY and SELL (\$50).

If investors apply BUY's P/E multiple, the common-stock price would be maximized, and since the market value of the combination (\$60) exceeds the \$50 hurdle, the net value change to both BUY and SELL is positive. The adjusted P/E multiple could, in fact, be any number greater than 25, and the combined shareholders would be better off.

Model Development

Let us now examine a quantitative approach to determine the adjusted P/E multiple. A basic theorem underlying the following development is: *A merger will be desirable if the earnings of the acquired company per share of common stock issued by the acquirer exceed the premerger earnings of the acquiring company.*

Thus,

$$\frac{E_{sell}}{(NS)_{buy\ 1}} > \frac{E_{buy}}{(NS)_{buy\ 2}}$$

where $(NS)_{buy\ 1}$ = number of shares of acquirer (BUY) issued to purchase candidate SELL Corp.

$(NS)_{buy\ 2}$ = number of shares of BUY Corp. outstanding prior to the merger

The question that then arises is which year or years of earnings to compare. One solution is to multiply this year's earnings by a growth factor, $(1 + g)^n$, where g equals expected average annual growth, and n is an index corresponding to the year to be evaluated: 0 for the current year, 1 for the next year, and so on. Thus, we have

$$\frac{E_{\text{sell}}}{(NS)_{\text{buy 1}}} (1 + g)_{\text{sell}}^n > \frac{E_{\text{buy}}(1 + g)_{\text{buy}}^n}{(NS)_{\text{buy 2}}} \tag{1}$$

where g = growth rate of earnings
n = number of years over which g is compounded

In an attempt to simplify this expression, we note that since

$$\text{Purchase Price} = (P_{\text{sell}})(NS_{\text{sell}}) = (NS_{\text{buy}})(P_{\text{buy}})$$

$$p = (P_{\text{sell}})(NS)_{\text{sell}} = (NS)_{\text{buy 1}}(P_{\text{buy}})$$

$$(NS)_{\text{buy 1}} = \frac{(NS)_{\text{sell}}(P_{\text{sell}})}{P_{\text{buy}}} \tag{2}$$

where P_{sell} = market price, SELL common
P_{buy} = market price, BUY common
NS_{sell} = shares of SELL outstanding prior to the merger

Substituting Equation 2 into Equation 1,

$$E_{\text{sell}}(1 + g)_{\text{sell}}^n > \frac{E_{\text{buy}}(1 + g)_{\text{buy}}^n}{(NS)_{\text{buy 2}}(P_{\text{buy}})} \tag{3}$$

Moreover, since

$$(P/E)_{\text{sell}} = \frac{P_{\text{sell}}}{E_{\text{sell}}}$$

it follows that

$$(P/E)_{\text{sell}} = \frac{P_{\text{sell}}}{E_{\text{sell}}/(NS)_{\text{sell}}} = \frac{(P_{\text{sell}})(NS)_{\text{sell}}}{E_{\text{sell}}}$$

or

$$\frac{1}{(P/E)_{\text{sell}}} = \frac{E_{\text{sell}}}{(P_{\text{sell}})(NS)_{\text{sell}}}$$

which, when substituted into Equation 3, yields

$$\frac{(1 + g)_{\text{sell}}^n}{(P/E)_{\text{sell}}} > \frac{(1 + g)_{\text{buy}}^n}{(P/E)_{\text{buy}}} \tag{4}$$

(Note that the right-hand side of the inequality is transformed in the same manner as the left.) Inverting, we have

$$\frac{(P/E)_{\text{sell}}}{(1 + g)^{n}_{\text{sell}}} < \frac{(P/E)_{\text{buy}}}{(1 + g)^{n}_{\text{buy}}} \tag{5}$$

It can now be said that the merger will be desirable by year n if the adjusted (for expected growth) P/E multiple of the acquired company (SELL Corporation) is less than that of the acquiring company (BUY Corporation).

Once again rearranging terms,

$$\frac{(P/E)_{\text{buy}}}{(P/E)_{\text{sell}}} \cdot \frac{(1 + g)^{n}_{\text{sell}}}{(1 + g)^{n}_{\text{buy}}} > 1 \tag{6}$$

If we inspect Equation 6, we see that a desirable candidate should have a higher growth rate and a P/E ratio that is lower than that of the buyer. (Both conditions tend to drive the left-hand side of Equation 6 to a value greater than 1.) A company with a higher P/E ratio may nevertheless be a good acquisition if its growth potential is greater than that of its acquirer. It can also be seen that although acquisition of a company with somewhat less growth prospects at a low P/E ratio may produce beneficial near- or intermediate-term effects, the growth factor will result in long-term dilution of earnings.

The P/E Adjustment Factor

From the preceding discussion it may be theorized that a quantitative approach to determine the adjusted P/E ratio for the buyer must account for the P/E multiples and growth rates of the buyer and candidate. Therefore, we introduce the symbol Z and define it as the adjustment factor by which the P/E ratio of the buyer will be changed as a result of the acquisition. That is,

$$(P/E)_{\text{buy}*} = (P/E)_{\text{buy}}Z$$

In words, the adjusted P/E ratio of the BUY Corporation is equal to the P/E ratio of the company prior to the merger, times the adjustment factor Z.

This model, in accord with the previous section, assumes that the Z factor is a function of the growth in earnings of the combination relative to the potential nonmerged growth in earnings of the acquirer (for an assumed 5-year period):

$$Z = \frac{E^5_{buy + sell}}{E^5_{buy}} \qquad (7)$$

where $E^5_{buy+sell}$ = combined earnings growth for 5 years

E^5_{buy} = the relative growth of E of the buyer for 5 years

E^5_{sell} = the relative growth of earnings of SELL Corporation for 5 years

$E^5_{buy+sell}$ is assumed to be the weighted average of E^5_{buy} and E^5_{sell}, weighted by the number of shares of common stock each has outstanding prior to the merger:

$$E^5_{buy + sell} = \left[\frac{(NS)_{buy}}{(NS)_{buy} + (NS)_{sell}}\right]E^5_{buy} + \left[\frac{(NS)_{sell}}{(NS)_{buy} + (NS)_{sell}}\right]E^5_{sell}$$

Thus,

$$Z = \frac{\{(NS)_{buy}/[(NS)_{buy} + (NS)_{sell}]\}E^5_{buy} + \{(NS(_{sell}/[(NS)_{buy} + (NS)_{sell}]E^5_{sell}}{E^5_{buy}} \qquad (8)$$

but

$$E^5_{buy} = (1 + g)^5_{buy} \qquad \text{and} \qquad E^5_{sell} = \frac{(P/E)_{buy}}{(P/E)_{sell}} (1 + g)^5_{sell}$$

where the compound growth factor of SELL Corporation has been adjusted for the change in P/E due to acquisition.

Substituting into Equation 8,

$$Z = \frac{[(NS)_{buy}/(NS)_{buy} + (NS)_{sell}](1 + g)^5_{buy} + [(NS)_{sell}/(NS)_{buy} + (NS)_{sell}]\left[\frac{(P/E)_{buy}}{(P/E)_{sell}}\right](1 + g)^5_{sell}}{(1 + g)^5_{buy}} \qquad (9)$$

The market value of BUY Corporation's stock after the acquisition is therefore

$$P_{buy*} = (E_{buy*})\left(\frac{P}{E_{buy*}}\right)(NS)_{buy*}$$

$$P_{buy*} = (E_{buy*})\left(\frac{P}{E_{buy}}\right)(Z)(NS)_{buy*}$$

where $(P/E)_{buy}$ is known prior to the merger, E_{buy*} and $(NS)_{buy*}$ are easily determined, and Z may now be calculated from Equation 9.

It may be noted that this approach does not incorporate the element of market psychology, which may have very real near-term influence on the final determination of the adjusted P/E multiple. Nevertheless, this approach does provide a fundamental base from which to make educated projections.

Returning to the BUY/SELL example where g_{buy} equals 3 and g_{sell} equals 1, we obtain

$$(1 + g)^5_{buy} = (1.3)^5 = 3.71 \quad \text{and} \quad (1 + g)^5_{sell} = (1.1)^5 = 1.61$$
$$(NS)_{buy} = 1 \quad \text{and} \quad (NS)_{sell} = 1$$
$$(P/E)_{buy} = 30 \quad \text{and} \quad (P/E)_{sell} = 20$$

Therefore,

$$Z = \frac{0.5(3.71) + 0.5(1.61)(30/20)}{3.71} = 0.83$$

For $Z = 0.83$ and $(P/E)_{buy} = 30$,

$$(P/E)_{buy*} = (30)(0.83) = 25$$

The total market value of BUY after the merger will be

$$P_{buy*} = (E_{buy*})(NS)_{buy*}(P/E)_{buy*}$$
$$= (1.20)(5/3)(25) = \$50$$

In this case, the postmerger value of the combination is equivalent to the premerger value of both BUY and SELL.

This example relates the effect of one set of relationships between the growth rate, P/E multiple, E, and number of shares outstanding on the value of Z, and subsequently on the postmerger P/E multiple. Experimentation with the set of relationships will help demonstrate the development of an acquisition strategy. In the example, $(P/E)_{buy} > (P/E)_{sell}$, or

$$\frac{(P/E)_{buy}}{(P/E)_{sell}} > 1$$

If all other factors in the example remain constant, but we change the relative values of $(P/E)_{buy}$ and $(P/E)_{sell}$ such that

$$\frac{(P/E)_{buy}}{(P/E)_{sell}} < 1$$

we find that $Z = 0.63$, which results in a postmerger $(P/E)_{buy*}$ less than in the original example; that is,

$$(P/E)_{buy*} = (Z)(P/E)_{buy} = (0.63)(20) = 12.6 < 25$$

Obviously this situation represents a less desirable result, since the postmerger value of BUY would be considerably less than the postmerger value in the original example ($50), where $[(P/E)_{buy} \div (P/E)_{sell}] > 1.0$:

$$P_{buy*} = (E_{buy*})(P/E)_{buy*}(NS)^{buy*}$$

where $\quad (P/E)_{buy*} = 12.6$

$$(NS)_{buy*} = (NS)_{buy} + \frac{(P/E)_{sell}}{(P/E)_{buy}}(NS)_{sell}$$

$$= 1 + (20/30)(1.0) = 2\tfrac{1}{2}$$

$$E_{buy*} = \frac{E_{buy*}}{(NS)_{buy*}}$$

$$= \frac{\$2}{2\tfrac{1}{2}} = \$0.80$$

Therefore,

$$P_{buy*} = (\$0.80)(12.6)(2\tfrac{1}{2}) = \$25.20 < \$50.00$$

The conclusion is that acquisition of a company at market value with a higher P/E multiple, lower growth rate, equivalent earnings after taxes and number of shares of common stock outstanding results in lower postmerger earnings per share and a considerable decline in the P/E multiple of the acquirer.

An Optimum Acquisition Strategy

Rather than trying to enumerate the infinite number of sets of relationships that exist, Figure 14-2 has been developed to illustrate graphically these relationships and to aid in understanding the proposed acquisition strategy. The acquisition-minded corporation could prepare a set of such curves for its unique conditions and use. In this case, $g_{buy} = 0.3$, $(P/E)_{buy} = 30$, $E_{buy} = 1.0$, and in the specific curve set shown, $(NS)_{buy}$ is assumed to equal $(NS)_{sell}$. A set of these curves should be developed for various $(NS)_{buy}$ to $(NS)_{sell}$ ratios.

To illustrate the use of the set of curves, assume the P/E multiple of a candidate is equal to 25; then the ratio of the P/E multiples is 1.2. Further, assume $g_{sell} = 0.10$; then $g_{buy}/g_{sell} = 3.0$. Reading Z from the left-hand scale at the intersection of a P/E multiple ratio of 1.2 and the growth rate ratio of 3.0, we can see that $Z = 0.76$.

But would this Z factor lead to a postmerger market value of the combination that would exceed the premerger values of both BUY and SELL? This may be determined by solving for a breakeven Z factor (Z_{BE}) and comparing $Z = 0.76$ with the Z_{BE} for that P/E multiple ratio. Consider the following relationship:

$$P_{buy} + P_{sell} \leq P_{buy*} = (P/E)_{buy*}(E_{buy})(NS)_{buy*}$$

If we let the left-hand side of the expression equal the right-hand side, we can solve for the breakeven P/E_{buy*} [or the implied Z factor, since $(P/E)_{buy*} = (P/E)_{buy}(Z)$]. Thus, at the breakeven point,

$$P_{buy} + P_{sell} = P_{buy*} = \left(\frac{P}{E_{buy}}\right)(Z_{BE})(E_{buy*})(NS)_{buy*}$$

where Z_{BE} is the breakeven value of Z. But

$$E_{buy*} = \frac{(E_{buy})(NS)_{buy} + (E_{sell})(NS)_{sell}}{(NS)_{buy*}}$$

Therefore,

$$P_{buy} + P_{sell} = \left(\frac{P}{E_{buy}}\right)(Z_{BE})[(E_{buy})(NS)_{buy}] + [(E_{sell})(NS)_{sell}]$$

FIGURE 14–2   Illustrated acquisition strategy.

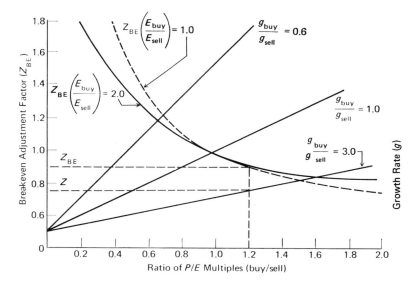

Rearranging,

$$Z_{BE} = \frac{P_{buy} + P_{sell}}{(P/E_{buy})[(E_{buy})(NS_{buy})] + [(E_{sell})(NS)_{sell}]}$$

$$= \frac{[(P/E_{buy})(E_{buy})(NS)_{buy}] + [(P/E_{sell})(E_{sell})(NS)_{sell}]}{[(P/E_{buy})(E_{buy})(NS)_{buy}] + [(E_{sell})(NS_{sell})]} \qquad (10)$$

Note that Z_{BE} is independent of the growth-rate ratio, but varies for different ratios of earnings after tax.

For the case where $Z = 0.76$, assuming $(E)_{buy}/(E)_{sell}$ equals 1.0, we find from Figure 14-2 that Z_{BE} equals approximately 0.92. Since $Z < Z_{BE}$, there will be dilution of market value in the fifth year as a result of the combination under this set of assumptions. Should the ratio of premerger earnings be equal to $2(E_{buy}/E_{sell} = 2)$, Z remains constant (0.76), but Z_{BE} increases slightly.

While development of these curves is computationally difficult relative to a simple calculation of Z and Z_{BE}, they do serve to illustrate the application of the strategy of selecting an acquisition candidate that will yield $Z > Z_{BE}$.

From Figure 14-2, it may be noted that, in general, for larger ratios of $(P/E)_{buy}$ to $(P/E)_{sell}$—and smaller ratios of g_{buy} to g_{sell}, where Z increases, the acquisition candidate becomes more favorable. For the range of P/E multiple ratios greater than 1.0, larger E on the part of the acquirer relative to the candidate is desirable. From this set of curves the following general acquisition strategy may be developed:

Acquirer (BUY)		Candidate (SELL)
$(P/E)_{buy}$	>	$(P/E)_{sell}$
g_{buy}	<	g_{sell}
E_{buy}	>	E_{sell}
$(NS)_{buy}$	<	$(NS)_{sell}$

While it is true that when $(P/E)_{buy} > (P/E)_{sell}$ and $g_{buy} < g_{sell}$ the optimum candidate will have less earnings per share $(E_{buy} > E_{sell})$, it is not universally true. From Figure 14-2, it can be seen that when $(P/E)_{buy} < (P/E)_{sell}$, the desirable candidate will have greater E than the acquirer.

Model usefulness. Rarely will a company follow an acquisition strategy that assures the maximum postmerger market value of common stock, but the ability to predict postmerger stock-value performance and to assimilate that performance into a graphic analysis of acquisition candidates is extremely helpful in managing a program of external expansion through acquisition. These financial screening criteria are vital, for unless synergism is expected to expand the postmerger growth rate of earnings above premerger expectations, a rejection of a candidate using these criteria is an explicit statement of the inability of the combination to meet the profit-maximizing goals of the common-stock holders.

PRIVATELY HELD COMPANIES—CAPITAL-BUDGETING APPROACH

The evaluation of a prospective acquisition candidate represents an extension of the concepts of capital budgeting. Acquisition candidates are evaluated in exactly the same manner as an internally generated capital-budgeting project. The acquisition requires an outlay (in cash or securities), a series of inflows, and an economic life.

Methodology

To illustrate this method of evaluation, assume the following: The ABC Corporation is currently considering the acquisition of XYZ Corporation. XYZ is currently reporting earnings after taxes of $850,000. Preliminary conversations indicate that XYZ would be willing to sell its fixed assets and inventories for $9 million. The $9 million price would mean a cost basis for depreciable assets of $7 million and $1.5 million for inventories. The average estimated remaining useful life of the fixed assets is 15 years. Therefore, depreciation charges for tax purposes after purchase would be $150,000 higher than the present $350,000 per year. If ABC acquires the fixed assets and inventories of XYZ, the financial manager estimates that an additional investment of $500,000 will be required for working capital (cash and accounts receivable). Thus, the total cash outlay for XYZ would be $9.5 million. Assume an income tax rate of 50 percent. If earnings remain at present levels and working capital is recovered at the end of year 15, what is the time-adjusted rate of return on XYZ? (Net cash outflow and inflow are calculated in Table 14-1.)

The rate of return is

$$\text{Net cash outlay} = (\text{net cash inflow})(A_{\overline{n}|i}) + (\text{one-time inflow})(S_{\overline{n}|i})$$

$$\$9,500,000 = (\$1,275,000)(A_{\overline{15}|i}) + (\$2,000,000)(S_{\overline{15}|i})$$

Thus, the rate of return is 11 percent:

$$\$9,500,000 = (\$1,275,000)(7.1909) + (\$2,000,000)(0.20900)$$
$$= \$9,168,397.50 + \$418,000$$
$$= \$9,586,397.50$$

TABLE 14-1   Net cash outflow and inflow.

NET CASH OUTFLOW

Fixed assets	$7,500,000
Inventory	1,500,000
Additional working capital	500,000
Total net outflow	$9,500,000

NET CASH INFLOW FOR EACH YEAR, YEARS 1 TO 15

	New	Old	Differential
Income before tax	$2,050,000	$2,050,000	0
Less depreciation expense	500,000	350,000	($150,000)
Taxable income	1,550,000	1,700,000	(150,000)
Less income tax, 50%	775,000	850,000	75,000
Income after tax	775,000	850,000	(75,000)
Plus depreciation expense	500,000	350,000	150,000
Total net inflow	$1,275,000	$1,200,000	$ 75,000

The preceding calculation assumes a zero rate of growth of cash inflows. If we assume a 10 percent compound annual rate of growth of cash inflows, the discounted rate of return becomes 21 percent (11 percent nongrowth plus 10 percent compound rate of growth).

Now let us assume that the net cash outlay has not been agreed upon. Since it is usually the subject of negotiation, the objective is to determine the maximum price to be paid for the acquisition candidate and still be acting in the best interest of the buyer's shareholders. The present value of the acquisition candidate represents the upper limit the company can pay for the candidate. Any price up to this amount represents a favorable acquisition; above this amount, the acquisition represents an unfavorable allocation of capital.

Let us now return to the preceding example, assume a weighted after-tax cost of capital of 6 percent for the ABC Corporation, and compute the present value of net cash inflows:

$$\begin{aligned}
\text{Net cash inflows} &= (\$1,275,000)(A_{\overline{15}|0.06}) + (\$2,000,000)(S_{\overline{15}|0.06}) \\
&= (\$1,275,000)(9.7122) + (\$2,000,000)(0.41726) \\
&= \$12,383,055 + \$834,520 \\
&= \$13,217,575
\end{aligned}$$

The present value of the acquisition candidate is $13,217,575. This represents the upper limit that the financial manager is willing to pay for the candidate. Since the XYZ Corporation can be acquired for a net cash outlay of $9.5 million this represents a favorable allocation of capital.

Cash inflows. In evaluating a prospective acquisition candidate, the after-tax inflows that the candidate is expected to generate must be anticipated. The inflows include the results of any synergistic effects, since we are concerned with the incremental impact of the acquisition. The task of estimating future cash inflows associated with an acquisition may appear difficult, but they are generally easier than for a capital-budgeting project because the firm being acquired is a going concern with a proven history of profits. Since a forecast of past results is being dealt with, the estimates of cash inflow and outlay are more accurate and subject to less fluctuation than a new capital-budgeting project. The most difficult part of the analysis is the estimate of the synergistic effects of the acquisition.

Cash outlays. The capital-budgeting approach to mergers and acquisitions treats a payment of cash or stock in the same manner. The primary concern of the financial manager is the cash equivalent of value paid for the company being acquired. The long-term payout situation, where the buying company agrees to pay the acquired company a specified sum over a period of years, is ideally suited to capital budgeting. The long-term payout situation has the effect of raising the rate of return on the acquisition. For example, if the XYZ Corporation agreed that the $9.5 million payment could be made over two years, with a net cash outlay of $3.5 million for year zero, $3 million for year 1, and $3 million for year 2, the rate of return on the acquisition would be increased to approximately 13 percent.

Likewise, if an additional investment were required in years 1 and 2, this could also be discounted back to year zero in the determination of net cash outlay. For example, if ABC Corporation estimated that an additional working capital investment of $500,000 would be required in years 1 and 2, the net cash outlay would be $9.5 million in year zero, $500,000 in year 1, and $500,000 in year 2. Since the additional investment would be nondepreciable, it would also affect the net cash inflow in year 15. The net cash inflow from working capital in year 15 would be $3 million rather than the $2 million used in the previous example. The rate of return on the acquisition would decline to approximately 10 percent.

If the buying company purchases both assets and liabilities of the selling firm, the maximum price the buyer should pay is the present value of the future net cash inflows, discounted at the after-tax weighted cost of capital, less the amount of debt of the acquired company. If the acquisition is for cash, as in the case of XYZ, the acquiring company must raise the necessary cash in the same manner as it would for any acceptable capital-budgeting project.

If the acquisition is financed with stock, the buying company issues stock (either preferred or common) in connection with the acquisition. Assuming that it is common stock, the explicit cost is higher than the weighted cost of capital. However, weighted cost of capital should not increase, since the additional common equity will increase the equity base and therefore the debt capacity of the firm. This, in turn, lowers the real cost of common equity. If we can assume that the firm is at its optimal capital structure, then the marginal real cost of common equity is equal to the weighted cost of capital, and weighted average cost of capital represents the appropriate discount rate for merger and acquisition evaluation.

APPENDIX

TABLE A-1   Present value of $1.00 due at the end of N years.   224

TABLE A-2   Present value of $1.00 received annually at the end of each year for N years.   228

TABLE A-3   Five-year compound interest $(1 + i)^n$.   233

TABLE A-1   Present value of $1.00 due at the end of N years.

$$S = \frac{x}{(1 + i)^N}$$

N	1%	2%	3%	4%	5%	6%	7%	8%	9%	10%	N
01	0.99010	0.98039	0.97007	0.96154	0.95238	0.94340	0.93458	0.92593	0.91743	0.90909	01
02	.98030	.96117	.94260	.92456	.90703	.89000	.87344	.85734	.84168	.82645	02
03	.97059	.94232	.91514	.88900	.86384	.83962	.81630	.79383	.77218	.75131	03
04	.96098	.92385	.88849	.85480	.82270	.79209	.76290	.73503	.70843	.68301	04
05	.95147	.90573	.86261	.82193	.78353	.74726	.71299	.68058	.64993	.62092	05
06	.94204	.88797	.83748	.79031	.74622	.70496	.66634	.63017	.59627	.56447	06
07	.93272	.87056	.81309	.75992	.71068	.66506	.62275	.58349	.54703	.51316	07
08	.92348	.85349	.78941	.73069	.67684	.62741	.58201	.54027	.50187	.46651	08
09	.91434	.83675	.76642	.70259	.64461	.59190	.54393	.50025	.46043	.42410	09
10	.90529	.82035	.74409	.67556	.61391	.55839	.50835	.46319	.42241	.38554	10
11	.89632	.80426	.72242	.64958	.58468	.52679	.47509	.42888	.38753	.35049	11
12	.88745	.78849	.70138	.62460	.55684	.49697	.44401	.39711	.35553	.31863	12
13	.87866	.77303	.68095	.60057	.53032	.46884	.41496	.36770	.32618	.28966	13
14	.86996	.75787	.66112	.57747	.50507	.44230	.38782	.34046	.29925	.26333	14
15	.86135	.74301	.64186	.55526	.48102	.41726	.36245	.31524	.27454	.23939	15
16	.85282	.72845	.62317	.53391	.45811	.39365	.33873	.29189	.25187	.21763	16
17	.84438	.71416	.60502	.51337	.43630	.37136	.31657	.27027	.23107	.19784	17
18	.83602	.70016	.58739	.49363	.41552	.35034	.29586	.25025	.21199	.17986	18
19	.82774	.68643	.57029	.47464	.39573	.33051	.27651	.23171	.19449	.16351	19
20	.81954	.67297	.55367	.45639	.37689	.31180	.25842	.21455	.17843	.14864	20
21	.81143	.65978	.53755	.43883	.35894	.29415	.24151	.19866	.16370	.13513	21
22	.80340	.64684	.52189	.42195	.34185	.27750	.22571	.18394	.15018	.12285	22
23	.79544	.63416	.50669	.40573	.32557	.26180	.21095	.17031	.13778	.11168	23
24	.78757	.62172	.49193	.39012	.31007	.24698	.19715	.15770	.12640	.10153	24
25	.77977	.60953	.47760	.37512	.29530	.23300	.18425	.14602	.11597	.09230	25

TABLE A-1 (continued)

N	11%	12%	13%	14%	15%	16%	17%	18%	19%	20%	N
01	0.90090	0.89286	0.88496	0.87719	0.86957	0.86207	0.85470	0.84746	0.84034	0.83333	01
02	.81162	.79719	.78315	.76947	.75614	.74316	.73051	.71818	.70616	.69444	02
03	.73119	.71178	.69305	.67497	.65752	.64066	.62437	.60863	.59342	.57870	03
04	.65873	.63552	.61332	.59208	.57175	.55229	.53365	.51579	.49867	.48225	04
05	.59345	.56743	.54276	.51937	.49718	.47611	.45611	.43711	.41905	.40188	05
06	.53464	.50663	.48032	.45559	.43233	.41044	.38984	.37043	.35214	.33490	06
07	.48166	.45235	.42506	.39964	.37594	.35383	.33320	.31392	.29592	.27908	07
08	.43393	.40388	.37616	.35056	.32690	.30503	.28478	.26604	.24867	.23257	08
09	.39092	.36061	.33288	.30751	.28426	.26295	.24340	.22546	.20897	.19381	09
10	.35218	.32197	.29459	.26974	.24718	.22668	.20804	.19106	.17560	.16151	10
11	.31728	.28748	.26070	.23662	.21494	.19542	.17781	.16192	.14756	.13459	11
12	.28584	.25667	.23071	.20756	.18691	.16846	.15197	.13722	.12400	.11216	12
13	.25751	.22917	.20416	.18207	.16253	.14523	.12989	.11629	.10420	.09346	13
14	.23199	.20462	.18068	.15971	.14133	.12520	.11102	.09855	.08757	.07789	14
15	.20900	.18270	.15989	.14010	.12289	.10793	.09489	.08352	.07359	.06491	15
16	.18829	.16312	.14150	.12289	.10686	.09304	.08110	.07078	.06184	.05409	16
17	.16963	.14564	.12522	.10780	.09293	.08021	.06932	.05998	.05196	.04507	17
18	.15282	.13004	.11081	.09456	.08080	.06914	.05925	.05083	.04367	.03756	18
19	.13768	.11611	.09806	.08295	.07026	.05961	.05064	.04308	.03669	.03130	19
20	.12403	.10367	.08678	.07276	.06110	.05139	.04328	.03651	.03084	.02608	20
21	.11174	.09256	.07680	.06383	.05313	.04430	.03699	.03094	.02591	.02174	21
22	.10067	.08264	.06796	.05599	.04620	.03819	.03162	.02622	.02178	.01811	22
23	.09069	.07379	.06014	.04911	.04017	.03292	.02702	.02222	.01830	.01509	23
24	.08170	.06588	.05322	.04308	.03493	.02838	.02310	.01883	.01538	.01258	24
25	.07361	.05882	.04710	.03779	.03038	.02447	.01974	.01596	.01292	.01048	25

TABLE A-1 *(continued)*

N	21%	22%	23%	24%	25%	26%	27%	28%	29%	30%	N
01	0.82645	0.81967	0.81301	0.80645	0.80000	0.79365	0.78740	0.78125	0.77519	0.76923	01
02	.68301	.67186	.66098	.65036	.64000	.62988	.62000	.61035	.60093	.59172	02
03	.56447	.55071	.53738	.52449	.51200	.49991	.48819	.47684	.46583	.45517	03
04	.46651	.45140	.43690	.42297	.40960	.39675	.38440	.37253	.36111	.35013	04
05	.38554	.37000	.35520	.34111	.32768	.31488	.30268	.29104	.27993	.26933	05
06	.31863	.30328	.28878	.27509	.26214	.24991	.23833	.22737	.21700	.20718	06
07	.26333	.24859	.23478	.22184	.20972	.19834	.18766	.17764	.16822	.15937	07
08	.21763	.20376	.19088	.17891	.16777	.15741	.14776	.13878	.13040	.12259	08
09	.17986	.16702	.15519	.14428	.13422	.12493	.11635	.10842	.10109	.09430	09
10	.14864	.13690	.12617	.11635	.10737	.09915	.09161	.08470	.07836	.07254	10
11	.12285	.11221	.10258	.09383	.08590	.07869	.07214	.06617	.06075	.05580	11
12	.10153	.09198	.08339	.07567	.06872	.06245	.05680	.05170	.04709	.04292	12
13	.08391	.07539	.06780	.06103	.05498	.04957	.04472	.04039	.03650	.03302	13
14	.06934	.06180	.05512	.04921	.04398	.03934	.03522	.03155	.02830	.02540	14
15	.05731	.05065	.04481	.03969	.03518	.03122	.02773	.02465	.02194	.01954	15
16	.04736	.04152	.03643	.03201	.02815	.02478	.02183	.01926	.01700	.01503	16
17	.03914	.03403	.02962	.02581	.02252	.01967	.01719	.01505	.01318	.01156	17
18	.03235	.02789	.02408	.02082	.01801	.01561	.01354	.01175	.01022	.00889	18
19	.02673	.02286	.01958	.01679	.01441	.01239	.01066	.00918	.00792	.00684	19
20	.02209	.01874	.01592	.01354	.01153	.00983	.00839	.00717	.00614	.00526	20
21	.01826	.01536	.01294	.01092	.00922	.00780	.00661	.00561	.00476	.00405	21
22	.01509	.01259	.01052	.00880	.00738	.00619	.00520	.00438	.00369	.00311	22
23	.01247	.01032	.00855	.00710	.00590	.00491	.00410	.00342	.00286	.00239	23
24	.01031	.00846	.00695	.00573	.00472	.00390	.00323	.00267	.00222	.00184	24
25	.00852	.00693	.00565	.00462	.00378	.00310	.00254	.00209	.00172	.00142	25

TABLE A-1 (concluded)

N	31%	32%	33%	34%	35%	36%	37%	38%	39%	40%	N
01	0.76336	0.75758	0.75188	0.74627	0.74074	0.73529	0.72993	0.72464	0.71942	0.71429	01
02	.58272	.57392	.56532	.55692	.54870	.54066	.53279	.52510	.51757	.51020	02
03	.44482	.43479	.42505	.41561	.40644	.39754	.38890	.38051	.37235	.36443	03
04	.33956	.32939	.31959	.31016	.30107	.29231	.28387	.27573	.26788	.26031	04
05	.25920	.24953	.24029	.23146	.22301	.21493	.20720	.19980	.19272	.18593	05
06	.19787	.18904	.18067	.17273	.16520	.15804	.15124	.14479	.13865	.13281	06
07	.15104	.14321	.13584	.12890	.12237	.11621	.11040	.10492	.09975	.09486	07
08	.11530	.10849	.10214	.09620	.09064	.08545	.08058	.07603	.07176	.06776	08
09	.08802	.08219	.07680	.07179	.06714	.06283	.05882	.05509	.05163	.04840	09
10	.06719	.06227	.05774	.05357	.04973	.04620	.04293	.03992	.03714	.03457	10
11	.05129	.04717	.04341	.03998	.03684	.03397	.03134	.02893	.02672	.02469	11
12	.03915	.03574	.03264	.02984	.02729	.02498	.02287	.02096	.01922	.01764	12
13	.02989	.02707	.02454	.02227	.02021	.01837	.01670	.01519	.01383	.01260	13
14	.02281	.02051	.01845	.01662	.01497	.01350	.01219	.01101	.00995	.00900	14
15	.01742	.01554	.01387	.01240	.01109	.00993	.00890	.00798	.00716	.00643	15
16	.01329	.01177	.01043	.00925	.00822	.00730	.00649	.00578	.00515	.00459	16
17	.01015	.00892	.00784	.00691	.00609	.00537	.00474	.00419	.00370	.00328	17
18	.00775	.00676	.00590	.00515	.00451	.00395	.00346	.00304	.00267	.00234	18
19	.00591	.00512	.00443	.00385	.00334	.00290	.00253	.00220	.00192	.00167	19
20	.00451	.00388	.00333	.00287	.00247	.00213	.00184	.00159	.00138	.00120	20
21	.00345	.00294	.00251	.00214	.00183	.00157	.00135	.00115	.00099	.00085	21
22	.00263	.00223	.00188	.00160	.00136	.00115	.00098	.00084	.00071	.00061	22
23	.00201	.00169	.00142	.00119	.00101	.00085	.00072	.00061	.00051	.00044	23
24	.00153	.00128	.00107	.00089	.00074	.00062	.00052	.00044	.00037	.00031	24
25	.00117	.00097	.00080	.00066	.00055	.00046	.00038	.00032	.00027	.00022	25

TABLE A-2 Present value of $1.00 received annually at the end of each year for N years.*

$$A = \frac{1}{i}\left[1 - \frac{1}{(1+i)^N}\right]$$

Year	1%	2%	3%	4%	5%	6%	7%	8%	9%	10%	Year
1	0.9901	0.9804	0.9709	0.9615	0.9524	0.9434	0.9346	0.9259	0.9174	0.9091	1
2	1.9704	1.9416	1.9135	1.8861	1.8594	1.8334	1.8080	1.7833	1.7591	1.7355	2
3	2.9410	2.8839	2.8286	2.7751	2.7232	2.6730	2.6243	2.5771	2.5313	2.4868	3
4	3.9020	3.8077	3.7171	3.6299	3.5459	3.4651	3.3872	3.3121	3.2397	3.1699	4
5	4.8535	4.7134	4.5797	4.4518	4.3295	4.2123	4.1002	3.9927	3.8896	3.7908	5
6	5.7955	5.6014	5.4172	5.2421	5.0757	4.9173	4.7665	4.6229	4.4859	4.3553	6
7	6.7282	6.4720	6.2302	6.0020	5.7863	5.5824	5.3893	5.2064	5.0329	4.8684	7
8	7.6517	7.3254	7.0196	6.7327	6.4632	6.2098	5.9713	5.7466	5.5348	5.3349	8
9	8.5661	8.1622	7.7861	7.4353	7.1078	6.8017	6.5152	6.2469	5.9852	5.7590	9
10	9.4714	8.9825	8.5302	8.1109	7.7217	7.3601	7.0236	6.7101	6.4176	6.1446	10
11	10.3677	9.7868	9.2526	8.7604	8.3064	7.8868	7.4987	7.1389	6.8052	6.4951	11
12	11.2552	10.5753	9.9539	9.3850	8.8632	8.3838	7.9427	7.5361	7.1607	6.8137	12
13	12.1338	11.3483	10.6349	9.9856	9.3935	8.8527	8.3576	7.9038	7.4869	7.1034	13
14	13.0038	12.1062	11.2960	10.5631	9.8986	9.2950	8.7454	8.2442	7.7861	7.3667	14
15	13.8651	12.8492	11.9379	11.1183	10.3796	9.7122	9.1079	8.5595	8.0607	7.6061	15
16	14.7180	13.5777	12.5610	11.6522	10.8377	10.1059	9.4466	8.8514	8.3125	7.8237	16
17	15.5624	14.2918	13.1660	12.1656	11.2740	10.4772	9.7632	9.1216	8.5436	8.0215	17
18	16.3984	14.9920	13.7534	12.6592	11.6895	10.8276	10.0591	9.3719	8.7556	8.2014	18
19	17.2261	15.6784	14.3237	13.1339	12.0853	11.1581	10.3356	9.6036	8.9501	8.3649	19
20	18.0457	16.3514	14.8774	13.5903	12.4622	11.4699	10.5940	9.8181	9.1285	8.5136	20
21	18.8571	17.0111	15.4149	14.0291	12.8211	11.7640	10.8355	10.0168	9.2922	8.6487	21
22	19.6605	17.6580	15.9368	14.4511	13.1630	12.0416	11.0612	10.2007	9.4424	8.7715	22
23	20.4559	18.2921	16.4435	14.8568	13.4885	12.3033	11.2722	10.3710	9.5802	8.8832	23
24	21.2435	18.9139	16.9355	15.2469	13.7986	12.5503	11.4693	10.5287	9.7066	8.9847	24
25	22.0233	19.5234	17.4131	15.6220	14.0939	12.7833	11.6536	10.6748	9.9226	9.0770	25

* For the derivation of A, see note following this table.

TABLE A-2 (continued)

Year	11%	12%	13%	14%	15%	16%	17%	18%	19%	20%	Year
1	0.9009	0.8929	0.8850	0.8772	0.8696	0.8621	0.8547	0.8475	0.8403	0.8333	1
2	1.7125	1.6901	1.6681	1.6467	1.6257	1.6052	1.5852	1.5656	1.5465	1.5278	2
3	2.4437	2.4018	2.3612	2.3216	2.2832	2.2459	2.2096	2.1743	2.1399	2.1065	3
4	3.1024	3.0373	2.9745	2.9137	2.8550	2.7982	2.7432	2.6901	2.6386	2.5887	4
5	3.6959	3.6048	3.5172	3.4331	3.3522	3.2743	3.1993	3.1272	3.0576	2.9906	5
6	4.2305	4.1114	3.9976	3.8887	3.7845	3.6847	3.5892	3.4976	3.4098	3.3255	6
7	4.7122	4.5638	4.4226	4.2883	4.1604	4.0386	3.9224	3.8115	3.7057	3.6046	7
8	5.1461	4.9676	4.7988	4.6389	4.4873	4.3436	4.2072	4.0776	3.9544	3.8372	8
9	5.5370	5.3282	5.1317	4.9464	4.7716	4.6065	4.4506	4.3030	4.1633	4.0310	9
10	5.8892	5.6502	5.4262	5.2161	5.0188	4.8332	4.6586	4.4941	4.3389	4.1925	10
11	6.2065	5.9377	5.6869	5.4527	5.2337	5.0286	4.8364	4.6560	4.4865	4.3271	11
12	6.4924	6.1944	5.9176	5.6603	5.4206	5.1971	4.9984	4.7932	4.6105	4.4392	12
13	6.7499	6.4235	6.1218	5.8424	5.5831	5.3423	5.1183	4.9095	4.7147	4.5327	13
14	6.9819	6.6282	6.3025	6.0021	5.7245	5.4675	5.2293	5.0081	4.8023	4.6106	14
15	7.1909	6.8109	6.4624	6.1422	5.8474	5.5755	5.3242	5.0916	4.8759	4.6755	15
16	7.3792	6.9740	6.6039	6.2651	5.9542	5.6685	5.4053	5.1624	4.9377	4.7296	16
17	7.5488	7.1196	6.7291	6.3729	6.0472	5.7487	5.4746	5.2223	4.9897	4.7746	17
18	7.7016	7.2497	6.8399	6.4674	6.1280	5.8178	5.5339	5.2732	5.0333	4.8122	18
19	7.8393	7.3658	6.9380	6.5504	6.1982	5.8775	5.5845	5.3162	5.0700	4.8435	19
20	7.9633	7.4694	7.0248	6.6231	6.2593	5.9288	5.6278	5.3527	5.1009	4.8696	20
21	8.0751	7.5620	7.1016	6.6870	6.3125	5.9731	5.6648	5.3837	5.1268	4.8913	21
22	8.1757	7.6446	7.1695	6.7429	6.3587	6.0113	5.6964	5.4099	5.1486	4.9094	22
23	8.2664	7.7184	7.2297	6.7921	6.3988	6.0442	5.7234	5.4321	5.1668	4.9245	23
24	8.3481	7.7843	7.2829	6.8351	6.4338	6.0726	5.7465	5.4509	5.1822	4.9371	24
25	8.4217	7.8431	7.3300	6.8729	6.4641	6.0971	5.7662	5.4669	5.1951	4.9476	25

TABLE A-2 (continued)

Year	21%	22%	23%	24%	25%	26%	27%	28%	29%	30%	Year
1	0.8264	0.8197	0.8130	0.8065	0.8000	0.7937	0.7874	0.7813	0.7752	0.7692	1
2	1.5095	1.4915	1.4740	1.4568	1.4400	1.4235	1.4074	1.3916	1.3761	1.3609	2
3	2.0739	2.0422	2.0114	1.9813	1.9520	1.9234	1.8956	1.8684	1.8420	1.8161	3
4	2.5404	2.4936	2.4483	2.4043	2.3616	2.3202	2.2800	2.2410	2.2031	2.1662	4
5	2.9260	2.8636	2.8035	2.7454	2.6893	2.6351	2.5827	2.5320	2.4830	2.4356	5
6	3.2446	3.1669	3.0923	3.0205	2.9514	2.8850	2.8210	2.7594	2.7000	2.6427	6
7	3.5079	3.4155	3.3270	3.2423	3.1611	3.0833	3.0087	2.9370	2.8682	2.8021	7
8	3.7256	3.6193	3.5179	3.4212	3.3289	3.2407	3.1564	3.0758	2.9986	2.9247	8
9	3.9054	3.7863	3.6731	3.5655	3.4631	3.3657	3.2728	3.1842	3.0997	3.0190	9
10	4.0541	3.9232	3.7993	3.6819	3.5705	3.4648	3.3644	3.2689	3.1781	3.0915	10
11	4.1769	4.0354	3.9018	3.7757	3.6564	3.5435	3.4365	3.3351	3.2388	3.1473	11
12	4.2785	4.1274	3.9852	3.8514	3.7251	3.6060	3.4933	3.3868	3.2859	3.1903	12
13	4.3624	4.2028	4.0530	3.9124	3.7801	3.6555	3.6381	3.4272	3.3224	3.2233	13
14	4.4317	4.2646	4.1082	3.9616	3.8241	3.6949	3.5733	3.4587	3.3507	3.2487	14
15	4.4890	4.3152	4.1530	4.0013	3.8593	3.7261	3.6010	3.4834	3.3726	3.2682	15
16	4.5364	4.3567	4.1894	4.0333	3.8874	3.7509	3.6228	3.5026	3.3896	3.2832	16
17	4.5755	4.3908	4.2190	4.0591	3.9099	3.7705	3.6400	3.5177	3.4028	3.2948	17
18	4.6079	4.4187	4.2431	4.0799	3.9279	3.7861	3.6536	3.5294	3.4130	3.3037	18
19	4.6346	4.4415	4.2627	4.0967	3.9424	3.7985	3.6642	3.5386	3.4210	3.3105	19
20	4.6567	4.4603	4.2786	4.1103	3.9539	3.8083	3.6726	3.5458	3.4271	3.3158	20
21	4.6750	4.4756	4.2916	4.1212	3.9631	3.8161	3.6792	3.5514	3.4319	3.3198	21
22	4.6900	4.4882	4.3021	4.1300	3.9705	3.8223	3.6844	3.5558	3.4356	3.3230	22
23	4.7025	4.4985	4.3106	4.1371	3.9764	3.8273	3.6885	3.5592	3.4384	3.3254	23
24	4.7128	4.5070	4.3176	4.1428	3.9811	3.8312	3.6918	3.5619	3.4406	3.3272	24
25	4.7213	4.5139	4.3232	4.1474	3.9849	3.8342	3.6943	3.5640	3.4423	3.3286	25

TABLE A-2 *(concluded)*

Year	31%	32%	33%	34%	35%	36%	37%	38%	39%	40%	Year
1	0.7634	0.7576	0.7519	0.7463	0.7407	0.7353	0.7299	0.7246	0.7194	0.7143	1
2	1.3461	1.3315	1.3172	1.3032	1.2894	1.2760	1.2627	1.2497	1.2370	1.2245	2
3	1.7909	1.7663	1.7423	1.7188	1.6959	1.6735	1.6516	1.6302	1.6093	1.5889	3
4	2.1305	2.0957	2.0618	2.0290	1.9969	1.9658	1.9355	1.9060	1.8772	1.8492	4
5	2.3897	2.3452	2.3021	2.2604	2.2200	2.1807	2.1427	2.1058	2.0699	2.0352	5
6	2.5875	2.5342	2.4828	2.4331	2.3852	2.3388	2.2939	2.2506	2.2086	2.1680	6
7	2.7386	2.6775	2.6187	2.5620	2.5075	2.4550	2.4043	2.3555	2.3083	2.2628	7
8	2.8539	2.7860	2.7208	2.6582	2.5982	2.5404	2.4849	2.4315	2.3801	2.3306	8
9	2.9419	2.8681	2.7976	2.7300	2.6653	2.6033	2.5437	2.4866	2.4317	2.3790	9
10	3.0091	2.9304	2.8553	2.7836	2.7150	2.6495	2.5867	2.5265	2.4689	2.4136	10
11	3.0604	2.9776	2.8987	2.8236	2.7519	2.6834	2.6180	2.5555	2.4956	2.4383	11
12	3.0995	3.0133	2.9314	2.8534	2.7792	2.7084	2.6409	2.5764	2.5148	2.4559	12
13	3.1294	3.0404	2.9559	2.8757	2.7994	2.7268	2.6576	2.5916	2.5286	2.4685	13
14	3.1522	3.0609	2.9744	2.8923	2.8144	2.7403	2.6698	2.6026	2.5386	2.4775	14
15	3.1696	3.0764	2.9883	2.9047	2.8255	2.7502	2.6787	2.6106	2.5457	2.4839	15
16	3.1829	3.0882	2.9987	2.9140	2.8337	2.7575	2.6852	2.6164	2.5509	2.4885	16
17	3.1931	3.0971	3.0065	2.9209	2.8398	2.7629	2.6899	2.6206	2.5546	2.4918	17
18	3.2008	3.1039	3.0124	2.9260	2.8443	2.7668	2.6934	2.6236	2.5573	2.4941	18
19	3.2067	3.1090	3.0169	2.9299	2.8476	2.7697	2.6959	2.6258	2.5592	2.4958	19
20	3.2112	3.1129	3.0202	2.9327	2.8501	2.7718	2.6977	2.6274	2.5606	2.4970	20
21	3.2147	3.1158	3.0227	2.9349	2.8519	2.7734	2.6991	2.6285	2.5616	2.4979	21
22	3.2173	3.1180	3.0246	2.9365	2.8533	2.7746	2.7000	2.6294	2.5623	2.4985	22
23	3.2193	3.1197	3.0260	2.9377	2.8543	2.7754	2.7008	2.6300	2.5628	2.4989	23
24	3.2209	3.1210	3.0271	2.9386	2.8550	2.7760	2.7013	2.6304	2.5632	2.4992	24
25	3.2220	3.1220	3.0279	2.9392	2.8556	2.7765	2.7017	2.6307	2.5634	2.4994	25

Note:

The symbol A is defined as the sum of present values of each item. For the general case, the present value of an ordinary annuity of $1 may be expressed as follows:

$$A = \frac{1}{1 + i} + \frac{1}{(1 + i)^2} + \frac{1}{(1 + i)^3}$$

Substituting values from our illustration in Chapter 11:

$$A = \frac{1}{1.06} + \frac{1}{(1.06)^2} + \frac{1}{(1.06)^3}$$

Multiplying by $\frac{1}{1.06}$:

$$A\left(\frac{1}{1.06}\right) = \frac{1}{(1.06)^2} + \frac{1}{(1.06)^3} + \frac{1}{(1.06)^4}$$

Subtracting:

$$A - A\left(\frac{1}{1.06}\right) = \frac{1}{1.06} - \frac{1}{(1.06)^4}$$

Factoring:

$$A\left(1 - \frac{1}{1.06}\right) = \frac{1}{1.06}\left[1 - \frac{1}{(1.06)^3}\right]$$

or

$$A\left(\frac{0.06}{1.06}\right) = \frac{1}{1.06}\left[1 - \frac{1}{(1.06)^3}\right]$$

Dividing by $\frac{0.06}{1.06}$:

$$A = \frac{1}{0.06}\left[1 - \frac{1}{(1.06)^3}\right]$$

The general formula for the present worth of an annuity is

$$A = \frac{1}{i}\left[1 - \frac{1}{(1 + i)^n}\right]$$

Solving:

$$A = \frac{1}{0.06}(1 - 0.840) = \frac{0.160}{0.06} = 2.67$$

TABLE A-3   Five-year compound interest $(1 + i)^n$.

Percentages	Amount	Percentages	Amount
1 %	1.05	24%	2.93
$1\frac{1}{2}$	1.08	25	3.06
2	1.10	26	3.17
$2\frac{1}{2}$	1.13	27	3.30
3	1.16	28	3.44
$3\frac{1}{2}$	1.18	29	3.57
4	1.22	30	3.71
$4\frac{1}{2}$	1.25	31	3.86
5	1.28	32	4.00
6	1 34	33	4.16
7	1.40	34	4.32
8	1.47	35	4.49
9	1.54	36	4.66
10	1.61	37	4.82
11	1.68	38	5.00
12	1.76	39	5.28
13	1.84	40	5.37
14	1.95	41	5.55
15	2.01	42	5.75
16	2.11	43	5.97
17	2.20	44	6.19
18	2.29	45	6.41
19	2.39	46	6.64
20	2.50	47	6.87
21	2.60	48	7.10
22	2.70	49	7.33
23	2.81	50	7.59

Index

acceleration principle, 12
Accounting Principles Board (of AICPA), 98, 99
accounts payable
  centralization of disbursements, 26–27
  deceleration of payments, 26
  discounts, trade, 45
  float, 27
  turnover, 120
  velocity, increasing, 22–23, 26–27
accounts receivable
  quick ratio, 117–118
  turnover, 115–117, 118–119
  velocity, increasing, 22–26
acquisitions, *see* mergers and acquisitions
Alchien, Armen A., 20n
Alleghany Corporation, 105
American and Foreign Power Company, 106
American Institute of Certified Public Accountants (AICPA), 98, 99
American Machine and Foundry Company, 94

analysis, financial, 109–129
  accounting methods and, 112, 113–114
  accounts payable turnover, 120
  accounts receivable turnover, 115–117, 118–119
  asset turnover, 121–122
  auditor's opinion, 113–114
  balance sheets, 111–112
  breakeven, 131–135
  capitalization rate, 128–129
  common-stock ratios, 109, 127–129
  cost-volume-profit, 130–143
  current ratio, 117
  debt to net worth ratio, 120–121
  dividend payout, 127
  dividend yield, 128–129
  earnings coverage, 121
  earnings, per share, 127
  earnings/price rate, 127–128
  equity, return on, 124–126
  financial statements, 111–112
  funds, source and application statements, 112–113
  income statements, 111–112

235

analysis, financial (*cont.*)
  information sources for, 115
  inventory turnover ratios, 115–117, 119–120
  investment, return on (ROI), 109, 121, 122–126
  judgment, need for, 115
  liquidity ratios, 109, 115–121
  per-share earnings, 127
  price-earnings ratio, 127–128
  profit margin, 121
  quick ratio, 117–118
  ratios, determination of, 114–115
  shares, book value of, 127
  turnover ratios, 115–117, 118–122
asset turnover, 121–122
assets
  liquidity ratios and, 109–121
  monetary, 17
  current ratio, 117
  net financial position and, 17–21
audits, postcompletion, of capital expenditures, 180
  implementing, 182
  model, 180–182
  project selection for, 183–184
  responsibility for, 183
  timing of, 183

Baker, Richard L., 92n
balance sheets, 111–112
  leases and, 186
  projected, and budgets, 154–155
  see also analysis, financial
Bankers Security Life Insurance Society, 81–83
banks and banking
  certificates of deposit, negotiable time (CD), 29–30
  compensating balances, 27, 45
  concentration banking, 25
  drafts, 25, 26
  float, 27
interest rates, 16–17
link financing, 45
loans, costs of, 45–46
lockboxes, 23–24
monetary policy and, 15–17
notes, short-term, of, 30
rediscount rates, 16–17
reserve requirements, 15, 16
short-term investments in, 29–30
Bladen, Ashby, 102n
bonds, convertible
  as "sweetener" of issue marketability, 99
  call policy, 101–104
  compared to warrants, 93–94, 104–105
  conversion value of, 100–101
  equity capitalization and, 96–99
  grade rating and, 104
  institutional buyers and, 98
  leverage, 99
  limitations of, 100
  margin requirements, 102
  premium, 103
  risk factor, 102, 103
  straight-debt value of, 103–104
  subscription price, 97
bonds, corporate
  convertible, 17, 93–106
  costs as capital, 48–49, 60–66
  net financial position and, 17–18
breakeven analysis, 131–135
Brigham, E. F., 102n, 103n
Brown Shoe, 88–89
budgets and budgeting, 147–162
  balance sheet, projected, 154–155
  capital, 165–185 (*see also* capital budgeting)
  cash, 148–151
  cash, centralization of disbursement and, 27
  correlation analysis, 158–161
  fixed, 148
  forecasting methods, 158–161

budgets and budgeting (*cont.*)
  nonmonetary considerations, 178–179
  periods, 148, 149
  preparation of budget, 148–151
  present-value tables used in, 184–185
  regression analysis, 158–161
  sales estimates, 149–151
  variable, 148
  variance from projections, 156–157
  volume vs. mix variance, 157–158
business cycle, 11
  acceleration principle, 12
  coincidental indicators, 13–14
  lagging indicators, 14

Cady, Roberts and Company, 92
capital budgeting, 165–185
  approach, in screening acquisition candidates, 219–222
  audits, postcompletion, 180–184
  capital expenditures, definition of, 165–166
  net present value and probability index, 171–172
  net-present-value method of evaluation, 167–179
  nonmonetary considerations, 178–179
  payback technique of evaluation, 179–180
  present-value tables used in, 184–185
capital, convertibles as source of, 96–99
capital, cost of, 7–8, 41–69
  bank loans, 45–46
  bonds, 48–49
  borrowed capital, 44–60
  breakeven point, 41
  capital structure and, 62–66

convertible securities, 59–60, 99
  discounts, trade, 45
  earnings, retained, 52–59
  equity capital, 48–60
  installment debt, 47–48
  intermediate-term debt, 47–48
  leverage and, 63–66
  long-term, 48–49
  marginal, 42–44
  notes payable, 46–47
  optimum, 41
  planning and, 145
  short-term debt, 45–47
  stock, common, 50–51, 60–66
  stock, preferred, 49–50, 60–66
  taxes, 44, 66–67
  weighted, 60–66
capital, definition of, 41
capital expenditures
  acceleration principle, 12
  audits, postcompletion, 180–184
capitalization rate, 128–129
Carleton, Willard T., 76n
cash budget, 148–151
  projected balance-sheet method, 154–155
cash management, 22–40
  centralization of disbursements, 26–27
  concentration banking, 25
  deceleration of payments, 26–27
  float, 27
  inflows, velocity control of, 22–26
  investments, 27–40 (*see also* investments, corporate)
  lockbox technique, 23–24
  outflow, velocity control of, 22–23, 26–27
cash velocity, *see* velocity
certificates of deposit, negotiable time (CD), 29–30
Clayton Act, 198
Colt Manufacturing Company, 89–90
Commerce Department, 115

compensating balances
 costs, 45
 credit and, 27
concentration banking, 25
conglomerates, 199–200
 see also mergers and acquisitions
consolidations, 202, 203
 see also mergers and acquisitions
control, dilution of in mergers and
  acquisitions, 204
convertible securities, 93–106
 as "sweetener" for issue marketability, 99
 callable, 95
 call policy, 101–104
 equity capitalization, and, 96–99
 forcing conversion of, 96, 103
 institutional investors and, 98
 limitations of, 100
 margin requirements, 102
 warrants, 93–94, 104–105
 warrants compared to, 96
correlation analysis, 158–161
costs
 capital, see capital, cost of
 operating, 41
cost-volume-profit analysis, 130–143
 applications of, 138–142
 breakeven analysis, 131–135
 leverage, combined, 142–143
 leverage, financial, 141–142
 leverage, operating, 140–141
 profit to volume ratio, 135–137
CPM (critical path method), 163–
 164
credit
 compensating balances and, 27
 monetary policy and, 15–17
 see also accounts payable; debt
current ratio, 117

debt
 bank loans, 45–46
 capital structure and, 62–66

convertibles and leverage, 99
 costs of, 44–67
 discounts, trade, 45
 equity capital, costs of, 48–60
 installment, 47–48
 intermediate, costs of, 47–48
 long-term, costs of, 48–49
 notes payable, 46–47
 ratio of, to equity, 42
 ratio of, to net worth, 120–121
 short-term, costs of, 45–47
discounts, trade, 45
dividend(s)
 cash, 70–73
 chart system for analysis of, 77–80
 convertible bonds, 101–102
 economic factors, 73
 extra, 71
 guidelines, legal, 72–73
 payout ratio, common stock, 127
 ratio of earnings per share to price
  per share, 128–129
 stability of, 71
 stock, 73–74
 stock price and, 70–83
 warrants, 104
drafts, 25, 26
Dravo Corporation, 79–81
Dun & Bradstreet, 115

earnings
 accumulation, taxes and, 67
 coverage, 121
 dilution of by mergers and acquisitions, 205
 ratio of operating income to interest earned, 121
 retained, opportunity cost of, 52–
  59
 per share, 127
earnings to price ratio, 127–128
 capitalization rate and, 128
 inflation and, 20–21

earnings to price ratio (*cont.*)
  merger of publicly held companies
    and, 207–218
  use of, in screening acquisition
    candidates, 209–216
economic factors, 11–21
  business cycle, 11–15
  dividends and, 73
  inflation and net financial position,
    17–21
  monetary policy, 14–16
equity
  capital, costs of, 48–60
  convertibles as source of, 96–99
  optimal capital structure and, 62
  ratio of, to debt, 42
  return on, 124–126
  statements, 112–113
  treasury stock reacquisition and,
    86–92

Federal Deposit Insurance Corpora-
    tion, 30
Federal Home Loan Bank, 29
Federal National Mortgage Associa-
    tion, 29
Federal Reserve Board Index, 13
Federal Reserve System
  monetary policy, 15–16
  open market operations, 16
  rediscounting, 16
  regulations of, 30
  reserve requirements, 15
FIFO vs. LIFO pricing, 119
finance lease, 191
financial leverage, 141–142
financial position, net
  inflation and, 17–21
  market valuation and, 20–21
  monetary items and, 17–18
financial statements, 111, 112
financing, *see* capital, cost of; *specific
    forms of financing*

First Boston Corporation, 30
First National Bank of Altoona v.
    U.S., 203n
fleet leasing, 187–188
  breakeven points, 191–193
  finance lease, 191
  financing methods, 188–191
  maintenance lease, 190–191
  mileage reimbursement to sales-
    men, 191
float, 27
Forbes magazine, 115
forecasting
  correlation analysis, 158–161
  scatter diagram, 161–162
Fortune magazine, 115

Gordon, Myron J., 74–77
Gordon stock evaluation model, 74–
    77
government securities
  monetary policy and, 16–17
  as short-term investment, 29–30,
    36
growth rate
  convertibles and grade rating, 104
  stock price and, 56–59
  treasury stock acquisition and, 87

Hess, A., 103n

income, operating
  ratio of, to interest earned, 121
  ratio of, to net sales, 121
  ratio of, to operating assets, 122–
    126
income statements, 111–112
inflation
  interest rates and, 20–21
  market valuation and, 20–21
  net financial position and, 17–21

installment debt, 47–48
interest
    convertible bonds, 99, 101–102
    earned, ratio of, to operating income, 121
    inflation and, 20–21
    installment debt, 47–48
    investment policy and yield, 31, 36–40
    monetary policy and, 15–17
    Treasury bills, 16–17
    warrants, 105
intermediate-term debt, 47–48
Internal Revenue Code and Service
    on capitalization, 66–67
    on earnings accumulation, 67
    on mergers and acquisitions, 85, 201–203
inventory
    LIFO vs. FIFO pricing, 119
    turnover ratios, 115–117, 119–120
investments, corporate
    bank notes, short-term, 30
    capital costs and, 41–42 (see also capital, cost of)
    certificates of deposit, negotiable time (CD), 29–30
    criteria, 31–32
    government securities, 29–30, 36
    liquidity or marketability of, 31
    maturities, 31–32
    models, 32–35
    net financial position and, 17–21
    policies, conservative vs. dynamic, 35–40
    repurchase agreements, 29–30
    return on (ROI), 7–8 (see also return on investment)
    safety, 31
    short-term, 27–30
    Treasury bills, 29–30, 36
    yields, 31–32

Justice Department, 198–200

Kessel, Reuben A., 20n
Kinney (G. R.) Corporation, 88–89

Lancey, Roderic C., 207n
leases and leasing, 186–193
    advantages vs. disadvantages of, 187
    balance sheet ratios and, 186
    fleet, model of, 187–193
    net financial position and, 18
    sale leaseback, 187
    taxes and, 187
Lerner, Eugene M., 76n
leverage, 140
    capital costs and, 63–66
    combined, 142–143
    convertibles and, 99
    financial, 141–142
    operating, 140–141
liabilities, monetary, 17
    current ratio, 117
    net financial position and, 17–21
LIFO vs. FIFO pricing, 119
link financing, 45
liquidity
    of corporate investments, 31
    financial analysis and, 109–121
    ratios, 109, 115–121
lockboxes, 23–24, 25
loss carry-overs in mergers and acquisitions, 204

maintenance lease, 190–191
margin requirements of convertible bonds, 102
market valuation, net financial position and, 20–21
market value concept of retained earnings and capital costs, 53–59
mergers and acquisitions, 197–205
    balance sheet presentation, 112
    candidates for, and capital-budgeting approach to screening, 219–222

mergers and acquisitions (*cont.*)
 candidates for, and *P/E* multiple approach to screening, 209–216
 conglomerate, 199–200
 consolidations, 202, 203
 dilution aspects of, 204–205
 direct purchase of assets, 203
 federal guidelines for, 198–200
 horizontal, 199
 legal aspects of, 198–201
 loss carry-overs, 204
 optimum *P/E* strategy, 216–219
 price/earnings (*P/E*) approach, 207–218
 privately held companies, 219–222
 problems, practical, 198
 publicly held companies, 207–219
securities laws and, 200–201
 statutory, 202, 203
 stock for assets, 202–203
 stock vs. cash acquisition, 84–86
 tax aspects of, 84–85, 197*n*, 201–204
 tax-free transactions, 201, 202–203
 treasury-stock model, 84–90
 valuing acquisitions, 206–222
 vertical, 199
 warrants in, 104–105
monetary policy
 business cycle and, 14–17
 Federal Reserve System and, 15–16
 theories about, 15
Morgan Guaranty Survey, 12*n*
Murphy, James T., 59

net-present-value method of evaluation, 167–179
 differential cash inflows, 169–171
 net cash outlay, determination of, 167–169
 nonmonetary considerations, 178–179
 and probability index, 171–172

used to appraise project risk, 172–178
net worth to debt, ratio of, 120–121
New York Stock Exchange treasury-stock transaction reports, 91–92
notes payable, costs of, 46–47

objectives, corporate
 organization of financial function and, 6–8
 planning, 147
open market operations, Federal Reserve, 16
operating assets
 ratio of, to net sales, 121–122
 ratio of, to operating income, 122–126
operating costs, breakeven point for, 41
operating income
 ratio of, to interest earned, 121
 ratio of, to net sales, 121
 ratio of, to operating assets, 122–126
operating leverage, 140–141
organization of financial function, 1–8
 decision-making, critical, 5–6
 evaluation, 1
 objectives, 6–8
 procurement of funds, 1–2

Paramount Pictures, Inc., 90–91
payback technique of evaluating capital expenditures, 179–180
payout ratio, common-stocks, 127
performance standards, planning and, 147
personnel relations
 capital expenditures and, 178
 planning and, 145–147
PERT analysis, 162–164
Phillips Petroleum, 94
Pilcher, C. J., 96*n*

planning, financial, 144–164
  advantages of, 145–147
  budgeting and, 147–162 (*see also*
    budgets and budgeting)
  CPM (critical path method), 163–
    164
  corporate objectives and, 147
  criteria for, 144–145
  effective, 147
  performance standards and, 147
  PERT analysis in, 162–164
pollution control, capital expenditures
  for, 178–179
present-value tables, 224–232
  usage of, 184–185
price-earnings (*P/E*) ratio, 127–128
  capitalization rate and, 128
  inflation and, 20–21
  merger or acquisition of publicly
    held companies and, 207–218
probability index, 171–172
profit
  margin, 121
  ratio of, to volume, 135–137
  relationship to volume, budgets
    and, 149–151
profitability, *see* return on investment
  (ROI)
profit-cost-volume analysis, 130–143

quick ratio, 117–118

ratios, determination of, 114–115
rediscounting, Federal Reserve System, 16
regression analysis, 158–161
Regulation Q, 30
rents and leases, 18
  see also leases and leasing
reorganization, warrants in, 104–105
repurchase agreements, 29–30
research, budgeting for basic, 178
return on investment (ROI), 7–8,
  109, 121, 122–126

budget preparation and, 149–151
  planning and, 145
  profit margin, 121
  return on equity and, 125–126
  risks and, 123–124
  share earnings and, 127
risk
  capital budgeting and appraisal of,
    172–178
  convertibles and, 102, 103
  return on investment and, 123–124
RKO, 106

sale leaseback, 187
sales estimates, cash budgets and, 149
sales, net
  ratio of, to operating assets, 121–
    122
  ratio of, to operating income, 121
sales volume vs. mix variance, budgeting and, 157–158
scatter diagram, 161–162
securities (corporate)
  convertible, cost of, 59–60
  dilution in mergers and acquisi-
    tions, 204–205
  flotation costs, average, 98
  see also specific types of securities
securities (as investments)
  criteria, 31–32
  government, 17
  net financial position and, 17–18
  repurchase agreements, 29–30
  short-term, 27–30
  see also investments; *specific types
    of securities*
Securities Exchange Act (1933), 200
Securities and Exchange Act (1934),
  91, 200
Securities and Exchange Commission
  and acquisitions and mergers, 197,
    200–201
  on securities flotation costs, 96
  securities laws and, 99, 200–201

on treasury stock transactions, 91–92

securities laws, 200–201

selling price, cost-volume-profit analysis and, 138–140

Small Business Administration, 115

Smalter, Donald J., 207n

Soldofsky, Robert M., 59

source and application of funds, statements of, 112–113

Southland Ice Company, 203n

speculation, warrants and, 105–106

Sperry Rand, 95

stock, common (corporate)
book value per share of, 127
convertible bonds and, 94–95
cost of, 50–51, 60–66
dividend payout ratio, 127
dividend policy and valuation of, 70–83
as dividends, 73–74
earnings per share, 127
ratios, 109, 127–129
of supernormal growth firms, 56–59
warrants, 93–94, 95

stock, common (as investments), net financial position and, 17–18

stock, preferred (corporate)
cost of, 49–50, 60–66
dividend guidelines, legal, 73
warrants, 104–105

stock, preferred (as investments), convertibility of, 17

stock, treasury (corporate), 84–92
acquisitions, corporate, 84–86
legal restrictions, 91–92
reacquisition, 86–92

Symington Gould Corporation, 105

tax-anticipation bills, 29

taxes
and accumulated earnings, 67
cost of capital and, 44, 66–67

leasing and, 187

loss carry-overs, 204

on mergers and acquisitions, 84–85, 197n, 201–204

trade discounts, 45

Treasury bills, 16–17
investments in, 29–30, 36

treasury stock, 84–92
acquisitions model, 84–90
equity retirement, 86–92
growth rate and, 87
securities laws and ethical problems, 91–92

turnover ratio
accounts payable, 120
accounts receivable, 115–117, 118–119
inventory, 115–117, 119–120

United Aircraft, 94

velocity, 22–30
centralization of disbursements, 26–27
concentration banking, 25
deceleration of payments, 26
float, 27
lockbox technique, 23–24
short-term investments and, 27–30

volume-cost-profit analysis, 130–143

warrants, 93–94
convertibles compared to, 96
dividends, 104
interest, 104
in mergers, 104–105
price of, 95
in reorganizations, 104–105
separately salable, 95
speculation and, 105–106

Wayne Pump Company, 105

Winn, W. J., 103n

wire transfers, 25

zero-balance accounts, 27